802
808
804 x
598
737
596

Ecology of
Salt Marshes
and Sand Dunes

Ecology of Salt Marshes and Sand Dunes

D. S. RANWELL

Head of the Coastal Ecology
Research Station (Nature Conservancy)
Norwich

LONDON
CHAPMAN AND HALL

First published 1972
by Chapman and Hall Ltd
11 New Fetter Lane, London EC4P 4EE
Printed in Great Britain by
Cox & Wyman Ltd., Fakenham

SBN 412 10500 4

Contents

PART 3   SAND DUNES

List of Plates

Preface

Some attempt has been made in this book to bring together recent knowledge of the ecology of salt marshes and sand dunes and to relate it to current work on associated subjects.

What could be a greater contrast than the flatness and wetness of a marsh and the hilliness and dryness of a dune? Yet in both there are interesting parallels in the ways in which plants and animals achieve mastery over these initially inhospitable environments as well as in the obvious contrasts.

The extreme differences in the two habitats have influenced approaches to the study of each in the past. This has led to emphasis on study of salinity in the salt marsh and lack of appreciation of the significance of drought near the upper limits of the marsh. Emphasis on the study of drought effects on the dunes has resulted in neglect of moisture effects in the damp slacks between them.

Individual habitats, or parts of them, have been studied in isolation in the past. Now, with increasing knowledge and better facilities, it is possible and essential to study whole systems and the relationships between salt marshes and sand dunes and their associated environments.

With the increasing pace of human activities on and near the coast it is vital for the coastal ecologist to gain a more balanced understanding of these habitats and to develop effective predictive models of the processes at work in them.

I hope that this book will help to encourage new studies where they are most needed, not only in existing marshes and dunes, but also in the design of the new coastal environments derived from the exciting coastal engineering schemes now on the drawing boards. We should no longer submit to a defensive protection of coastal wildlife resources, but insist that due regard for a rightful place for these be built into the new environments to come and ensure that adequate stepping stones are preserved to allow them to take this place alongside their human neighbours.

The book is planned in four parts: the first (Chapters 1 to 3) and last (Chapters 12 and 13), synthetic in character; the two central parts (Chapters 4 to 11) analytical. The first part concerns general relationships of both habitats, the second and the third parts contain separate treatments of the ecology of salt marshes and sand dunes, while the fourth part deals with human influences and management.

Coastal Ecology Research Station,   D.S.R.
(Nature Conservancy),
Norwich

February 1972

Acknowledgements

I am very much aware of the dependence of this book on the guidance and help I have received from teachers and colleagues in the past, but I should make it clear that the responsibility for opinions expressed is solely my own.

In particular I am grateful to Professor W. T. Williams and Professor T. A. Bennet-Clark F.R.S., who taught me respect for the discipline of plant physiology; Dr G. Metcalfe and Dr J. M. Lambert who encouraged my initial ecological interest; Professor J. A. Steers who encouraged my interest in coastal physiology; and especially Professor P. W. Richards who supervised my first studies in coastal ecology with a wisdom which I still appreciate. I would like to thank also colleagues who helped with my work and influenced my thinking: Dr M. V. Brian, Dr D. A. Ratcliffe, Mrs B. Brummitt, Mr R. E. Stebbings, Mr J. C. E. Hubbard and Dr E. C. F. Bird. I am especially grateful to Dr R. L. Jefferies for much helpful advice on Chapter 3 and to the many others too numerous to mention who have helped in many ways. Special thanks are due to Miss E. J. Reeve and Mrs S. van Piere for help in typing the manuscript, and to Mr P. G. Ainsworth, Miss S. S. Anderson and Mr B. H. Grimes for assistance with a number of the illustrations and photographs.

I should also like to thank the following for permission to use various quotations: Dr A. J. Brereton; the American Society of Limnology and Oceanography; the British Entomological and Natural History Society; the Institution of Civil Engineers; the New York Botanical Garden; Academic Press Inc. (London) Ltd.; G. Bell and Sons Ltd.; Blackwell Scientific Publications Ltd.; and the University of Chicago Press. Grateful acknowledgement is made to those who have granted permission to reproduce figures and tables; the source in each case is given at the end of the caption or table title.

Finally I would like to record my gratitude to the editor, Mr D. C. Ingram, for much helpful advice and to my wife for her constant encouragement throughout.

D.S.R.

PART ONE General Relationships

1 Climatic Restraints

Distributions and Climate

World patterns

There is a certain similarity in the appearance of the vegetation of salt marshes or of sand dunes in whatever part of the world they are found. Each is subjected to two overriding physical restraints which control the type of growth they can support. For the salt marsh these are silt and saline water; for the dune, sand and wind.

Given these physical restrictions, the kinds of plants and animals which can survive in any particular part of the world is then largely governed by prevailing climate. Whether they actually occur there or not depends on chance factors of migration or introduction. Opportunities for widespread dispersal are in fact much better for coastal plants than for other kinds because the transporting powers of the sea, migratory birds and ships all help to promote this.

It follows that we might expect to find among coastal plants some of the most widely distributed species in the world; species whose distribution most nearly reflects the absolute climatic limits they can withstand. So, we find for example that *Phragmites communis*, accredited to be perhaps the most widely distributed species in the world (Ridley 1930), is an element of the coastal flora on moderately saline coastal soils. The submerged coastal aquatics *Ruppia maritima* and *Zostera marina*, which occur respectively at the upper and lower limits of estuaries, and the brackish marsh species *Scirpus maritimus*, are among the most widely distributed species in the northern hemisphere. The recent discovery of *Zostera marina* beneath 1 m of winter ice at nearly 65°N in the Bering Sea, Alaska, is a remarkable further extension of the known range of this species (McRoy, 1969).

B

But we must bear in mind the limitations of the species concept when considering widely distributed species spanning major climatic zones. Such widely distributed plants as *Phragmites*, though relatively uniform in appearance and behaviour throughout its range, will undoubtedly be broken down eventually into a complex of closely related forms each adapted to special conditions. For example coastal *Phragmites* of the Red Sea area is known to tolerate a much higher soil salinity than temperate forms of *Phragmites* (Kassas – in litt.).

The absence of large accumulations of blown sand on tropical coasts was noted by Hitchcock (1904). He concluded that in these latitudes the long growing season is especially favourable to vegetation allowing it to colonize closer to high water mark than in more temperate zones. It therefore covers up sites from which sand dunes would normally receive their sand supply. Jennings (1964) has recently reached a similar conclusion from a study of literature on tropical coasts, but adds that the humid climate may also limit the extent to which sand can be blown. Special local conditions may account for exceptions such as the large dune accumulations in south Java. On corraline strands, the angularity of fragments may lock them into a more wind resistant surface (Oosting 1954). It seems likely that, as Van Steenis (1958) claims, genuine dunes tend to be restricted to regions with a seasonal climate in the more temperate parts of the world.

While it is true that salt marshes throughout the world are generally similar in appearance, even a layman would place himself in the tropics if set down in a mangrove marsh. These coastal marsh trees form a very distinctive group of some half a dozen genera whose main distribution falls neatly within the tropic zone. Their absolute limits are at 28°N and 25°S in the New World and 28°N and 38°S in the Old World (MacNae 1968, Good 1966, Clark and Hannon 1967, and Chapman and Ronaldson 1958). Frost damage occurs both at their north limit in Florida (Webber 1895 and Davis 1940) and at their south limit (Chapman 1911) in New Zealand. Their restriction to these limits is thought to be controlled largely by frost incidence.

The mangrove (*Rhizophora mangle*) forms dense growths on mainland and island shores as far north as Ormond (29° 22′N), Florida. It was killed during the 1894–95 winter (minimum temperature Ormond 29 December 1894, −7.7°C) as far south as Lake Worth (26° 40′N), except in cases where plants grew on the south side of large stretches of water. On the west shore of the Florida peninsula at Myers (26° 40′N) mangroves *were* killed on the south shore of the Calosabatchee river estuary (Webber 1895). The points of interest here are the width, over 200 miles (320 km), of the damage belt at the mangrove northern limit, and the pockets of survival related to local topography lying within it. This illustrates the difficulty of applying precision to the concept of a climatic limit although it may be clearly significant for the plant or animal concerned.

The latitudinal temperature gradient in the sea is very gradual because here fluctuations in climate are literally damped down. Work on the distribution of marine Angiosperms in relation to temperature has suggested that the distribution of these plants is likely to be controlled by temperature and the following main world zones have been distinguished on this basis. (Table 1)

Table 1. Marine temperature zones (after Setchell 1920).

Zone	Mean maximum temperature range °C
Upper Boreal	0–10
Lower Boreal	10–15
Temperate	15–20
Subtropical	20–25
Tropical	25–30

Crisp (see Johnson and Smith 1965) observes, 'Our success in relating intertidal population changes to climatic fluctuations may result from the fact that the main factor, temperature, is easily measured. The lack of comparable evidence from land plants may perhaps be due to the intervention of interaction of other factors (such as rainfall, sunlight, day length) which tend to obscure correlations. Are we clear about what limits the distribution of land plants?'

The answer to this is certainly no at the present time, but it does suggest that we may have a better chance of finding limits which are climatically controlled in intertidal salt marsh plants than in dune plants beyond tidal influence.

Assumptions about climatic limits are best tested by transplants to find out potential range. This is a useful preliminary to more critical work in the growth cabinet and field. Success and failure results for world-wide transplants of the salt marsh grass *Spartina anglica* probably give a true indication of the climatic limits of this species (Fig.1). The northern limit of *S. anglica* in the northern hemisphere (57°N), like mangrove, seems to be controlled by frost frequency. Frost killed 99 per cent of transplants in plantations in northern Holland; those in southern Holland were virtually unaffected. The northern limit of the species in the southern hemisphere

(35°S) may be controlled by day length as the plant does not flower under short day conditions (Hubbard 1969). However, Chapman (1964 *in litt.*) has suggested that winter temperatures may be too high at 35°S for normal development and notes that little seed is set at this latitude in New Zealand.

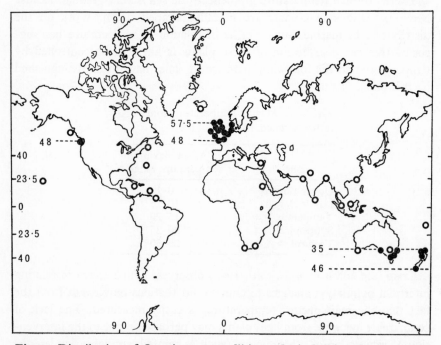

Fig. 1. Distribution of *Spartina townsendii* (*sensu lato*). Solid circles show sites where plants were known to be established in 1965. Open circles show sites where plantings are known to have failed. There are records of many other introductions, but the fate of these is unknown (from Ranwell 1967).

Ammophila arenaria, the principal dune-building grass native to European coasts, has been planted successfully in N. America, South Africa, New Zealand. It thrives from the boreal to subtropical zones (Cooper 1958). No similar study of its world distribution and climatic requirements seems to have been made in spite of its acknowledged success as a foredune builder and aid to coastal protection.

Regional patterns

We are so ignorant of what limits individual species of plants and animals to particular parts of the world that great care must be taken not to make any assumptions about the extent to which climate controls the individual components of regional floras and faunas. Indeed the very constitution of the coastal dune and salt marsh floras (let alone faunas) of many parts of the world are still very incompletely known. This does not only apply to the remoter shores of South America or Asia, but also in surprising measure to shorelines like the Mediterranean close to major centres of civilization.

Chapman (1960) distinguishes nine major regional salt marsh floras adapted to the particular climate conditions where they occur:

Arctic	Chinese, Japanese and Pacific Siberian
North European	South American
Mediterranean	Tropical
Eastern North American	Australia and New Zealand
Western North American	

Within each group are certain characteristic species of relatively wide range which impart some degree of inherent homogeneity to the group as a whole (e.g. *Puccinellia phryganodes* in Arctic salt marshes).

No similar attempt has been made to classify the dune floras of the world. These are much more variable in species composition than salt marshes partly because their distribution tends to be much more discontinuous and less freely linked by any major agent of dispersal like the sea.

Matthews (1937) showed how the British flora could be clumped into recognizable geographical groups. He found that some 600 species out of 1500 native or well naturalized species could be classified in distinctive geographical groups. The rest were generally distributed. Since his analysis was based on the known absolute distribution of the species concerned it seemed reasonable to assume that climatic factors were predominant in determining the flora of these groupings.

In fact an analysis of species reaching coastal limits in the British Isles (based on data from Perring and Walters 1962) shows a background of continuous replacement with evidence of disjunction at certain points clearly related as much to geographical barriers as to climatic zones (Fig. 2). Further analysis of the species reaching limits at points of concentration shows that less than half of them fall into Matthew's groups, the remainder being presumably capable of much wider distribution round the coast and to that extent relatively independent of climatic restraints.

Mörzer-Bruijns and Westhoff (1951) have shown how the Netherlands can be divided into climatic areas using indices based on extremes of climate over the course of a decade. These climatic areas can be correlated with biogeographical regions as determined by the distribution of insects

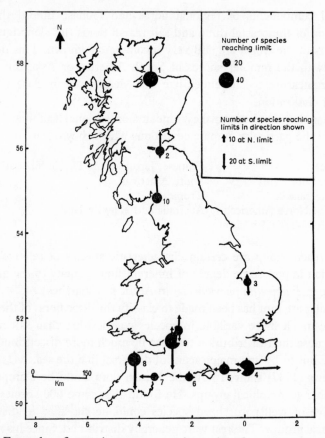

Fig. 2. Examples of some important meeting points for geographical elements of the Coastal flora in Great Britain.

1. Moray Firth
2. Forth of Firth
3. Wash
4. Bridgwater Bay
5. Arun

6. Poole Harbour
7. Exe
8. Taw Torridge
9. Devern
10. Solway Firth

Results are derived from records of all species recorded in coastal 10 Km squares in the Atlas of the British Flora (1962) and show numbers of species reaching north and south limits on east and west coasts, and north, east and west limits on the south coast, for only those squares in which 20 or more species reach such limits. There are two exceptions: (1) Beachy Head to Sussex Ouse, two contiguous squares each with more than 20 species at limits which have been combined to make the map record clearer. (2) Exe estuary with only 16 species at limits, included because other evidence, not considered here, suggests it is an important meeting point of eastern and western elements of the flora (from Ranwell 1968).

and plants. Beeftink (1965) has produced a comprehensive classification of European halophytic higher plant communities related to geographic regions.

Studies of this type help to narrow down the field to specific locations and particular species where intensive study of the biology of the plants or animals concerned in relation to key climatic factors is likely to prove rewarding (Plate 2). They do not in themselves tell us exactly how climatic factors control survival.

Oceanicity

Troll (1963) points out that: 'the greatest modification of the latitudinal zonation of thermal seasons in temperate latitudes is due to the distribution of oceans and continents'. Reduction of annual fluctuation of temperature is a measure of oceanicity. It is achieved by the greater heat storage capacity of water compared with land and the possibilities of convective heat exchange between warm water surface and colder land surface.

Thermophilous species such as *Samolus valerandi* are capable of surviving in inland localities of England and Wales but are restricted to the coast in Scotland (Fig. 3) and in Scandinavia. The more oceanic climate of the north-west coast of the North American continent allows *Spartina anglica* to survive at least 2° of latitude further north than on the north-east coast where the incidence of frost in the more continental climate prevents its survival.

Faegri (1958 and 1960) gives useful discussions of the climatic demands of oceanic plants. He concludes that many oceanic or maritime plants are sensitive to winter frosts, and that summer warmth for the successful ripening of seeds may be an additional limiting factor. The northernmost limit of oceanic species frequently follows winter isotherms closely up to a certain point then crosses them to follow particular summer isotherms. This suggests that a point has been reached where summer temperature has become more critical than that of winter. Rising lower altitude limits towards the south (such as *Dryas octopetala* shows in Britain) suggest that humidity may be critical for certain species. Ratcliffe's (1968) studies of Atlantic bryophytes also stress the importance of humidity and demonstrate interaction with varying soil tolerances. The concept of oceanicity is not a simple one and involves the interaction of at least three important climatic factors (temperature, wind and humidity) together with other environmental restraints.

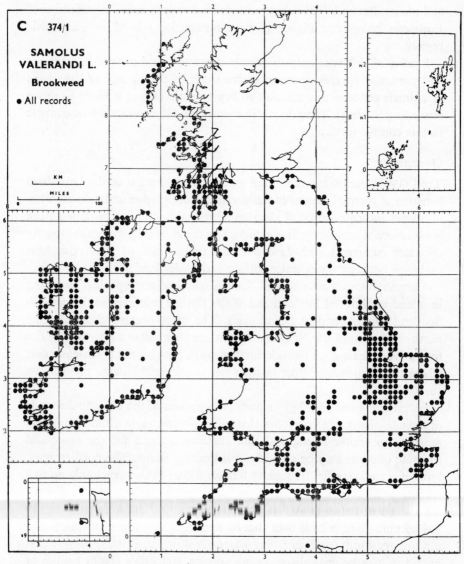

Fig. 3. Distribution of *Samolus valerandi* in the British Isles showing trend to strictly coastal distribution in the northern part of its range (from *Atlas of the British Flora*, F. H. Perring and S. M. Walter, T. Nelson & Sons Ltd., 1962).

Specific Climatic Factors

Local variations

It will be useful at this point to consider the effects of sunlight, temperature, rain and wind on dune and marsh, because they differ profoundly in each habitat. In particular, climatic factors operate much more uniformly over the flat surface of a marsh than over the broken terrain of a dune system. Climatic variability tends to be unidirectional across a marsh surface from seawards to landwards and is a contributory factor to the marked zonation of vegetation apparent in this direction (Fig. 4). Much greater diversity of microclimate is detectable in the different parts of a dune system according to local shelter effects and proximity to the water table (Fig. 5). This is reflected in much more complex mosaic patterns of the vegetation.

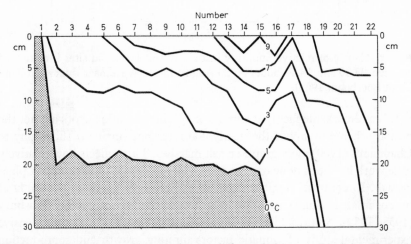

Fig. 4. Soil temperature 0–30 cm deep in different habitats at Liminka, Finland. 18. V. 1968 at 12–14 o'clock. The shaded area is below 0°C. No. 1. *Carex nigra* var. *juncea*, 2. *Phragmites communis*, 3. *arable land*, 4. wood of *Vaccinium – Myrtillus* type (VMT), shaded by spruce, 5. *Juncus gerardii – Odontites litoralis*, 6. *Carex aquatilis*, 7–9. *Carex mackenziei*, 10. *Salix phylicifolia* shrubs, 11. *Juncus gerardii – Primula finmarchica*, 12. *Eleocharis palustris*, 13. *Alnus incana* wood, 14 – 15. *Phragmites communis*, 16. *Eleocharis palustris*, 17. VMT wood (open location), 18. *Triglochin maritimum* (a depression in the Carices distigmaticae zone), 19–20. *Deschampsia caespitosa*, 21. *Betula pubescens* wood, 22. field drainage ditch. All readings correspond to littoral zones, except numbers 3, 4, 17, 19 and 22, which were taken on the epilittoral 5 km from the water boundary (from Siira 1970). N.B. Communities not in zonal sequence.

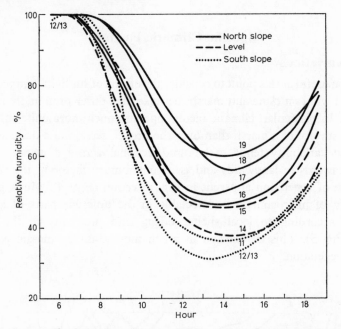

Fig. 5. Course of relative humidity just above soil surface at sites investigated between 05.30 and 18.40 hours on 23 August in the Wassenaar dunes, Holland (from Boerboom 1964).

It is a remarkable fact that climate or specific climatic factors are not the primary theme in any of the nearly 400 references in the bibliography to Chapman's (1960) monograph on salt marshes. This reflects how relatively little work has been done on climatic factors in relation to salt marsh plant growth. In contrast, significant advances have been made in the study of microclimate in dune vegetation by a number of authors, notably Salisbury (1933, 1952), Stoutjesdijke (1961) and Boerboom (1964). Comprehensive experimental study of climatic factors limiting growth and reproduction still remains to be carried out for the majority of the commoner salt marsh and dune species which make up the bulk of the floras of these two habitats.

Stoutjesdijke (1961) discusses thermo-electric measuring techniques suitable for use on dunes and in dune vegetation. He obtained simultaneous measurements of temperature and absolute humidity of the air, wind velocity, radiation intensity and soil temperature in dune grass and scrub vegetation.

Miniaturization at the sensor end and direct linkage to computer analysis at the other would be the best way to reveal the complex micro-meteorological patterns prevailing in salt marsh and sand dune communities.

Light

Cottam and Munro (1954) record that *Zostera marina var. latifolia* survives at the 'almost incredible' depths of 100 ft (30m) on the slopes of La Jolla submarine canyon in the clear waters off southern California. Beneath the relatively turbid waters over mudflats around European shores *Zostera marina* is usually confined to water depths of less than 20 ft (6m). Transplants of *Zostera marina var. angustifolia* made in the upper reaches of Poole Harbour a few years ago died gradually *in situ* at levels normally within the tidal range of this species, apparently for lack of adequate light. Johnson and York (1915) have shown that the anatomical leaf structure of *Zostera* and *Ruppia* is similar to that of shade tolerant plants. Day (1951) notes that in the turbid waters of the Berg estuary, South Africa, *Zostera* (*Z. capensis*) is limited to inter-tidal banks, but in the clear waters of the Knysa estuary it extends at least 3 ft (1m) below low tide mark. He summarizes techniques of measuring turbidity and gives a useful brief discussion of this factor.

Much work has been done to show how salt marsh plant zonation may be correlated with duration of tidal submergence (Chapman 1938, Adams 1963, Hinde 1954), but practically none on the survival of individual species subjected to submergence experimentally. *Spartina anglica* has been shown to survive continuous submergence in clear sea water in greenhouse conditions without apparent harm for $4\frac{1}{2}$ months. This is far beyond the maximum possible duration of submergence it receives in its normal intertidal habitat. Growth chamber studies have demonstrated that this species tillers but does not flower in short days (Hubbard 1969) and flowering may be inhibited by limitations on the supply of light during submergence at its lower limit. Flowering is generally poor at this limit, but this may be due to mechanical damage as well as reduced light.

The effects of reduced light on salt marsh plants is very noticeable beneath the shade of overhanging oaks in estuaries like the Fal, Cornwall or Beaulieu estuary, Hampshire. Here the growth of *Glaux maritima*, *Aster tripolium* or *Triglochin maritima* becomes very straggly and attenuated. It would be interesting to measure light values, morphological responses and the sequence of survival as shade increases in such situations.

Not all salt marsh plants require high light intensities, however, and *Althaea officinalis* appears to thrive best in the half shade of oaks near high water mark on wooded shores of Hampshire and Sussex. Lack of light may limit growth at both ends of the salt marsh. At the seaward end turbidity may be operative, and at the landward end the growth of taller plants shades out shorter plants where the marshes are ungrazed.

Thus in a mixed boundary where *Phragmites* was invading *Spartina anglica* marsh in Poole Harbour, it was found that *Spartina* was first drawn up in the taller growth, then ceased to flower, then lost its ability to tiller, became aetiolated, and finally died out some 25 m landward of the seaward limit of *Phragmites*. Merely cutting the stems of *Phragmites* near the extinction point of *Spartina* in no more than 1 metre square was sufficient to enable *Spartina* to recommence both tillering and flowering again.

It might be assumed that the light requirements of pioneer plants on the open sand of dunes would be high. In fact this is not necessarily so. It is intriguing to find for example that *Carex arenaria*, which we associate with the very high light conditions of open sand, is one of the last species to survive beneath the quite dense shade of mature pines on the dunes at Holkham in Norfolk. Once again no study appears to have been made of the shade-tolerance of dune plants and this would be of particular interest in view of the current trend towards scrub on dunes since 1954 when rabbit populations in Britain were greatly reduced by the virus disease known as myxomatosis.

Temperature

Little information is available about the field temperature controls on the germination, establishment, growth and flowering of salt marsh plants. There must certainly be far lower temperature ranges and smaller rates of fluctuation in lower marshes subject to regular inundation by the sea than in higher marshes free from its influence for days or even weeks at a time. Duff and Teal (1965) provide evidence supporting this in *Spartina alterniflora* marsh. *Cochlearia anglica* grows on both lower and higher shore in the Orne estuary, France. Binet (1965a) shows that on the lower shore seed germination is delayed and growth slowed down in mature in this species compared to germination and growth on the higher shore, but he does not relate these differences to temperature differences. Species like *Halimione portulacoides* and *Agropyron pungens* are often generally abundant in English and Welsh salt marshes, but absent from Scotland north of a line from the Solway to the Forth and in the more northerly parts of Europe. The abrupt disappearance of common species such as these at certain latitudes strongly suggests that their limits are controlled by some climatic factor, but just how and at what stage in the life cycle this happens we do not know. Iverson (1954) records the rapid spread of *Halimione portulacoides* at Skallingen, Denmark between 1931 and 1954 and this may be partly in response to ameliorated climatic conditions. The species was clearly damaged by frost in Holland in 1963. *Limonium vulgare* on the other hand is not particularly frost sensitive (Boorman 1968) and it seems more likely that day length requirements for flowering may be a controlling factor near its northern limit in Scandinavia.

Binet (1965*b*) has shown that seeds of *Cochlearia anglica* germinate best at relatively low temperatures between 5° – 15°C while those of *Plantago maritima* will scarcely germinate at all at these temperatures, but will do so at 25°C, though even better in diurnal alternations of 5°C and 25°C.

It is extremely difficult to get a clear indication of the way in which temperature may limit survival because of its complex interactions with photoperiod and salinity which is itself affected by rainfall. Tsopa (1939), Chapman (1942) and more recently, Binet (1964 *a* and *b*, 1965 *a, b, c, d, e,* and 1966) have made important contributions in this field in relation to germination requirements of salt marsh species, while Seneca (1969) has studied the germination responses of dune grasses. Chapman (1960, p. 315) points out that the germination of seeds of most salt marsh species occurs at times of reduced salinity, that is when low temperatures combine with high rainfall.

Stubbings and Houghton (1964) have shown that the cooling effect in winter and heating effect in summer which takes place in the harbour shallows of Chichester Harbour, Sussex, is of the order of 2°C below or above the open surface water temperature of the Harbour.

In contrast to the ameliorating effect of more or less permanently moist ground on temperature fluctuation in salt marshes, extremely wide and rapid temperature fluctuations are characteristic of the dune habitat. For example at Newborough Warren in Anglesey the temperature of the sand surface rose 14°C between 4.30 and 10.0 a.m. on a clear day in August. Salisbury (1952) notes that temperatures of over 60°C occur at the surface of bare sand on a hot summer day and diurnal fluctuations of 30°C were common. Such fluctuations are much reduced in damp dune slacks compared with dunes. In the generally cooler climate of damp slacks leafing of *Salix repens* may be delayed up to a fortnight after that on nearby dunes. Boerboom (1964) noted the persistence of late frosts in dune slacks in Dutch dunes in June 1957. *Juncus acutus* suffered over 80 per cent mortality in open drier slacks, but less than 50 per cent mortality locally in closed wetter slacks to landward in the 1962–1963 cold winter at Braunton Burrows, Devon (Hewett 1971).

Soil temperature fluctuation is markedly reduced beneath dune scrub, compared with bare sand (Fig. 6). Stoutjesdijk (1961) notes that the heat storage capacity of the soil beneath open sand was able to compensate for the net radiation loss from the surface during the night and there was no dew formation. By contrast, beneath *Hippophaë* scrub the much lower heat storage of the soil was only able to compensate for about one third of the net radiation loss so that the remainder was compensated by heat taken up from the air either as sensible heat or as heat of condensation resulting in strong dew formation on the *Hippophaë* surfaces. Further studies related to dew formation are considered in Chapter 9.

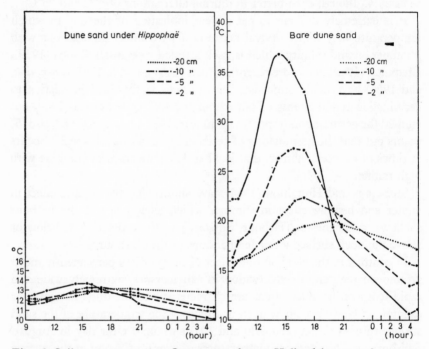

Fig. 6. Soil temperatures on Oostvoorne dunes, Holland between 9 a.m. on 16 June and 5 a.m. on 17 June (from Stoutjesdijke 1961)

The sand dune flora is notable for its high proportion of annual plants. These, unlike those of arable land, tend to pass through the hot summer period as seed and grow during cooler months, some germinating in autumn to grow as winter annuals. Salisbury (1934) has shown that the air close to leaves of annual dune species in April may be around 10°C higher in temperature than that of the general ambient air temperature. This could allow rapid photosynthesis in annuals at a time when low temperature was preventing photosynthesis in other species. Following the earlier work of Salisbury there is renewed interest in the temperature and light controls on the germination and growth of these species at the present time (Bakker *et al*, 1966). The variable topography of dunes produces striking climatic contrasts according to aspect. For example *Tortula ruralis* carpets may differ in temperature as much as 9°C on north and south aspects of Dutch dunes (Boerboom 1946). Such contrasts provide a juxtaposition of almost regionally distinct climatic zones in the form of mosaic units a few metres apart.

Rainfall

There is a very characteristic difference in the appearance of salt marsh vegetation as one goes south from North Europe to the sub-tropics. This is shown by the increasing openness of the vegetation dependent on the degree to which evapo-transpiration exceeds precipitation for substantial periods of time. In general the vegetation of north European marshes forms a more or less continuous sward (except in the pioneer zone), interrupted only by discontinuities in the surface. In the Camargue, France, Bigot (1958) notes that cover in the main salt marsh areas is often less than 80 per cent and some times as low as 50 per cent and here evapo-transpiration exceeds precipitation during much of the summer (Plate 1). On the borders of the Red Sea vegetation cover rarely exceeds 70 per cent and is mostly below 50 per cent, though this is partly due to the incidence of grazing in addition to the desert-type climate (Kassas 1957). In Gambia (in the tropical zone) where the rainy season is confined to June to October, the remaining months are in general hot and very dry and Giglioli and Thornton (1965) note that this results in extensive areas of barren mud within the mangrove swamps. There is marked interaction between seasonal and season to season rainfall and salinity. Indeed it is the incidence and amount of rainfall and not tidal influence which dominates salinity concentrations in upper salt marsh levels (Ranwell *et al* 1964).

Plants of the higher salt marsh are generally tolerant of the highest salinities likely to obtain in the climate of north European coasts. Growth room studies have shown that *Spartina anglica* for example can survive salinities up to twice that of sea water, a value much in excess of any recorded in 162 field samples measured. *Glaux maritima* and *Limonium vulgare* are also known to be tolerant of salinities in excess of sea water. Yet, in periods of summer drought these plants may die back extensively as they did on the northern Irish coast for example in the dry summer of 1968. Little study seems to have been made of the drought tolerance of salt marsh plants and this would be well worth investigation for it might help to explain the successive replacement of species in progressively higher zones of marsh. Boorman (1967) has demonstrated by transplant experiments that drought is a limiting factor of growth for *Limonium vulgare* on sandy soil at the upper levels of a marsh.

As mentioned earlier, species characteristic of the montane element in the British flora such as *Dryas octopetala, Trollius europaeus* and *Saxifraga aizoides* descend to the coast and are able to survive on north and west Scottish dunes. Further south they are confined to montane regions. These plants are characteristic of high rainfall in their mountain habitats and it is probably the more humid climate on the northern dunes which allows them to survive there.

Mosses normally found in dune slacks further south, grow on dunes at Luskentyre in the Outer Hebrides and Gimingham *et al* (1948) suggest this may be correlated with the relatively uniformly rainy climate of the area. Similar moisture-loving mosses occur in *Ammophila* tussocks in north-west Sutherland. In both of these sites the average annual potential water deficit is less than 0·5 ins (13 mm), among the lowest for any coastal site in Great Britain, one of the wettest parts of Europe (Green 1964).

Wind

There is much historical evidence (from the burial of human settlements), of pronounced dune activity on European coasts in Mediaeval times during periods of exceptionally stormy weather, e.g. from Penhale, Cornwall (Steers 1964); South Wales (Higgins, 1933); Newborough, Anglesey (Ranwell, 1959); Forvie, Aberdeenshire (Barkley, 1955), and many other sites on the European coast from the Baltic dunes to those of The Landes in France. Attempts have been made to link exceptional periods of storminess with recurrent astronomical events affecting tidal maxima (Petterssen, 1914; Brooks, 1949) and there does seem to be some evidence in the above of pronounced dune activity at times of major (1700 year cycle) and minor (90 year cycle) tidal maxima. According to Petterssen's hypothesis the last major maximum was in 1433 A.D. and we should be reaching the next minor maximum in the 1970 to 1980 period, when it might be expected that the storminess noted at the end of the nineteenth century may be repeated. Lamb (1970 *a* and *b*) has recently drawn together evidence of climatic periodicity which suggests that cycles of 5, 10, 20, 90, 200 years may also be operative.

The direct effect of wind on plant growth in salt marshes has not been investigated, but it must curtail both height and extent of growth in more exposed sites. There is a noticeable reduction in height of *Phragmites* growth at the windward edge of clones invading *Spartina* marsh in Poole Harbour, Dorset, but this may be partly due to competition for water or nutrients. Lines (1957) has shown how wind exposure may be compared from site to site using tatter flags.

Wind exerts a profound influence on the growth of dune plants, on the redistribution of organic and inorganic nutrients, on the amount of salt received, on the distribution of propagules, and above all shapes the very ground on which they grow. These different influences are discussed in Chapter 8 and subsequently.

Response to Climatic Changes

While it is true as Major (in Shaw 1967) points out that: '. . . ecologists ascribe to climate major importance in differentiating the kinds of vegetation on earth' it is also paradoxically true as he says, '. . . it is difficult even to rank the relative importance of a climatic difference in relation to other site factors.'

The problem becomes less acute perhaps if individual species rather than vegetation types are considered. Especially those species which by their powers of regeneration, superior height or dominating influence in one form or another gain ascendancy and exert such influence as to control to a large extent the type of habitat and even survival of accompanying plants and animals. In fact one searches the literature in vain for critical studies of the performance of such species near the limits of their range. Experimental transplants beyond such limits have scarcely been attempted let alone monitored to see how prevailing climate affects their growth.

Many botanists are reluctant to deliberately move plants outside their existing range. They are keenly aware of the risks of liberating potentially invasive species in a new environment. However the case against introductions is frequently based on the argument that they may interfere with studies on geographical distributions. In fact such studies often reveal only correlations of doubtful significance between range and climatic factors. Properly controlled introductions provide information of real predictive value and are a powerful tool for those who are asked to make a practical contribution to advice on vegetation management.

Lethal and sub-lethal damage.

Wholesale damage to *Spartina anglica* and *Halimione portulacoides* was noted in Holland near the northern limit of range of these species after the cold winter of 1963. But in fact despite this setback *Halimione* has apparently extended its range northwards in Denmark.

The 1963 winter froze *Spartina anglica* marsh soil to a depth of 10 cm

C

(the main rooting level) at the height of the frost, and surface growth was much diminished in the following summer at Poole Harbour, Dorset. There was full recovery in lower *Spartina* marsh in 1964, but near the upper limit of *Spartina* growth species such as *Agropyron pungens* and *Aster tripolium* invaded and persisted, occupying much of the ground formerly covered by *Spartina*. This differential effect of severe frost on plants in optimum, compared with sub-optimum growth conditions, underlines the need to examine climatic effects on the same species in different habitats.

Suaeda fruticosa near the northern limit of its range in Europe at Blakeney Point, Norfolk lost all its leaves after the 1962–1963 cold winter, but some buds on higher twigs survived to put out new growth which however mostly came from the base of plants (White 1967). This illustrates how extremely local even severe climatic effects can be.

Zoologists use the level at which 50 per cent of the population is killed by any particular factor operating over unit time as an indication of lethal dose (L.D. 50). Crisp (1965) for example gives L.D. 50's for low temperature operating for 18 hours for a range of shore organisms many of which were severely affected by 1962–1963 frosts. It would be of great interest to have similar information on low temperature lethal limits for salt marsh and dune plants of predominantly southern distribution in the British Isles. *Festuca arundinacea*, though by no means confined to these habitats, does occur in dune grassland and in upper estuarine brackish marsh grassland. It also shows a marked coastal trend in northern Scotland. Recent work by Robson and Jewiss (1968) demonstrates an inverse relationship between winter growth and winter hardiness in forms of this species. In culture the L.D. 50 for Mediterranean varieties occurs at temperatures of $-13°C$ and for more northerly varieties at $-16°C$. Their work illustrates the further complexity of interaction between climate and genetic adaptation.

Population response to climatic changes

The nature of the limit in relation to a plant population must be considered as the combination of internal and external environmental factors which regularly result in L.D. 50, rather than in reference to any one factor in particular.

As we saw in the case of the Florida mangrove, local pockets of the species may persist in sheltered refuges (perhaps for a century or more), so a frequency value needs to be added to the L.D. 50 to make it meaningful for a climatically controlled limit.

Study of microclimates at refuge limits could characterize climatic tolerances where these are believed to be limiting to growth, reproduction or survival. They would be representative of the effective adaptive limits but not necessarily of the potential adaptive limits of the species as a whole. For example, Sakai (1970) has recently drawn attention to the latent genetic potential of tropical willows to withstand freezing to very low temperatures.

There is little evidence of climatically induced population changes in the British sand dune flora, with a few notable exceptions. Prior to 1930 *Otanthus maritimus* occurred as far north as Anglesey and Suffolk, but now survives only in Cornwall in Great Britain. *Eryngium maritimum*, formerly in the Shetlands, now survives only south of a line from the Hebrides to south Yorkshire, while *Glaucium flavum* appears to have retreated south from its Scottish habitats. The latter is a continental southern species which may require hot dry summers and therefore not be favoured by the increasing trend towards higher rainfall evident up to at least the 1950's, (Lamb in Johnson and Smith, 1965). *Parnassia palustris* on the other hand, a plant of the continental northern flora, has disappeared from several coastal habitats including dune slacks in southern England, possibly in response to the generally warmer winters which have characterized our climate in the first half of the twentieth century.

It is now becoming evident (Lamb 1969) that climatic trends may be quite short-lived and that records over periods as short as a decade may give a better indication of current trends, than longer runs of records. We are only beginning to see how rapidly there may be an adaptive adjustment in species populations where other factors related to establishment and selection operate in favour or against a species. Adaptation to climatic change is clearly a product of inherent variability and where this is low in a rare species, ground lost by the species may not be regained for very long periods of time, even though climatic trends once more favour its growth in the site.

2 Physiography and Hydrology

As the sum of knowledge grows in different disciplines it becomes possible to break down the isolation between them, to see relevant connections and work towards a synthesis which in turn opens up new lines of study and unsuspected possibilities for the practical use of knowledge gained. Understandably in the past both ecological and physiographic studies have tended to concentrate on the immediate influences at work in particular sites, and this has led to a distinctly piecemeal approach to advice on problems of coastal protection or coast land reclamation. For example the benefits in terms of raised shore levels obtained by groyning at one site may be gained at the expense of lowered shorelines in another. Again, a low water training bank to hold a deep water channel for shipping on one side of an estuary may result in silting on the other side of the estuary and loss of beach recreational facilities.

Now there are welcome signs that we are moving towards a synthesis of coastal physiographic knowledge and in this chapter some attempt is made to link up the complex of forces which controls the disposition, type and development of salt marshes and sand dunes on the British coast as a whole. Sources of sediment supply come from erosion of the land surface, the edge of the coast or the sea bed mainly during periods of high wind or high rainfall; deposition occurs mainly in calm weather conditions.

Physiographic Influences

Rock-type influences

Primary geological effects on the distribution of marshes and dunes are particularly evident in a country like Great Britain because its small size and unusually diverse series of rock types bring out striking differences between one part of the coast and another.

There is an obvious natural division for example between highland and lowland Britain. To the north and west of a line from the Tees to the Exe hard rocks predominate in relatively high-lying country. To south and east of this line soft rocks predominate in relatively low-lying country. This is reflected in the predominance of coarse sediment deposits in the north and west which form the building material of dunes. Finer sediments have accumulated to form the extensive marshlands of the south and east and also in the three isolated soft rock outlets on the west coast: the Bristol Channel, the Dee-Mersey area, and the Solway.

Apart from any contributions of sedimentary material brought down by rivers which we shall consider shortly, the erodibility and lime status of coastal rocks partly governs the particle size and particle type of adjoining sedimentary deposits. It is not easy to sort out the various contributions from country rock, glacial material and soil erosion which go to make up marsh and dune sediments and this is a field that would repay much further study. Clues to the origins of sediments can be obtained from heavy mineral analysis, X-ray diffraction and differential thermal analysis of clay minerals (Guilcher and Berthois, 1957), and more recently from electron micrography studies of particle surface textures (e.g. Biederman, 1962; Porter, 1962 and Krinsley and Funnell, 1965). There are one or two sites where direct connections between adjoining rock strata and dune type can be made with some confidence. The Spurn Head dunes, Yorkshire, are clearly influenced in their high lime status by the extensive exposures of chalk on the Yorkshire coast. The lime deficient dunes of Studland, Dorset (an area not subject to glaciation), must owe their relatively recent origin to erosion of the adjoining lime-deficient Bagshot sand deposits of Poole Bay.

Indented cliff coasts of lime-deficient rocks, though not themselves a source of lime, provide innumerable sites for molluscs which derive lime for their shells from the adequate supplies in sea water. Much of the beach material for building dunes on these hard coasts is therefore in the form of broken shell material often comprising more than 50 per cent of the sand, as at Penhale, Cornwall, the dunes of the Outer Hebrides, or the shell sand beaches of the west coast of Scotland.

The legacy of glacial deposits

Superimposed on the rock formations of northern Europe are varying quantities of glacial material of mixed and derived origin. Its deposition occurred rapidly in the form of out-wash fans from the main centres of glaciation as the glaciers themselves began to melt and retreat northwards some 20,000 years ago. These glacial deposits, re-worked by the sea at the time of the last major land and sea level adjustment some 7,000 years ago, probably form the structural basis of many of our present-day marshes and dunes. They also form a bank of material, easily eroded at the coast and in the immediately offshore zones, from which supplies are drawn to help feed accreting coastal systems today. We do not know the size of this bank, nor, what is more important, its capacity to supply withdrawals, but both are clearly limited.

Long term changes in the relationship of land and sea level modify the distribution of salt marshes and sand dunes by exposing or submerging the foreshore deposits from which they are built according to varying amounts of wind or wave action. The pattern of the present configuration of the coast and its adjoining inter-tidal flats was established about 6,000 years ago when sea level is believed to have attained its present level. Since that time there have been only minor oscillations (Fairbridge 1961). Land subsidence or elevation operates more locally and it may increase or reduce the relative sea level rise in any particular part of the coast.

It is not certain whether the sand in Caernarvon Bay is of glacial or pre-glacial origin, but there is evidence (Ranwell 1955) that there has been a steady deepening of the bay during the past 250 years. During that time very considerable quantities of sand have been blown from the shore onto land beyond reach of tides. This clearly must have come from the bay.

Studies in the Danish Waddensea have shown that there is a net input of sedimentary material to the system and the bulk of this is believed to be derived from off-shore deposits of glacial or pre-glacial material. The movement of submarine material can be studied indirectly by means of sea bed drifters (Perkins *et al* 1963), or more directly by the use of radio-active tracers (Perkins and Williams (1965)), but much of this work has been confined to littoral deposits and we are largely ignorant about the extent to which storms can stir up and transport deeper sea bed deposits, and incidentally, potential pollutants dumped off-shore.

Topographic relationships

Coastal sedimentary material derives ultimately from aerial or marine erosion of the land surfaces and forms a discontinuous belt of various thickness and width on either side of the shoreline.

The disposition of material is related to the vertical angles and horizontal distributions of the 'rocks' across and along the shoreline which in turn is governed by the nature of these rocks. These topographical relationships control rates of river and sea-water flow in which loose sediments are carried when it is fast, or deposited when it is slow.

The type of material available for transport or deposition varies according to the texture of the rocks eroded: harder rocks producing coarser-particled material and softer rocks finer-particled material.

It follows that of the two habitats with which we are concerned, sand deposits are characteristic of the inlets and embayments of the hard rock cliffed coast of Northern Scotland; silt deposits of the graded soft coastline of south and east England. Elsewhere the conjunction of both types of rock provides both sand and silt for deposition side by side according to local shelter and the sorting action imposed by differential rates of water flow.

Only at the extreme heads of the most sheltered inlets on the rugged north and west coasts of Scotland (e.g. Kyle of Tongue, Sutherland), can one find vestigial salt marshes on silt. This contrasts with the widespread occurrence of salt marsh in the estuaries of lowland coasts further south and even extending onto the open coasts of Essex shores (e.g. at Dengie and Foulness). These are the two extremes. More commonly estuaries are found with silt in the sheltered upper reaches and sand accumulations in the form of various types of spits and cusps on one or both sides of the estuary mouth.

Before considering the different types of dune and marsh systems we need to consider external hydrological factors operating on them from the larger systems of which they form a part: on the landward side, the catchment area, and to seawards, its effective counterpart, the tidal basin.

Hydrological Influences

Influences from the land catchment

In the past, as we have seen, the bulk of European coastal deposits are believed to have derived from glacial deposits distributed by glacial melt-water erosion of the land surface. At the present time available evidence and deductions from river volume and flow rates, suggests that relatively small amounts of material are derived from the land surface (excluding for the moment the contribution from coastal erosion), and these mainly at times of bank-full river conditions during heavy rain. Nevertheless catchment type, size, vegetative cover and management, together make discernible contributions, particularly to upper estuarine marshes. The catchment influences deserve much fuller study than they have yet received, and a few examples will help to make this clear.

Catchment types with predominantly basic rocks and soils derived from them in the south of England provide nutrients which favour the growth of *Artemisia maritima*, *Carex divisa*, *Inula crithmoides* and many other species absent from salt marsh soils deficient in lime. At Langstone Harbour, Hampshire, chalk bed-rock outcrops in the inter-tidal zone and freshwater springs from it help to keep the chalk surface exposed and free from mud locally. These lime-rich waters, quite brackish at low tide, favour growths of *Zostera angustifolia* and some of the biggest marsh populations of *Inula crithmoides* found in Britain. Permeable sandy marshes and those with only a thin layer of silt overlying permeable deposits or bedrock may be strongly influenced in this way by sub-surface fresh water drained from the catchment.

A relatively high-lying catchment commanding high rainfall such as that of the River Tay in Scotland, which produces a greater discharge than any other in Britain, markedly reduces the estuarine salinity. This allows species such as *Scirpus maritimus* (normally a pioneer of upper estuarine muds), to extend its range as a pioneer to much nearer the estuarine mouth than normal.

A large catchment like that of the Mississippi produces great quantities of silt and characteristic deltaic marshes. Some tendency towards deltaic marsh development is evident in the Thames with its reclaimed marsh islands (Canvey, Grain), lying at the mouth.

Vegetative cover in the form of blanket bog and hard rocks resistant to erosion provide little sediment in the rivers of north and west Scotland. Much more sediment is transported from catchments with a high proportion of agricultural land, notably catchments from the Humber to the Thames. Little quantitative information is available in this country on catchment erosion, but Gottschalk and James (1955) estimate that soil loss from arable land is about 500 times that from grassland. Recent estuarine barrage feasibility studies (Anon 1966 a, b, and c) for freshwater reservoirs provide rough comparative estimates of the river-borne sediment supplies to the Solway and Morecambe Bay. Those to the Solway are sufficiently high to influence decisions in favour of selecting Morecambe Bay as a potential barrage site rather than the Solway.

Currently the enormous increase in the use of fertilizers, herbicides and pesticides in agricultural catchments is also changing the chemical quality of water and silt coming from the land. Westlake (1968) calculates that 500 metric tons per year of nitrate nitrogen at an average concentration of 2 mg/1, and about 20 metric tons per year of phosphate phosphorus at an average concentration of 0·09 mg/1, are currently discharged to the sea by the River Frome, Dorset, a small well-graded river. Relationships with catchment activities on the one hand and contributions of silt and nutrients from these sources to the marshes on the other, have yet to be made. However it is recorded that the amount of nitrogen applied as fertilizer to agricultural land in England and Wales has doubled in the 7 years from 1962 to 1969 (Anon 1970 c).

Tidal basin influences

One way of considering the marine contribution to the hydrology and physiography of marsh and dune systems is to think in terms of the tidal basin. Like the catchment for the land, this is a convenient, though much less discrete unit of the sea. Superimposed on both, of course, are the effects of aerial weather systems and one can foresee that with better understanding it may eventually be possible to relate contributions from land, sea and air in some unit form to the modelling of coastal systems.

As an example of this type of approach, Phillips' (1964) studies on the Yorkshire coast is of outstanding interest. She studied beach features known as 'ords' which develop on the Yorkshire coasts between Flamborough Head and Hornsea. Where protection of Flamborough Head is no longer effective, strong northerly winds directly on shore generate big waves which may initiate upper beach erosion to form an 'ord'. 'Ords' are about 45 to 55 m long and may lower the top beach by as much as 3 m. They travel southwards as units at an average rate of about 1·6 km per year and enable storm waves to erode embryo dunes or coast defence works, whichever is present. Their movement as a unit is only initiated when winds of over 15 knots (7·7 m/s) blow from the northerly quarter for at least several hours. Such winds are usually associated with a deep depression centred over southern Scandinavia. These conditions produce not only powerful waves developed in the long fetch available to the north west, but also a storm surge which causes a temporary oscillatory rise in sea level in the North Sea basin. Under most other wind conditions the beach tends to become built up in form. Once developed, 'ords' and the higher sections of beach between them, move as a unit since, as Phillips points out, the rate of longshore movement on this only slightly curving stretch of coast would tend to be uniform. The importance of this work lies in the link-up and interaction of major environmental systems, the distinctive threshold effect that produces such beach features, and the very short time periods that may be involved in beach re-structuring. Concerning the latter, Groves (in Steers 1960) records that even under relatively calm conditions

en found that the level of a shore feeding a dune system may alter
uch as 0·3 m over the greater part of the profile within as little as
rs. Clearly beach profiles should be sampled in relation to weather
itions rather than at regular time intervals.

Tides are produced in the oceans by the gravitational pull of planetary
bodies, primarily the sun, the moon and the earth. Because these are
moving in relation to each other the gravitational forces change. Constraints
to movement formed by land boundaries result in water basins within
which oscillations are set up and rotated by Coriolis forces about nodal or
amphidromic points, points or areas of no significant tidal rise or fall
(Defant, 1964). Around these points tidal range increases concentrically.
Fig. 7 shows the distribution of tidal basins around British coasts. The
minimum tidal ranges of the Solent area are, as one might expect, close to
an amphidromic point in that region. Maximum tidal ranges on the west
coast in the Bristol Channel region lie towards the outer edge of the much
larger Atlantic Ocean tidal basin.

The vertical range in level of a salt marsh is primarily related to tidal
range and secondarily to turbidity of the water. If the turbidity of the
water is high, this reduces the potential vertical range of growth of salt
marsh plants. In the maximum tide range of 12 m in the Bristol Channel,
salt marsh growth ranges vertically over 4 m; in the small tidal range of
1·8 m in Poole Harbour salt marsh growth is telescoped into a vertical
range of about 1 m. Marshes within a large tidal range tend to be more
steeply sloping and consequently have more clearly zoned vegetation and
sharper drainage systems normal to the shore. Marshes within a small
tidal range have less clearly zoned vegetation and sluggish drainage on the
ebb which produces a more complex network of winding and much-
branched creeks. The Poole Harbour to Chichester Harbour salt marshes
in a minimum tide zone have these distinctive features of complex drainage
patterns and mosaics of indistinctly zoned vegetation. It is true, also that
long established high level marshes tend to flatten near the limit at which
tidal submergence (and therefore silting), becomes insignificant. In such
regions zonation again becomes indistinct and vegetation mosaics are
common.

Water in the tidal basin moves in response to tidal streams and currents
which may have their origin within or outside the basin and, to winds
which generate waves. While the former may transport material in the
vicinity of coasts, it is waves under the influence of wind which predominate
in moving material along the shore or add material to the shore from
supplies immediately off-shore or by erosion of the coastline (Steers, 1964).

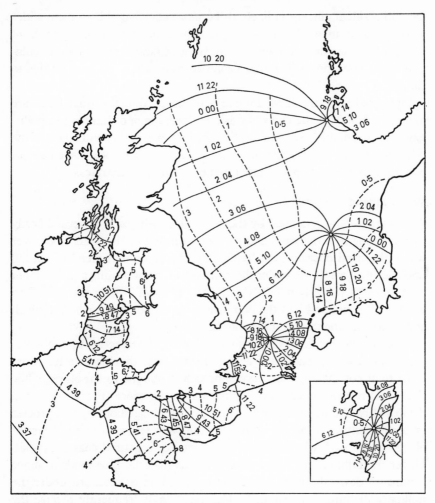

Fig. 7. Co-tidal and range lines for the North Sea tides. (Based on BA chart no 5058 with the sanction of the Controller, H.M. Stationery Office and of the Hydrographer of the Navy, from *Beaches and Coasts*, C. King, Edward Arnold Ltd. 1972.)

Robinson (1966) concluded from marine surveys, observations of current movements and drogue runs, that residual ebb/flood currents were important in determining off-shore bottom topography on the East Anglian coast. In addition to waves, tidal streams also influenced coastal topography. The tidal basin of the southern North Sea gives a decrease of tidal range along the Norfolk coast southwards leading to a tendency for the flood residual to be dominant. South of Yarmouth the situation is reversed and the ebb residual current is likely to be more effective. These inequalities of tidal range affect the tidal streams which have velocities capable of transporting the sea-bed sediment. In this area sand is in constant circulation throughout the shallow water zone down to at least 18 m according to Robinson.

Compared with the land, human activities within the tidal basin are minimal, though in the cases of offshore dredging and dumping of pollutants, not negligible. By contrast, human activities at the land edges of the tidal basin may have profound effects on the longshore movement of beach material as a glance at any groyne system demonstrates.

Wave action

Waves are usually generated by the wind, and their size is governed partly by the strength of the wind and partly by the size of the water body over which the wind operates, the 'fetch', e.g. the Atlantic 'rollers' which fall upon our western shores under the influence of the prevailing and dominant west or south-westerly winds. On the east coast of Britain the prevailing wind is off-shore and it is the dominant winds from the north-east which occur most frequently on these shores.

When a wave breaks upon the shore it has a forward action up the shore, the 'swash', and a backward action downwards, the 'backwash'. More often than not the angle of wave approach is oblique to the shore, while that of its retreat under gravity is normal to the shore (Fig. 8). Material disturbed by the wave is consequently carried along shore by this process of beach drifting. Material carried in this way tends to pile up against objects in its path whether this be a groyne or a natural coastal deposit. Under the influence of north easterly winds material thus tends to move southward down the east coast or on the south coast eastward under the influence of south-westerly drift. Contrary winds frequently reverse the directional flow.

Certain types of waves throw up more material than they comb down off the beach (constructive waves), others remove more material than they supply (destructive waves). The conditions under which these different types of waves occur are not yet fully understood, further discussion of the subject is given in King (1972) and Steers (1964). Certainly storm waves can be of either type, and undoubtedly the shore profile on their approach path (whether well or poorly stocked with material) must influence this. Efficient sampling methods for estimating mean particle size of beach samples, are discussed by Krumbein and Slack (1956). Where the whole sample population is used, careful choice of size grades enables the results

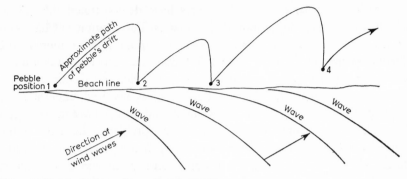

Fig. 8. Beach-drifting (from Steers 1964).

to be plotted on a logarithmic basis and departures from the smooth curve
give clues to the presence and possible origins of unsorted material newly
deposited on the shore.

Kestner (1961) points out that two groups of processes, sorting and
mixing are continually going on in estuaries. Suspended load travel sorts
particle sizes so that fine material is transported up or downstream in tidal
flow and can only settle in fairly still water. Mixing processes include side
erosion, scour and bed movement. From his studies on the Lune estuary,
Lancashire and elsewhere, Kestner distinguishes three types of loose
boundary transport.

Silt (particles below 0·1 mm diameter) forms loose boundary surfaces
which are flat and unrippled. The material has arrived in suspension, is
highly cohesive and resistant to surface scour; it is most likely to be eroded
by some form of side erosion.

Fine sand between 0·1 and 0·2 mm can be very highly mobile and capable
of moving with equal ease either in suspension or along the bed. Changing
current velocities rather than high velocity itself may be responsible for
starting this material into movement. Since more of this material is carried
in the flood than on the ebb tide it may be responsible for rapid upstream
shoaling especially where fresh water flow is reduced.

Medium and coarser sands above 0·2 mm may not be in suspension and
sand banks of this material tend to move along the bed as units.

Kestner (1963) has demonstrated from suspended load sampling in the
Wash that the important material for mudflat and therefore salt marsh
development is a coarse silt or fine sand around 0·64–0·128 mm particle
size. He notes that quite a small addition of finer particles makes it very
cohesive. Clearly these threshold effects are highly relevant to both animal
and plant establishment.

Experiments with radio-active tracers have demonstrated the rate at which silt or sand can be moved in estuaries. For example silt has been shown to move 10 miles (16 km) downstream in a matter of hours in the Thames estuary (Inglis and Allen 1957). Sand may move upstream up to 500 ft (152 m) per tide in the Mersey estuary (Price and Kendrick 1963). The speed of such changes and the distances involved underline the difficulties of investigating these movements and the need to extend studies (and plans for dealing with coastal erosion problems) far beyond the immediate vicinity of the coastal area being investigated. Just as whole catchment studies are necessary to understanding changes in an estuary, so studies based on whole tidal basins are likely to be needed to understand forces moulding estuary mouths and adjoining open coasts.

Habitat Series

The salt marsh series

Both salt marsh and dune physiographic series are best classified in relation to their maritime or terrestrial affinities.

The most maritime of all salt marshes are those which develop on relatively open coast conditions. Those in the lee of small islands offshore from low coasts backed by low hills are bathed in almost full strength sea water since the island fresh water catchment is negligible and drainage from the land catchment minimal. Some of the best examples of these marshes in Europe are found in association with the shingle and dune islands and spits off the north Norfolk coast, e.g. at Scolt Head Island. Marshes attached to the open coastline are developed on relatively coarse-particled sediments, as one might expect in the conditions of relatively strong water flow. They occur where broad expanses of inter-tidal sediments are found e.g. off the North Norfolk coast or on the Danish, German and Dutch Waddom coasts.

Next in the series are estuarine mouth marshes. These usually form in the lee of coastal spits, tend to be more coarse-particled than those further up estuary, and subject to stronger saline influence though less so than the open coast marshes. Estuarine mouth marshes such as those on the Dovey or Burry estuaries in Wales occupy about one fifth of the marsh area in any estuary.

Marshes of the more maritime type are characteristically rich in algae including free-living diminutive forms of *Fucus* species derived from normal forms attached to rocks or stones in the neighbourhood of the marshes.

Embayed marshes themselves form series according to the depth of the embayment and degree of fresh water flushing they receive. Shallowly embayed marshes are often extensive in area and developed on relatively freely-draining sandy silt of relatively high salinity as at Morecambe Bay in Lancashire for example. Marshes at the head of lochs tend to be small in area and subject to much fresh water flushing for silt is in short supply, but land drainage water abundant in the rocky terrain where they occur. Narrow-mouthed deep embayments are more sheltered and allow deposition of finer particles, producing salt marshes with intricate drainage systems on poorly drained clay and silt soils as at Hamford Water, Essex, Poole Harbour, Dorset or Chichester Harbour, Sussex. The salinity of embayed marshes depends on the amount of fresh water inflow. At Hamford Water and Chichester Harbour very little surface-drained fresh water reaches the marshes. At Poole Harbour two sizable rivers enter the upper reaches and reduce marsh salinity.

This brings us to the final group of marshes associated with the mid and upper reaches of estuaries which are progressively more terrestrial in affinity and increasingly influenced by fresh, rather than salt water tidal flooding.

Mid estuary marshes are extensive in area, occupying some three fifths of the total marsh area of an estuary. They are usually developed on silt and much subject to alternate periods of advance or retreat on any mid-estuarine shore under the influence of swings of the low water channel where this has not been trained in a particular direction. Studies on the Wyre-Lune estuary provide evidence that these fluctuations are self maintaining (Kestner and Inglis 1956). The important thing to bear in mind here is the relative impermanence of at least the lower levels of mid-estuarine marshes.

Upper estuarine marshes are the most sheltered of all and develop on clay-silt in regions of reduced salinity.

Any particular marsh may be intermediate in character between the three main types distinguished: spit-associated marshes; embayed marshes; estuarine marshes. So long as the various gradients: exposure; soil particle size; salinity; are kept in mind there should be no difficulty in placing the marsh in the ecosystem of which it forms a part. It is essential to consider the system as a whole when interpreting results obtained from the study of any part of it.

Transitional habitats

Before considering the dune series it is logical at this point to refer briefly to habitats transitonal between salt marshes and dunes, and between either of these two and any other coastal habitats.

The important point to bear in mind is that special conditions obtain in the transition zone dependent on interactions between the two or more coastal habitats represented.

Take the case of the horizontal transition between high level sand flats and high level mudflats. The primary colonist of such regions on European coasts is *Puccinellia maritima* which characteristically forms dome-shaped hummocks under the joint influence of contributions of wind-borne sand and water-borne sand and silt (Plate 3). These transitions usually occur either in sand-floored bays with silt deposits in the more sheltered inlets to landward (e.g. Morecambe Bay, Lancashire or Baie de la Frenaye, Côtes du Nord, France) or near the mouths of estuaries where the mud deposits of upper and mid estuary give way to sand deposits at the estuary mouth (e.g. Burry estuary, Glamorgan or the Dovey estuary, Cardiganshire). In all these cases the resultant marshes are rich in pans whose development is clearly traceable to a primary origin dependent on the formation of *Puccinellia maritima* hummocks, and the associated hollows between them.

The development of vegetation on these transitional tidal flats increases surface roughness, reduces rates of flow of tidal water and encourages deposition of increasing amounts of fine-particled material. Consequently the original sandy flat becomes overlaid with silt and gradually converted to a more uniform level salt marsh. In the early stages when only a thin layer of silt overlies sand the habitat is transitional not only in the horizontal, but also in the vertical plane and certain species (e.g. *Armeria maritima*), favoured by relatively well-aerated marsh soil conditions, are characteristic of this phase. In open bays with limited supplies of silt, marshes of the transitional type may persist through to maturity. In estuaries, gradually increasing silt accretion insulates the marsh from soil surface sand effects (e.g. improved drainage, aeration, and percolation of fresh water from land drainage) and a typical silt or silt and clay marsh flora develops.

Similar horizontal and vertical transitions occur between salt marsh or sand dune and shingle to produce special relationships of drainage and aeration and characteristic floras and faunas. The tendency to fresh water flooding in dune slacks is usually presumptive evidence of an impermeable silt or clay sub-surface below the sand. However, in the case of island dunes on shingle there may be a tidal influence on the water table due to the high permeability of the underlying shingle.

Study of these transitional habitats and the complexities resulting from interaction of different coastal habitat systems is still in its infancy but it is central to an understanding of much of the pattern of diversity which distinguishes minor variants in the salt marsh or sand dune series.

In the case of the sand-silt flat transition one useful line of laboratory investigation would be to study seedling displacement from sand and silt mixtures in relation to rates of water and wind flow. In the field it might be possible to estimate strain forces at work using anchored fibres of different breaking-strain strengths attached to seedlings.

The dune series

Six main physiographic types of dune system are distinguished on the basis of position in relation to the shoreline. Three of these types: offshore islands, spits, and nesses, project seawards from the shoreline and are generally of a prograding nature. They are best collectively described as Frontshore systems and are more characteristic of sheltered shores including those where the prevailing and dominant winds are at least partially in opposition.

The other three types of dune systems distinguished here are bay dunes, hindshore dunes (usually with well developed slacks) and hindshore sand plains, or 'machairs' as they are known in western Scotland where the latter characteristically occur. These last three systems, progressively more terrestrial in position, may be collectively called Hindshore systems though their point of origin is of course on the shoreline itself. Bay dunes may have equally developed frontshore and hindshore components and form an intermediate link between the more maritime frontshore systems and the more terrestrial hindshore systems. The latter are particularly associated with more exposed shorelines where prevailing and dominant winds reinforce each other.

For a dune to form at all there must be some obstacle, natural or artificial around which wind blown sand can accumulate. In the absence of significant amounts of tidal litter or other wind-stilling barriers, but where abundant supplies of sand at the backshore level occur, the backshore flats may become colonized *in situ* and the whole system develops as a rapidly prograding vegetated sand plain with minimal dune formation. Where sections of lower-lying backshore levels become enclosed by higher-lying backshore levels to seawards, primary slacks develop in parallel with the shore line and they often carry elements of the sandy salt marsh facies due to occasional incursions of sea water or a brackish water table. The low-relief vegetated sand plain, Morrich More, Ross is a good example of this rather unusual rapidly prograding Frontshore system.

D

The effect of a solitary obstacle placed on backshore flats just high enough to accommodate the growth of strandline plants is well illustrated at Holkham, Norfolk. Here an abandoned military vehicle left on the backshore is said to have accumulated an isolated dune some 5 or 6 m high in about 20 years.

More usually tidal litter initiates sand accumulation at the top of backshore. This becomes colonized first by annual species and then by perennial grasses capable of growing up through sand accretion to form dunes of varying height according to the level at which sand loss exceeds sand supply.

Dunes up to 100 m high occur in the Coto Doñana, Spain. On British coasts they rarely exceed 30 m though sand may be blown to higher levels over rock outcrops in the hinterland e.g. at Penhale in Cornwall. Dunes with low relief may either occur in more sheltered areas with rapid progradation and stabilization, or in sites so exposed that strong winds never allow growth of high dunes at all e.g. Shetland Island dunes.

Sand or shingle spits built by beach drifting form a foundation on which dunes can accumulate, fan-wise by apposition of new material to seawards, or terminally as the spit lengthens alongshore. Storm conditions may throw material at the exposed tip landwards intermittently so that the linear growth alongshore is interrupted by a series of spur-like recurves. Systems such as these at Scolt Head Island or Blakeney, Norfolk tend to achieve stabilization in the position of formation of main dune ridges. This results in a series of dune zones of increasing age from the distal to the proximal end of a spit, or in the case of nesses, a series of apposition ridges of increasing age from seaward to landward.

This tendency to stabilize *in situ* is dependent on reduced wind strengths found on sheltered coasts and reduced frequency of higher wind strengths in any one particular direction. In other words coasts where the stronger winds tend to cancel out each others effects.

Bay dunes frequently occur as a narrow strip of dunes at the head of the bay with some penetration back onto the land surface. Relatively small bay systems set in cliffed coast are much influenced by fixed shelter factors of the surrounding topography. This greatly modifies the prevailing and dominant wind pattern of the general area so that dune systems only a few miles apart may be controlled by dominant winds from totally different directions. Ritchie and Mather (1969) have calculated the Exposure Index (pattern of wind incidence and direction) for a number of Scottish dune sites (Figs 9 and 10). Melvich Bay and Strathy Bay, both facing north on the north shore of Sutherland and, only 5 km apart, have dominant winds from the south and north west respectively. Sand supply

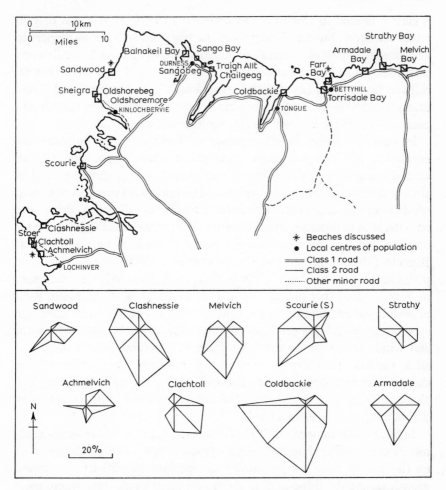

Fig. 9. Location of beaches in Sutherland, Scotland where Ritchie and Mather calculated exposure index as given in Fig. 10. (After Ritchie and Mather 1971)

Fig. 10. Exposure index for a selection of sites in Sutherland, Scotland as given in Fig. 9 (from Ritchie and Mather 1969)

is clearly limited in small bays in cliffed coast such as this, not only in actual resources, but also in supply as the bay headlands act as barriers to longshore transport of material. In large shallow open bays (virtually open coastline), growth of a dune system, may be limited to a single coastal ridge by limited supplies of backshore and high level foreshore sand. Good examples of this type of system are found along the Northumberland coast e.g. Druridge Bay and on the Scottish east coast.

In contrast, where broad expanses of backshore and foreshore are exposed in the inter-tidal zone opportunities exist for the largest of all sand dune systems to develop. In addition to the prograding systems already discussed, such shores orientated so that prevailing and dominant winds reinforce each others influence in an onshore direction, drive sand onto the land to form hindshore systems. The mechanics of vegetated dune building and movement are much in need of study along the lines that Bagnold (1941) has explored for un-vegetated desert dunes, but some preliminary work on this is given in Chapter 8. Here it is only necessary to bear in mind that just as Bagnold showed that sand movement itself profoundly alters the state of the wind, so the dune system itself alters the state of the wind. This produces continuous feedback between dune form and wind regime which expresses itself in differentiation of dune and slack, the basic land form units of all large hindshore dune systems. Note the contrast here between the effects of *fixed* topography as referred to above in small bay systems in cliffed coast and the *plastic* topography within a large dune system itself.

In effect what happens with abundant sand supplies but onshore winds too strong to allow significant progradation is that dune building grasses on the coastal dune are provided with optimum conditions for upward growth raising the dune level to the height limit for the area where more sand is lost than gained at the crest from wind erosion, and at the seaward too, from wave erosion. Thereafter, the mature coastal dune, unable to repair the continuously eroding vertical faces on its seaward side, is eroded back to make way for new embryo dunes to develop on tidal litter cast to the limit of storm tides. Such a dune once set in motion continues inland until it is sufficiently flattened and sheltered to stabilize while a new coast dune builds vertically again. Between the two, erosion persists to the damp sand level where it stops and a slack surface is available for colonization. The ridge structure may be broken up into a series of parabola-shaped mobile dunes. Landsberg (1956) has developed formulae which give good correlation between orientation of the long axis of these parabolas and calculated wind resultant.

Perhaps the most significant distinction between these active hindshore systems and prograding systems stabilized *in situ* is the periodic re-exposure of bare sand at intervals in the mobile part of the system and the tendency to cyclic alternation of dune and slack at any particular point within it. Braunton Burrows, Devon, Newborough Warren, Anglesey and Ainsdale, Lancashire are among the best examples of hindshore systems in Britain. Full stabilization is only achieved when the landwardmost ridges are deflated to an almost flat plain at the dry slack level.

The last system in the dune series is really an extreme example of the hindshore system and has close affinity with its stable stage. Under extreme conditions of exposure on the north west coast of Scotland where the full force of Atlantic gales reach low lying islands, the height limit of dune building is so low that much of the sand from the shore is swept inland to form low lying sandy plains. The universal influence of open range sheep grazing or of cultivation of the lime-rich sandy pastures further limit the possibilities of dune development. Towards the landward side of these sandy plains or 'machairs' lime-rich sand thinly overlies lime-deficient moorland peat providing contrasting conditions for great variety of plant species.

Many salt marshes and sand dune systems are of course intermediate between the types distinguished on the maritime to terrestrial gradient. Familiarity with the series as a whole soon enables intermediate and apparent anomalies to be placed in the general framework described. We begin to see these plastic deposits of the coast moulded into recognizable forms by the four great agents, wind, water, land and living things, operating simultaneously upon them.

3 Mineral Nutrient Relations

The essential nutritional problem for plants that grow on salt marsh or calcareous dune soils is one of adaptation to growth on soils, with elevated levels of certain ionic species. Such adaptation is intimately concerned with osmotic effects. These partly control ionic concentrations either side of cell membranes and also the capacity of plants to function in the presence of elevated ionic levels, particularly of sodium. Although these adaptations can be studied at a variety of organizational levels; within the cell, within the whole plant, or within the community, they must be related to the capacity of a plant to survive, grow and reproduce in the habitat where selection operates at all levels in the life cycle; on individuals, populations and at the species level.

While elevated levels of sodium ions are the main problem for salt marsh plant growth, there is increasing evidence that high levels of calcium ions in addition exert profound effects on the tolerance of certain species to sodium and on the actual species composition of the salt marsh flora.

The sodium ion problem is only critical for a small but important element of the dune flora near the coast where significantly most of the species confined to the dune habitat occur. Elsewhere in the dune system the main nutritional problems for dune plants are either, growth in elevated levels of calcium ions or, the more widespread problem of general mineral deficiency.

The presence of high ionic levels makes it essential to discuss a number of soil physical parameters related to soil evolution, development, and structure since they have big effects on availability of ions for plants. It must be remembered also that ionic exchange is not confined to the soil and root boundary, but also to the leaf and water, or leaf and air boundaries. For example ionic exchange in *Zostera* occurs primarily through the leaf cuticle and salt may be exuded through leaf glands as in *Spartina* in addition to exchange through cuticle and stomata. Consideration of osmotic effects follows logically discussion of soil physical parameters. This in turn sets the scene for discussion of chemical parameters associated with nutrient uptake, salt tolerance mechanisms and ionic balance. This chapter concludes with a brief account of nutrient levels and availability in the two habitats. Nutrient supply and nutrient cycling at the community level are mentioned in passing but considered in more detail in appropriate places in the sections dealing with salt marshes and sand dunes separately.

Physical Constraints on the Chemical System

Effects of particle size composition

Kelley (1951) notes that the amount of growth of plants is much more seriously affected by exchangeable sodium in the soil than by equal amount in true solution. The yield of beans (*Phaseolus vulgaris*) for example has been shown to be much reduced by quite low levels of exchangeable sodium in the soil, but is maintained in the presence of soluble sodium at much higher concentrations (Bernstein and Pearson 1956). Now Lopez-Gonzales and Jenny (1959) have demonstrated with the aid of cation-exchange resin discs in contact and apart, that contact exchange of ions occurs much more rapidly than that by mass transfer of ions through the solution when discs were separated. As Heimann (1958) points out this suggests an explanation for the different effects of sodium in soil and solution on plant growth. In soil it seems likely that contact exchange mechanisms may operate additionally to mass flow under the influence of transpiration or diffusion mechanisms. If so, then ionic readjustments of equilibrium disturbed at the root surface by selective uptake may well be more rapidly compensated by the common pool of ions where solution mechanisms are at work than where less readily compensated contact exchange mechanisms are in operation. The ecologist might advance knowledge in this field by comparing the salinity tolerance of clonal material of different species in mud, sand and culture solution. It is clear that we should beware of concluding that tolerances in culture are immediately relevant to field conditions. Equally, in reporting field tolerances it is evidently important to specify the clay and organic matter content of the soil. The lengthy procedures associated with mechanical analysis have been a barrier to this, but water holding capacity of the soil can be quite rapidly measured and Glopper (1964) has shown this is closely correlated with the clay and organic matter content.

It is relevant at this point to recall the early experiments of Joseph and Oakley (1929) on the structural improvements to soil with impeded drainage produced by charging their exchange complexes with calcium or potassium ions. With either, this results in at least a halving of the water retaining capacity and a capillary rise of water increased by at least a factor of 40 compared with sodium-charged exchange complexes. These effects may not be important in lower salt marshes subject to regular inundation by sea-water, but they are likely to be important in improving both the nutrient environment and the amelioration of salinity at higher marsh levels.

Soil macrostructure

Salt marsh and sand dune soils form an extreme contrast so far as texture is concerned. Improvements in texture (and nutrient availability) in the salt marsh soil depend on factors *increasing* pore space; in contrast in sand dune soil factors *decreasing* pore space are instrumental in improving texture and nutrient availability.

Reduced incidence of flooding in higher marsh levels does not automatically improve texture as dried out sodium clays are mechanically difficult for roots to penetrate. Cracking of the surface helps, but only in a very localized way. Far more important are the biological effects of roots and the larger soil animals in opening up cavities. Green and Askew (1965) have investigated the activities of roots, ants, and earthworms in reclaimed marsh soils at Romney Marsh, Sussex, using infiltration techniques. They attribute the high fertility of these soils to improvements in drainage caused in this way.

Olson (1958 *a*) notes the improvements of exchange capacity with buildup of the clay fraction in an inland dune system and incidentally notes the value of dune soils for studies on dust fall and weathering.

Dust exchange characteristics of salt marsh and sand dune soils

In young salt marsh muds there may be very little organic matter (less than 5 per cent) and the bulk of adsorbed ions will be associated with the clay mineral lattices which would be fully saturated with ions, presumably mainly sodium ions. The cation exchange capacity of different clay minerals varies considerably. For kaolinite it is approximately 3 to 15 mE; for illite and chlorite 10 to 40 mE; for montmorillonite 80 to 150 mE. (Grim 1953). Equivalence (E) is defined here as 1 mole of electronic charge (i.e. 96 487 coulombs) on the clay lattice complex. There have been very few analyses of the clay mineral composition of salt marsh muds, but Guilcher and

Berthois (1957) investigating the possible origin of salt marsh muds in Brittany showed that illite was the dominant clay mineral in that area. Unpublished work by Stebbings and Ball indicated that in muds at Poole Harbour, Dorset, and Bridgwater Bay, Somerset, illite and chlorite were dominant while in the upper reaches of the Fal estuary, Cornwall, the fine clay fraction was practically pure kaolinite. Now it is interesting that on the Fal estuary, *Scirpus maritimus* exhibits much poorer growth and flowering than in Bridgwater Bay, and Poole Harbour. At Bridgwater Bay it is true that the exceptionally strong growths there are also no doubt influenced by greatly increased nutrient supply and abundant calcium both of which may be limiting factors in the other two environments. However, the point to be made is that salt marsh muds do differ by as much as a factor of 10 in cation exchange capacity and this may well be partly responsible for differences in productivity.

Nutrient-deficient muds like those of the Fal estuary, could profitably be used as an experimental medium for studies on the effects of adding nutrients in relation to salt marsh plant growth. It would also be interesting to know the total cation exchange capacity of these muds in relation to the amount of organic matter as this might shed light on that part of the exchange capacity dependent on organic matter.

Sand dune soils with free carbonate are invariably base-saturated, but the total cation exchange capacity is itself low due to the very low clay and organic matter contents of the soil. In dune soils it is of the order of 10–15 mE. per 100 g and in dune slacks from 15–30 mE. per 100 g (Ranwell 1959). In dune sands devoid of free carbonate, either initially or through leaching, the exchange complexes are frequently partly unsaturated and this may occur even where the soil reaction is neutral (Table 2). We can see these figures in perspective against Renger's (1965) observations derived from over 1,500 soil samples estimating the mE. per 100 g of: organic matter (168 to 249); clay (38 to 51); silt (2 to 22) and sand (0·7 to 6·5).

Ecologists can make a useful contribution by studying field sites where a particular environmental factor is likely to exert an extreme influence. So far as nutrient deficiencies are concerned, the kaolin muds of the Fal estuary, Cornwall and the base deficient dunes of Winterton, Norfolk or Studland, Dorset are therefore recommended for study.

Osmotic Effects

Plant cells must maintain internal osmotic potential lower than the external osmotic potential or they lose water. The osmotic effect only becomes

Table 2. Base status of stable dune and slack soils at Newborough Warren, Anglesey beneath *Salix repens* associes. Equivalence (E) is defined as 1 mole of electronic charge (i.e. 96,487 coulombs) on the soil/organic complex (from Ranwell 1959).

Sample site	Sample depth (cm)	Exch. bases in mE/100 g oven-dry soil	Exch. H_2 in mE/100 g oven-dry soil	Total cation exch. cap. in mE/100 g oven-dry soil	% Base saturation	CaO as % of total exch. bases	CO_3 as % of weight of oven-dry soil	pH value Water	pH value KCl	Water table (free) depth (cm)
Fixed dune	8	12·02	0	12·02	100	79·07	0·03	7·8	7·3	>200
Salicetum	30	19·09	0	19·09	100	60·82	0·23	8·8	8·2	104
Fixed dry slack	8	2·76	0·61	3·37	81·9	67·11	0	5·3	5·0	72
turf	30	7·10	0·08	7·18	98·9	89·04	0	7·1	7·2	84
Fixed dry slack	8	1·85	4·38	6·23	45·7	61·58	0	4·4	4·1	
Salicetum	30	17·78	0·76	18·54	95·9	7·71	0	4·9	4·7	
Fixed wet slack	8	18·84	0	18·84	100	63·16	0·22	7·2	7·1	64
Salicetum	30	27·36	0	27·36	100	39·66	0·77	7·3	8·1	
Fixed wet-dry	8 (i)	17·09	2·46	19·55	87·4	86·22	0	6·1	6·3	
slack Salicetum	(ii)	18·58		18·58	86·8	89·76				
(+ *Calluna*)	30 (i)	27·54	0	27·54	100	48·51	0·61	7·5	8·0	79
	(ii)	32·75		32·75	100	59·91				

serious for non-halophytes at high external concentrations of salt in the order of 0·05 M (e.g. one tenth sea water strength) or more, corresponding to osmotic potentials around two bars (Epstein 1969). It is of interest that concentrations of salt of this order occur in the water flooding the seaward limit of tidal woodland in Europe marking a major change in the flora from few halophytes to many non-halophytes (see Stebbings 1971). Obligate halophytes subject to salinities at full strength sea water need to develop osmotic pressures greater than 20 bars to survive. Arnold's (1955) results (Table 3) show in fact that they do. The two exceptions (*Glaux maritima* and *Scirpus maritimus*) are facultative halophytes and persist for centuries in effectively non-saline habitats e.g. in dune slacks or old reclaimed marshland.

Table 3. Osmotic pressures of cell-sap of various halophytes and proportion due to chloride ion. One atm. is equal to $101325 \ Nm^{-2}$ (from Arnold 1955).

Species	No. of determinations	O.P. sap (atm.)	Proportion O.P. sap due to Cl⁻ (atm.)	Cl⁻ as per cent O.P. sap
Atriplex patula var. *hastata*	6	31·6	13·3	42
Suaeda fruticosa	15	35·2	15·3	43
Glaux maritima	2	14·6	7·4	51
Distichlis spicata	10	29·3	15·1	52
Juncus gerardi	3	27·8	15·5	56
Iva frutescens var. *oraria*	4	23·9	13·8	58
Suaeda nigra	2	41·1	24·7	60
Spartina glabra	4	27·0	16·9	62
Triglochin maritima	10	24·6	16·1	66
Scirpus maritimus	2	14·7	10·4	71
Salicornia rubra	11	44·3	31·5	71
Limonium carolinianum	4	29·2	21·4	73
Spartina patens	4	20·9	15·7	75
Salicornia ambigua	6	42·5	34·1	80
Salicornia stricta (*herbacea*)	10	39·7	35·9	91
Salicornia mucronata	3	34·0	31·5	93
	Av.	32·6	21·1	65 ± 11·2

There are four main effects of high external osmotic potential according to Slatyer (1967).

(1) It depresses growth and therefore yield of either the whole plant or parts of it and this effect occurs even with halophytes.

(2) It may depress transpiration initially, but not to the extent that growth is depressed. The extent to which this occurs depends in part on stomatal behaviour.

(3) It may have similar effects to low soil water content and reduce water availability.

(4) It induces excess ion accumulation in tissues which may combine with reduced uptake of essential mineral elements.

In the past workers have tended to give undue weight to the effect of osmotic pressure of the soil solution and pay little attention to the effect of soil matric pressure. The soil water potential (soil water stress) is now recognized to be a combination of these forces. However, the osmotic relations within the plant are modified by uptake of soil solutes and entry of excess salts. Therefore the effects of osmotic pressure of the soil solution and those of the soil matric pressure do not have equivalent effects on the internal osmotic relations of the plant tissue.

Experimental studies suggest that some reduction of metabolic function may be attributable to direct osmotic effects on internal water deficits, but this does not appear to be as pronounced as that caused by a similar reduction in substratum water potential caused by a reduction in soil water content. However these are short term responses to imposed salinity. The main long term effects of salinity are associated with ion accumulation (and therefore mineral uptake disturbance or toxic ion effects) in the plant rather than with reduced water availability in the substratum, as earlier workers tended to assume.

It follows that tolerance to elevated ionic levels therefore requires a high degree of selectivity in ion uptake. Excess accumulation of electrolytes in plant cells, particularly of sodium or chloride ions, is likely to result in progressive changes in protein hydration and conformation and enhancement or depression of enzyme activity resulting in gradual dislocation of metabolism.

Less tolerant species with less efficient discriminatory mechanisms may expend more respiratory energy, resulting in reduction of net assimilation rate and growth suppression, than more tolerant species with more efficient discriminatory mechanisms.

There is faster recovery from soil water stress than from salinity stress not only because of the more serious metabolic disturbances induced by the latter, but also as a result of the time required for excess ion accumulation within the plant to be diluted by new growth.

Mannitol has a large organic molecule which enters the cells of higher plants extremely slowly. A solution of mannitol can therefore be used to simulate osmotic effects similar to those produced by a solution of electrolytes, but without an immediate direct chemical effect on cell physiology.

However, mannitol is slowly metabolized and this must be kept in mind in the interpretation of experimental results. Parham (1970) has used solutions of mannitol to separate osmotic and ionic effects of saline solutions on the germination of halophyte seeds and this seems a very promising application of the technique. His results indicated that germination of *Plantago coronopus*, *P. lanceolata* and *P. major* seeds was inhibited by high ionic concentrations rather than high osmotic pressures. Germination of the halophytes *Plantago maritima* and *Triglochin maritima* and the non-halophyte *Triglochin palustris* occurred in high ionic concentrations, but was apparently inhibited by osmotic effects at salinities equivalent to a 70 per cent solution of sea water. However, it was shown that continued growth of the halophyte seedlings was better in solutions of sodium chloride than mannitol, while the reverse was found with the non-halophyte *Triglochin palustris*.

Chemical Problems of Nutrition in Elevated Ionic Environments

Nutrients essential for the growth of plants

At least 16 elements are required for the growth of all higher plants. They include: hydrogen, oxygen, carbon, potassium, calcium, magnesium, nitrogen, phosphorus, sulphur, iron, manganese, zinc, copper, chlorine, boron and molybdenum.

Cobalt is required for symbiotic nitrogen fixation in root nodules of legumes (Bollard and Butler 1966), and also for nitrogen fixation in blue-green algae. Diatoms have a specific requirement for silicon and there is evidence that the presence of silicon increases resistance to blast fungus disease in rice (Okuda and Takahashi 1965).

This is not the place to consider specific roles of mineral nutrients and Evans and Sorger (1966) have produced an excellent review of this subject. However, it is of some interest to see how concentrations of physiologically important elements are distributed in marine organisms compared with their distribution in sea water and Kalle's (1958) results for this are given in Table 4.

Other elements may be accumulated by sand dune or salt marsh plants without having any obvious nutritional role. For example *Lycium* species which occur on dunes and in other coastal habitats though not confined to the coast, accumulate especially high levels of lithium even when lithium is not abundant in the soil and the levels remain high throughout the growth period (Bollard and Butler 1966).

Table 4. Distribution of physiologically important elements in sea water organisms (from Kalle 1958).

Plastic Elements	Content of 100 g organism (dry) N	Content of 1 ml sea water 35% S, A	Ratio A/N
Hydrogen	7 g	10·75 kg	
Sodium	3 g	390 g	3,600
Potassium	1 g		390
Magnesium	0·4 g	1·3 kg	3,300
Calcium	0·5 g	416 g	830
Carbon	30 g	28 g	1
Silicon a	0·5 g	500 mg	1
Silicon b	10 g	500 mg	0·05
Nitrogen	5 g	300 mg	0·06
Phosphorus	0·6 g	30 mg	0·05
Oxygen as O_2 and CO_2	47 g	90 g	2
Sulphur	1 g	900 g	900
Chlorine	4 g	19·3 kg	4,800

Catalytic elements	Content of 100 g organisms (dry) N	Content of 1 ml sea water 35% S, A	Ratio A/N
Copper	5 mg	10 mg	2
Zinc	20 mg	5 mg	4
Boron	2 mg	5 g	2,500
Vanadium	3 mg	0·3 mg	0·1
Arsenic	0·1 mg	15 mg	150
Manganese	2 mg	5 mg	2·5
Fluorine	1 mg	1·4 g	1,400
Bromine	2·5 g	66 g	26,000
Iron a	1 g	50 mg	0·05
Iron b	40 mg	50 mg	1·3
Cobalt	0·05 mg	0·1 mg	2
Aluminium	1 mg	120 mg	120
Titanium	100 mg		
Radium	$4 \cdot 10^{-12}$ g	10^{-10} g	25

Iodine has been shown to be incorporated in amino acids in *Salicornia perennis* and *Aster tripolium* (Fowden 1959) and it is well known that iodine often accumulates in marine algae, but it is not known to be essential for growth. The mangrove *Rhizophora harrisonii* accumulates aluminium and up to 10 per cent of the aluminium in the mud is in the form of a complex with organic matter beneath stands of this species.

Certain halophytes have been shown to have a specific requirement for sodium. *Atriplex vesicaria* grown in the absence of sodium in water culture showed severe growth retardation and chlorosis but recovered when sodium was added to the culture solution (Brownell 1965). *Salicornia perennis* and *Suaeda maritima* grow larger with sodium well in excess of amounts needed by non-halophytes (Pigott in Rorison 1969). These effects seem to be characteristic of mature plants for, as mentioned in Chapter 1, in general halophytes germinate more freely in lower than in high salinities.

Salt tolerance mechanisms

The study of nutrition in coastal plants is still in its infancy. Much more work has been done on the nutrition of crop plants grown with the aid of irrigation in the very extensive salinized soils of central continental areas. A vast literature on this subject exists and perhaps because of this, the problem of salinity in relation to coastal plants tends to be given undue prominence at the expense of other nutritional aspects equally vital to their growth.

Much of the work on crop plants is not directly relevant to halophytes, because the crop species have only a marginal as opposed to full salinity tolerance. Much of the crop plant work also rests on short period studies and does not shed light on the adaptive phenomena associated with halophytism. Of far greater relevance is work associated with extreme forms of salt tolerance.

There are certain bacteria (*Halobacteria*) which cannot survive in sodium chloride concentrations *less than* 2 M and show optimum growth at the extremely high concentration of 4·3 M sodium chloride. They have been the subject of intensive study and it is of particular interest that even these highly specialized organisms are believed to have metabolic pathways not basically different from those in non-halophilic bacteria (Larsen 1967). It follows that we would not expect to find the basic metabolism of salt marsh plants very different from that of plants in non-saline environments and this seems to be so. But it is remarkable the number of ways in which halophytes have become adapted to high salinity environments. Since they shed light on the central problem of nutrition, the maintenance of balanced ionic environment in the plant cell in the face of temporary or permanent imbalance with relation to the external medium, they are worth considering in more detail. Without this background, the ecologist cannot fully appreciate for example the significance of measurements of salinity tolerance in relation to soil physical and chemical structure, or narrow down his selection of field situations for experimental study to sites where nutritional factors are paramount for the survival of particular species.

There are at least four ways in which halophytes have become adapted to enable normal metabolic functioning in high sodium environments: ion selection; ion extrusion; ion accumulation and ion dilution. Many halophytes exhibit more than one of these adaptations simultaneously and the relative importance of each in any particular species may vary according to the stage of growth and environmental conditions.

As we have seen, the extreme form of adaptation in which organisms can only function in the presence of abnormally high sodium levels occurs in the *Halobacteria* and marine algae, both of which are capable of a high degree of selective ion absorption (of potassium for example) in the presence of high sodium concentrations in the external medium.

Recently Parham (1970) has shown that in this respect certain flowering plant halophytes exhibit such marine algal-type properties. Maximum uptake of potassium into the roots of *Triglochin maritima* was shown to occur only when the concentration of both sodium and potassium in the external solution was high and moreover this uptake was shown to be metabolically mediated. This species, like *Salicornia* and *Suaeda maritima*, is therefore in the true sense an obligate halophyte.

Many species such as *Avicennia* and *Spartina* have long been known to practise ion extrusion via special salt glands on the shoots and there is evidence of sodium ion 'out pumps' in submerged halophytes and algae (Dollard and Butler 1966).

Ion accumulation in parts of the plant where concentrations may be stored away from active metabolic sites is probably a feature of most halophytes. For example *Agropyron elongatum* accumulates chlorides in the roots which, as in most grasses, are shed annually together with accumulated ions. Similarly it is commonly observed that in periods of drought on high marsh levels the leaves of *Limonium* die off prematurely shedding accumulated ions as they do so.

The development of succulence is another feature common to many halophytes (e.g. *Aster*) and this has the effect of increasing ion dilution by increasing the volume to surface area ratio of the plant.

Ionic balance

Gutnecht and Dainty (1968) suggest that the evolution of a sodium 'out-pump' may have developed in the earliest living systems in response to the need to control osmosis and that subsequently, with the development of a mechanically resistant cell wall, the sodium pump remained primarily for nutritional purposes. With elegant reasoning they go on to postulate that since extrusion of sodium ions results in high intracellular concentrations of potassium ions this would lead to enzyme adaptation to a high potassium ion environment and evolution of the inward potassium ion pumps. Sodium may also stimulate the growth of many organisms under conditions where potassium is deficient (Evans and Sorger 1966).

Several recent authors have drawn attention to the importance of calcium in enabling plants to grow in saline conditions (e.g. *Avicennia* (Macnae 1966) and *Agropyron* species (Elzam and Epstein 1969)). The sodium concentrations in leaves of *Phaseolus* fell by a factor of 16 over a range of calcium sulphate from 1×10^{-4}M to 3×10^{-3}M in 5×10^{-2}M sodium chloride solutions indicating a massive breakthrough of sodium to leaves in calcium sulphate concentrations below 3×10^{-3}M (i.e. 0·01 per cent calcium). It is suggested that calcium is essential for the maintenance of the integrity of selective ion transport mechanisms (especially selective absorption of potassium in the presence of sodium) at the surface of the absorbing cells of the roots where the entry of ions into the roots is governed.

Ionic balance and hydrogen ion concentration

In salt marsh soils the ionic balance is dominated by sodium. In dune soils landward of significant sea spray influence, the concentration of cations in solution is determined, either by a dominant calcium inflow (from shell fragments) or (in calcium-deficient sands), by the concentrations of nitrate, sulphate and bicarbonate anions resulting from (in part) microbial activity (Black 1968). The salt spray effect imposes a very localised nutritional regime at the dune coast well illustrated by the results of Gorham (1958), Willis *et al* (1959) and Sloet van Oldruitenborgh (1969) in respect of sodium, magnesium, and chloride (Tables 5 and 6). Its effects on the dune flora are masked by the severe limitations on the number of species that can occur because of high soil mobility. The nutritional effect of salt spray is much more readily appreciated on low coastal cliffs on acid soil where heath is replaced by a narrow band of grassland in the spray-dominated zone (e.g. in low offshore islands like the Isles of Scilly).

The salt effect is negligible in dune soils further inland from the coast.

E

Table 5. Soluble materials in fine sands from Blakeney Point, Norfolk. Equivalence (E) is defined as 1 mole of electronic charge (i.e. 96,487 coulombs) (From Gorham 1958 a).

	1 Embryo dunes	2 Sand hills (Ammophila)	3 Face of main ridge (Ammophila)	4 Laboratory dunes (Ammophila-Festuca)	5 (Carex arenaria)	6 Long Hills (Ammophila-Festuca)	7 The Hood (Ammophila-Carex arenaria)	8 Lifeboat House well 1957	9 1955 (analysed 1957)
pH (original)	8.2	8.1	7.9	6.2	5.7	6.1	5.7	7.9	8.6
(aerated)	7.9	7.9	7.8	7.7	7.0	7.6	7.1	8.6	8.7
Specific conductivity (micromhos at 20°C)	110	53	54	45	28	51	50	551	656
Sum of cations	1.18	0.60	0.61	0.52	0.29	0.57	0.52	6.57	7.73
Sodium	0.46	0.08	0.08	0.04	0.04	0.07	0.15	3.65	4.94
Potassium	0.05	0.03	0.04	0.04	0.04	0.07	0.11	0.20	0.24
Calcium	0.49	0.42	0.43	0.21	0.08	0.23	0.08	1.53	1.30
Magnesium	0.06	0.07	0.05	0.15	0.07	0.09	0.08	1.18	1.25
Ammonium	0.006	0.004	0.008	0.08	0.06	0.11	0.10	0.009	nil
Bicarbonate	0.49	0.47	0.47	0.35	0.12	0.29	0.15	3.56	3.95
Chloride	0.42	0.05	0.06	0.01	0.02	0.04	0.08	2.16	2.91
Sulphate	0.21	0.07	0.06	0.07	0.08	0.12	0.17	0.80	0.87
Phosphate	0.004	0.004	0.006	0.05	0.05	0.11	0.11	0.004	<0.001
Nitrate	0.011	0.005	0.004	0.001	<0.001	<0.001	<0.001	0.019	0.009
Silica (p.p.m. SiO_2)	5	1.6	1.5	1.0	1.0	1.1	1.0	8.1	8.1
Optical density (log $\frac{I_0}{I}$ at 320 mμ, 10 cm cells)	0.6	0.5	0.6	2.0	2.4	2.7	3.9	0.5	0.5
Na/Cl ratio	1.1	1.6	1.3	4.0	2.0	1.8	1.9	1.7	1.7
Mg/Cl ratio	0.1	1.4	0.8	15.0	3.5	2.3	1.0	0.6	0.4
Ca/HCO2 ratio	1.0	0.9	0.9	0.6	0.7	0.8	0.5	0.4	0.3
*CaCO3 (% dry wt. of soil)		0.28–0.61		nil–0.64		nil–0.05	nil–0.05		
*Ignition loss (% dry wt. of soil, corrected for carbonates)		0.2–0.5		0.3–0.9		0.6–2.7	0.6–6.3		

(The rows from "Sum of cations" to "Nitrate" are expressed in mE/200 g dry sand.)

*Soil data from Salisbury (1922).

Table 6. Chemical analyses of the soils from different types of vegetation at Braunton Burrows, Devon (from Willis *et al* 1959)

The results are expressed per gm dry weight of soil.

		Dry dunes							Slacks and hollows						
		Ammophila fore dunes	Pure Ammophiletum (main dunes)	Mixed Ammophiletum	Dry dune pasture	Stable pasture with lichens	Pteridietum	Dune scrub	Slack near sea	*Plantago-Leontodon* community	*Festuca-Agrostis* pasture	*Festuca-Carex flacca* pasture	Caricetum nigrae	Salicetum repentis	Salicetum atrocinereae
pH		9·05	9·06	8·79	8·70	8·66	8·60	8·18	8·99	8·73	8·42	8·22	8·12	8·11	8·06
Organic Carbon	mg	0·52	0·19	0·94	0·74	2·44	4·47	12·60	0·41	1·39	5·82	9·23	22·93	13·55	19·47
Total Nitrogen	mg	0·18	0·11	0·20	0·23	0·41	0·67	2·15	0·15	0·26	0·81	1·36	2·38	1·38	2·82
Calcium	mg	70·4	69·5	62·3	57·3	60·6	49·2	33·9	64·4	66·1	49·1	62·0	46·8	50·4	45·2
Magnesium	μg	2,270	990	1,070	1,060	880	980	220	1,570	1,470	770	970	570	280	240
Sodium	μg	528	14	11	6	11	14	55	15	25	17	24	50	26	81
Potassium	μg	50	6	9	7	7	12	13	11	14	18	6	26	15	17
Carbonate	mg	119·6	115·4	103·9	92·8	98·2	78·4	51·0	109·7	112·1	75·9	96·6	73·5	78·3	68·4
Phosphate-P	μg	109	110	98	107	59	91	148	112	110	103	108	133	110	131
Chloride	μg	845	14	7	3	3	3	10	10	25	14	17	29	22	39

In these regions, the hydrogen ion concentrations of the soil solution exerts profound effects on both nutrient availability and on concentrations of ions which may have toxic effects in the soil solution.

At high pH values for example there may be a decrease in availability of potassium, phosphorus and iron due in part to competition for sites on soil ion exchange complexes. The solubilities of metallic cations vary markedly at different hydrogen ion concentrations (Sparling 1967). In general they tend to increase with increasing hydrogen ion concentrations (i.e. at lower pH values). This effect is particularly marked with aluminium which may be released in soluble form in toxic concentrations at pH values around 4. There is also a marked increase in the solubilities of many other metallic cations around pH 7.

High levels of soluble aluminium may interfere with uptake of calcium, phosphorus and iron at low pH values. In toxic concentrations aluminium inhibits root growth, particularly in seedlings (Bollard and Butler 1966), so it would be interesting to experiment with calcicole members of the dune flora to see how their seedlings respond to varying aluminium levels where these species become eliminated from the more leached parts of a dune system.

Nutrient Levels and Availability

We are now in a better position to appreciate the significance of the general nutrient levels in salt marsh and dune soils in relation to availability. It must be stressed however that much of the older data is of limited value because of inadequacies of sampling and methodology. In view of this, emphasis is given to more recent work.

General levels of the commoner nutrients in salt marsh soils are given by Chapman (1960); Zonneveld (1960); Goodman and Williams (1961); Ranwell (1961 a, b) and Pigott (in Rorison 1969), and in sand dune soils by Gimingham (1951); Gorham (1958 a); Olsen (1958 a); Ranwell (1959); Willis et al (1959); Willis and Yemm (1961); and Freijsen (1964). The nutrient supply from rainfall, a source of particular importance to dune plants, has been analysed by Gorham (1958 b), Allen et al (1968), and Parham (1970).

Macro-nutrients

Both sea water and shore sand are very deficient in nitrogen, but so far as pioneer salt marsh plants are concerned this may be a distinct advantage as lush, brittle growth induced by high nitrogen levels would be subject to severe damage from wave action. Supplies in marsh mud are probably augmented by fixation of atmospheric nitrogen by blue-green algae the precursors of salt marsh growth. Gorham (1958 *a*) shows that nitrate nitrogen is distinctly higher in the embryo dunes subject to spray than further landward, but organic matter in tidal litter is undoubtedly an important source of nitrogen in this region. Also, Metcalfe (*pers. comm.*) has shown that *Azotobacter* is widely distributed in dune soils and again fixation of atmospheric nitrogen by this means is probably an important nitrogen source for the younger dune communities (see Chapter 9).

It is well known that organic carbon, and with it total nitrogen, augments with increasing age and increasing density of plant cover on dunes. The rate of increase in damp slacks due to inflow of nutrients from leaching and reduced rate of organic matter breakdown in the wetter soils, is faster than on dunes (Ranwell 1959; Willis *et al* 1959). Little is known about the changes in total nitrogen from seaward to landward in salt marshes, but evidence from newly accreted surface layers at Bridgwater Bay show an increasing trend in nitrogen (Table 7) from bare mud to marsh levels near high water mark. A similar trend was also found in Poole Harbour marshes. Since both marshes are dominated by *Spartina anglica* we can see also how the much higher soil moisture levels at Poole dependent on a high clay content result in almost twice as much organic carbon and total nitrogen compared with the more freely draining coarser-particled marsh soil at Bridgwater Bay.

Table 7. Nutrient content of newly accreted silt, 0 to 0·5 cm depth, from *Spartina anglica* marsh, Bridgwater Bay, Somerset, sampled 7 Nov. 1962 (from Ranwell 1964 *b*).

Sampling site	Distance seaward (m)	% oven dry weight of silt					% volume of wet silt				
		K	Ca	P	N	Organic carbon	K	Ca	P	N	Organic carbon
Level Spartina	30	2·2	5·11	0·11	0·30	5·66	1·27	2·94	0·06	0·17	3·26
Level Spartina	150	2·1	5·17	0·10	0·29	6·39	1·26	3·11	0·02	0·17	3·85
Spartina on ridge	230	1·3	5·62	0·08	0·14	4·68	1·38	5·55	0·08	0·14	4·63
Bare mud on ridge	230	1·1	6·11	0·07	0·11	3·80	1·03	5·74	0·07	0·10	3·57

Hesse (1961) however has shown that organic matter type may override soil conditions, for example he finds greater accumulation of organic matter beneath *Rhizophora* than *Avicennia* even though the soil of the latter had a higher clay content.

Total nitrogen does not of course tell us much about availability and inorganic nitrogen added to *Rhizophora* mud was rapidly immobilized (Table 8), presumably through bacterial consumption since the carbon/nitrogen ratio of 36 was extremely high. In dune soils the C/N ratio is usually less than 10 (Willis *et al* 1959) though Olson (1958) did find a ratio of 20 in ancient inland dune forest soils. In salt marsh soils the ratio usually lies between 10 and 20 but it may be higher at least for short periods where tidal litter accumulates. In spite of the frequent references to nitrophilous species being associated with tidal litter deposits, one of the commonest (*Atriplex hastata*) has been shown to grow on highly nitrogen-deficient substrata (Weston 1964).

Table 8. The immobilization of nitrogen by fibrous mangrove-swamp soil. Results on an oven-dry basis (from Hesse 1961).

Soil	ppm NH$_4$-N		ppm NO$_3$-N	
	Initial	After 15 days	Initial	After 15 days
Mud alone	12·5	14·0	0	1·6
Mud + (NH$_4$)$_2$SO$_4$ at 2 cwt/acre 6″	32·0	10·2	0	2·2

Some extremely interesting studies have been carried out recently on nitrogen availability to *Suaeda maritima* in Conway estuary marshes, North Wales (Stewart *et al* 1972). They have shown that total nitrogen, soluble amino acids, and nitrate show a well marked gradient which decreased in *Suaeda* tissue from seaward to landward up the marsh. Using an enzyme bio-assay technique they showed that nitrate reductase levels in *Suaeda maritima* were found to be as much as 40 to 50 times higher in plants from low-lying seaward parts, as opposed to higher-lying landward parts, of the salt marsh (Table 9). This adaptive behaviour of the enzyme system is an intriguing example of physiological plasticity. We know very little about this in salt marsh plants. The results also suggest that the actual through-put of nitrate as a result of daily incursions of the tide in lower marsh levels is very much higher than the supply at higher marsh levels rarely reached by the tide, even though the total nitrogen values of the soil are highest in the latter.

Table 9. Nitrate reductase activity in samples of *Suaeda maritima* from different levels in a salt marsh on the Conway estuary, Caernarvonshire. Figures in brackets refer to number of samples taken randomly at each site (from Stewart *et al* 1972).

| | μ moles NO_2/h/g fresh wt. | | μ moles NO_2/h/mg protein |
Site	Average value	Range of values	Average value
1 (Seaward)	5·55 (8)	4·86–6·14	0·62
2	2·45 (6)	2·01–2·69	0·40
3	1·84 (12)	1·09–2·49	0·21
4	0·81 (5)	0·41–1·19	0·11
5 (Landward)	0·11 (8)	0·08–0·16	0·01

Hesse (1963) has studied the forms in which phosphate occurs and their distribution in mangrove swamp mud (Fig. 11). He gives a useful discussion of the complexities associated with phosphate availability in saline muds.

The responses of salt marsh species from low marsh and high marsh levels to nitrogen and phosphate fertilisers have been examined by Pigott (in Rorison 1969). *Salicornia* species and *Suaeda maritima* grown on their own marsh soils with and without fertilizer all showed response to nitrogen

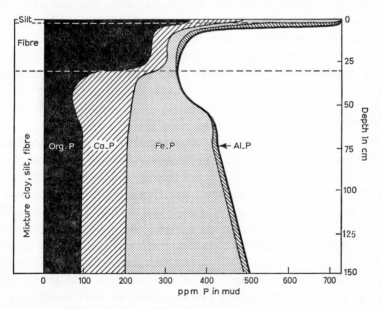

Fig. 11. Vertical distribution of phosphorus in mangrove-swamp mud (from Hesse 1963).

and phosphate fertilizer at higher marsh levels. In the case of the pioneer species *Salicornia dolichostachya,* growth on cores of bare mud was rapid with or without the addition of nitrogen. It was also shown that *Halimione portulacoides* taken from sub-optimal growth sites responded to nitrogen and phosphate. The apparent nutrient deficiency symptoms found in high marsh plants might be due in part to deficient water supply and soil mechanical restrictions on rooting since high marsh levels may dry out considerably in summer as Pigott points out.

Willis and Yemm (1961) used turf transplants and tomato culture to reveal that nitrogen, phosphate, and potassium were deficient in the soils of a calcareous dune system. Big responses to complete fertilizer applications were also found in both dune and slack vegetation resulting in a marked increase in grasses at the expense of lower-growing herbs and bryophytes (Willis 1963). The changes were in fact remarkably similar to those occurring in dune vegetation following myxomatosis, (Ranwell 1960 *b*). This illustrates the improved nutritional status that conservation of organic matter beneath taller vegetation can bring to these relatively arid soils. One notable effect of mineral deficiency is to restrain growth of fast growing species resulting in the maintenance of high species diversity.

Both Brown and Hafenrichter (1948) and Augustine *et al* (1964) found that ammonium compounds were the most effective nitrogen fertilizers in experiments concerned with promoting growth of *Ammophila* plantations on dunes. The controlled release fertilizer magnesium ammonium phosphate with potassium added, gave highly significant increases in growth over controls in *Ammophila arenaria* and *A. breviligulata*. (Augustine *et al* 1964).

Micro-nutrients

Willis (1963) found no significant response to trace element fertilization (iron, sodium, manganese, zinc, copper or molybdenum) in dunes.

Gorham and Gorham (1965) record that ash from salt marsh plants was 2 to 10 times greater than in plants from other habitats. However, iron was from $\frac{1}{3}$ to $\frac{1}{15}$, and manganese from $\frac{1}{7}$ to $\frac{1}{25}$ that of plants from other habitats. It is suggested that ion antagonism may prevent iron and manganese ions, mobilized in the reduced state, entering salt marsh plants freely in an ion-rich environment. Adams (1963) found that plants of *Spartina alterniflora* became chlorotic in iron-deficient soils where high level marsh species such as *Distichalis spicata* and *Juncus roemerianus* were unaffected. The *Spartina* responded to experimental foliar applications of ferrous sulphate or the addition of iron to a saline nutrient solution. Now *Spartina alterniflora* is restricted to low marsh where the mean soluble iron content is in excess of 4 p.p.m. Adams suggests that iron deficiency may limit the growth of *Spartina* in high level marsh. He also notes that iron becomes available through the action of anaerobic iron-reducing bacteria and observed that *Spartina alterniflora* shows the greatest tendency towards chlorosis in better-drained, rather than wetter sites at the high marsh level.

PART TWO   Salt Marshes

4 Salt Marshes: Tidal Influence

Salt marsh formation normally begins at a level subject to salt water tidal inundation twice daily. The upper level of the tidal influence, where salt marsh is replaced by fresh-water marsh, is subject to tidal inundation only a few times a year at the spring and autumn equinoxes, and then by almost fresh water. Between these two extremes organisms are zoned according to the range of conditions they can withstand; conditions dominated by the tide at lower levels, but almost independent of them at the highest levels.

It follows that efforts to explain zonation as a whole in relation to any one factor such as duration of tidal submergence or salinity is bound to fail not only in relation to different species, but even in relation to upper and lower limits of the same species where these have wide vertical ranges.

So far as survival, growth and reproduction of organisms in the intertidal zone is concerned, tidal factors of particular importance include: intensity and frequency of *mechanical disturbance* due to tidal action; the *vertical range* over which the tide operates which controls tidal flooding depths and the vertical extent of salt marsh; the *form of tidal cycle* which controls frequency and duration of submergence and emergence, and *water quality* which controls the amount of light reaching submerged growths and the salinity to which they are subjected.

Tidal Parameters

Tidal disturbance

Forward colonization of a salt marsh only takes place in relatively sheltered inlets or behind broad expanses of tidal flats where much of the energy of waves has already been dissipated. Under these conditions waves are relatively low in height and do not exert much force in their downward plunge on breaking. On these relatively level shores the swash, or landward motion of the water, tends to be more powerful than the backwash. The aerial parts of a pioneer plant are first pulled landward strongly and then pulled seaward less strongly as a wave completes its breaking.

There is much evidence (Ragotskie 1959, Møller 1964 and Pestrong 1965) that ebb flow reaches higher velocities than flood flow and controls drainage patterns in tidal channels on salt marshes and this is a subject we shall return to in Chapter 5. However, it is of interest to note here that Bradley (in Ragotskie 1959) found that tidal velocities of flood currents 3 cm above a tidal flat were consistently 15 to 20 per cent higher than those of the ebb.

No attempts appear to have been made to measure the strength of the water-borne forces required to break salt marsh plants or uproot them and this would be a profitable line of study of fundamental importance to an understanding of conditions required for salt marsh formation.

Clearly, as well as the force, the frequency with which a plant is rocked back and forth by the water affects its chances of survival. Wave force and frequency varies with both distant and local weather conditions but the maximum incidence of wave break tends to occur on a salt marsh at the

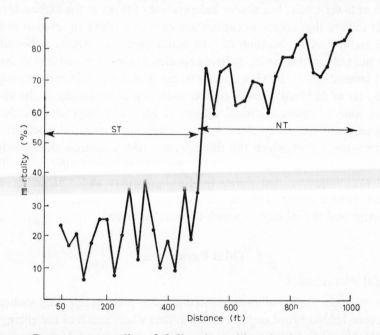

Fig. 12. Percentage mortality of *Salicornia* seedlings in the spring tide (ST) zone and the neap tide (NT) zone (From Chapman 1960, after Wiehe 1935).

level of mean high water neap tides because most tides pass over or reach this point and more waves have time to break there while the tide is on the turn.

Wiehe (1935) has shown that the density of *Salicornia* seedlings in the spring tide zone increases from 2 to 6 times that in the neap tide zone and that a two fold increase in density occurs within a 30 m distance above the top of the neap tide zone. In his work on the Dovey estuary in Wales he found *Salicornia* seedling mortalities of 60 per cent or more in the neap tide zone but less than 40 per cent in the spring tide zone (Fig. 12). As Chapman (1960) points out in relation to these observations, the sharp rise in seedling mortality occurs at the level flooded daily by the tides and mortality is a direct result of tidal water washing out a high percentage of the seedlings.

Brereton (1965) found that during the first half of the period March to June *Salicornia* seeds continue to germinate at a rate sufficient to offset losses due to up-rooting by the tide so that seedling density increases. In

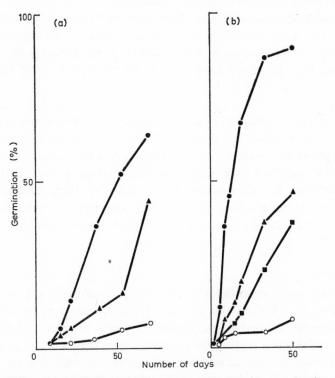

Fig. 13. Effect of (a) light and (b) temperature on the germination of seed of *Spartina anglica*. Light: ●, dark; ▲, 8 h; ○, 16 h. Temperature: ●, 25°C; ▲, 20°C; ■, 15°C; ○, 7°C. (from Hubbard 1970).

the second half of this period the rate of germination falls off but the uprooting effect of the tide does not and seedling density decreases.

Chapman (1960) suggests that pioneer species need a specific period of time of continuous emergence of the marsh surface so that seedlings are not swept away by the tides. In fact newly germinated seedlings of *Spartina anglica* at the seaward edge of the marsh at Bridgwater Bay, Somerset were invariably found with seed cases and/or stem collars from 2 to 10 cm below the mud surface. The seeds must have germinated below the surface and Hubbard (1970) has shown that both rate and amount of germination of this species is greater in the dark than in the light (Fig. 13). It follows that the period of continuous submergence is more likely to be related to the light requirements of the emerging seedling shoot than to mud surface stability given that wave action is sufficiently moderate to allow establishment to occur at all. Experimental work on the establishment of pioneer species from ripe seed buried at different depths and on the light requirements of newly emerged seedlings is indicated.

It is interesting to note that Stevenson and Emery (1958) obtained germination of *Salicornia bigelowii* in seeds completely submerged in sea water. Also tests on the seeds of five Australian salt marsh species showed that none were prevented from germination beneath 5 cm of tap water (Clarke and Hannon 1970).

The density of *Spartina anglica* seedlings in the neap tide zone at the seaward edge of a marsh in Bridgwater Bay, Somerset was at a maximum opposite the centre of the marsh and diminished regularly towards the more exposed and disturbed ends of the marsh. This again suggested that mechanical disturbance was regulating seedling density. Even in the most favourable zone for establishment 40 per cent of seedlings marked in July 1964 were missing after one month. Of the young plants wintering 50 per cent survived to become established clumps by the following August (Table 10).

Tide range

Tidal range varies enormously in different parts of the world from a few centimetres (e.g. in the Baltic and the Mediterranean) to nearly 19 metres (e.g. in the Bay of Fundy, Nova Scotia). However, the period of tidal cycle from one high water level to the next has a fixed period of about 12 hours predetermined by regular astronomical events. Consequently the vertical range in which salt marsh formation can take place is very much greater in the big tide range areas than in the smallest ones. Further in the big tide range areas there is room for a series of communities zoned according to the tidal conditions. In the smallest tide range (e.g. in the Baltic) tidal movements may be strongly modified by over-riding weather effects, nevertheless distinctive vegetational zonation related to duration of submergence is still found in such situations (Tyler 1971). Changes in atmospheric pressure alone are sufficient to depress or increase water level by as much as 30 cm in the Danish Wadden sea (Jacobsen, N.K. *pers. comm*); on west Swedish coasts where the tidal range is about 30 cm, changes in wind direction and atmospheric pressure give non-periodic water level ranges up to 170 cm (Gillner 1965).

Table 10. Survival of newly germinated *Spartina anglica* seedlings on open mud at the seaward limit of the Bridgwater Bay marsh, Somerset. Seedlings were searched for within a mudflat area 450 × 150 m (long axis parallel to the shore) and marked with a bamboo cane 1 m away.

Date	No. of marked sites (out of 50 originally marked) located	No. of marked seedlings still present	Survival %
13/7/64	50	50	100
17/8/64	48	30	62
23/9/64	47	22	46
14/6/65	45	10	22
27/8/65	45	9	20

Tide curve modifications

It is an observed fact that the tidal curve steepens up estuary though its ultimate amplitude of course diminishes eventually to zero. It was noted that the lower limits of *Spartina anglica* marsh in Poole Harbour, Dorset were higher at successive intervals up estuary (Ranwell *et al* 1964), though the differences were small and only just significant. However, Beeftink (1966) has shown on the Scheldt estuary in Holland that different species do retreat to higher levels upstream apparently proportionate to the steepening of the tidal curve.

Contrasted Habitats in Submergence and Emergence Zones

Tidal submergence

If the duration of tidal submergence per annum is plotted against vertical level within the tide range, the curve obtained is typically S-shaped (Fig. 14). In Poole Harbour, Dorset a difference in marsh level of 10 cm near high water spring tides gives difference of only about 100 hours submergence per year. In contrast, a difference in marsh level of 10 cm near high

F

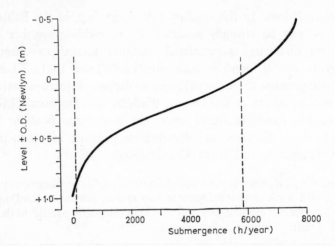

Fig. 14. Duration of submergence per annum in relation to O.D. levels. Broken lines mark upper and lower limits of *Spartina*. Derived from tide gauge records at Poole Bridge, Poole Harbour, July 1962 to July 1963 (from Ranwell *et al* 1964).

water neap tides gives a difference of about 700 hours submergence per year. In other words level is much more sensitively related to submergence at the marsh seaward limit than at its landward limit.

Now it is common knowledge that many salt marsh plants can survive much longer periods of submergence in the quiet waters of sheltered brackish lagoons than they are ever likely to experience at their seaward limits of growth in open marsh conditions. Hubbard (1969) has shown that *Spartina anglica* may be submerged throughout daylight hours during certain neap tide periods (Fig. 15) and it can also withstand submergence in the laboratory for at least $4\frac{1}{2}$ months. So submergence itself is not critical for survival of this. The lowest growing salt marsh species

Apart from any mechanical effect, the big difference between quiet saline water and tidal water flooding an open marsh is that the former tends to be clear while the latter is turbid with silt in suspension and this cuts down the length of time available for photosynthesis. It is remarkable that virtually no work seems to have been done on light as a limiting factor for establishment, growth, and survival of salt marsh plants, though shading effects are obvious wherever a salt marsh is overhung by trees.

The most turbid non-toxic tidal waters in Britain are found in Cornish estuaries clouded by sediment derived from china clay mining activities in the catchment. In the upper estuary of the River Fal this results in a

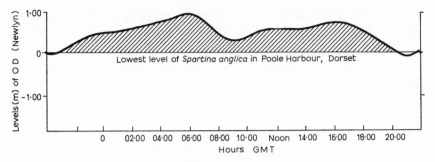

Fig. 15. Tidal curve showing the lowest level of *Spartina anglica* in Poole Harbour and the extent of its immersion (hatched area) by a neap tide on 5 November 1962. Readings obtained from the tide gauge on Poole Harbour, Dorset (from Hubbard 1969).

truncation of salt marsh zonation which precludes entirely the development of lower marsh levels. *Puccinellia maritima* growth is confined to the extreme upper limit of its vertical range where it shares a pioneer role with *Triglochin maritima* and other species of higher marsh levels.

Effects of turbidity on photosynthetic activity might be investigated using algal culture techniques (see Hopkins 1962).

Pioneer salt marsh plants capable of withstanding regular submergence must also withstand extremely low oxygen levels especially in marsh soils with a high clay content. However even in the exceptionally poorly drained soils associated with 'die-back' in *Spartina anglica* marsh, Goodman and Williams (1961) were unable to find direct evidence of damage primarily due to anaerobiosis.

Submergence and Emergence marshes

From extensive studies in British and American marshes on frequency and duration of submergence, Chapman (1960) concludes there is a fundamental distinction between lower marshes and higher marshes with the line of demarcation at about mean high water level. He notes that 'lower marshes commonly undergo more than 360 submergences per annum, their *maximum* period of continuous exposure never exceeds nine days, whilst there is more than 1·2 hours submergence *per diem* in daylight. Upper marshes on the other hand undergo less than 360 submergences annually, their *minimum* period of continuous exposure exceeds ten days, and there is less than one hour's submergence daily during daylight.'

However, as Chapman points out, this does not hold for the San Francisco Bay marshes studied by Hinde (1954). Moreover data on zonation and numbers of both algae and phanerogams given by Chapman (in Steers 1960) in his study area at Scolt Head Island, Norfolk, show no really significant disjunction at the proposed demarcation line (Figs 16 and 17).

Numbers of phanerogam species augment rapidly from seaward to landward, because only very few are adapted to regular submergence.

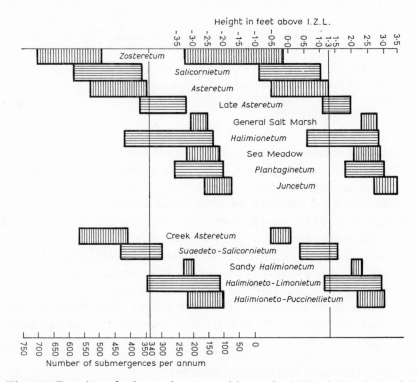

Fig. 16. Zonation of salt marsh communities at Scolt Head Island, Norfolk. Levels and numbers of mean submergences per annum (height 1.2 L. O.D. Newlyn). The lines at 1·30 ft and 340 submergences per annum mark the approximate division between Submergence and Emergence marsh (from Chapman in Steers, 1960).

It is of particular interest that Chapman (1940) found that it was characteristic of American salt marsh species that 'the further south they spread on the continent the more tolerant they are of submergence (i.e. the lower they go in the tidal plane).' Although he adduces temperature as the factor possibly responsible for this it seems more likely that stronger light intensities and temperature act together to allow photosynthesis at deeper levels of submergence further south.

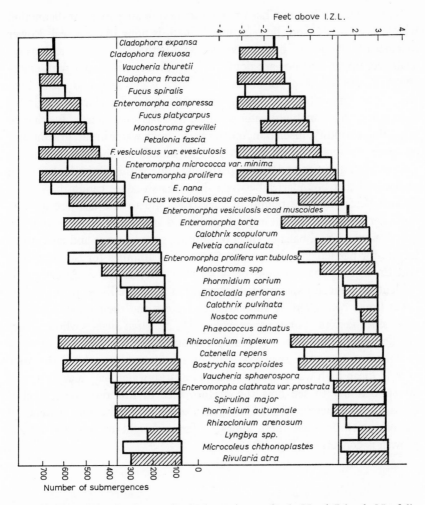

Fig. 17. Zonation of salt marsh algal species at Scolt Head Island, Norfolk. Levels and number of tidal submergences per annum (0·0 ft I.Z.L. = + 7 ft O. D. Newlyn). The lines at 1·30 ft and 340 submergences per annum mark the approximate division between Submergence and Emergence marsh (from Chapman in Steers 1960).

Nevertheless, Chapman has drawn attention to an important distinction which, even if it cannot be critically defined, is none the less real. Lower marshes are dominated by factors associated with submergence and, as we shall see, upper marshes are dominated by factors associated with emergence. Lower marsh from about mean high water neaps to mean high water is best described as *Submergence marsh*, and upper marsh from mean high water to mean high water springs, as *Emergence marsh*. Bearing in mind that turbidity, insolation, temperature, fresh water input, grazing and adaptive ecotypes will all play a part in modifying the exact limits of species both at a site and at any particular time within a site it should be recognized that boundaries between these marsh zones cannot be exactly defined since they are bound to vary from site to site and are anyway oscillatory in nature. What might be achieved and would be most useful in practice would be a balance sheet of limiting submergence and emergence factors for particular species so that their true affinities for Submergence and Emergence marsh could be more effectively assessed. Already it is evident that species spanning the transition zone are likely to have their lower limits controlled by submergence factors and their upper limits by emergence factors. The extreme example is *Spartina anglica* whose clones are known to persist for at least 50 years without significant seedling recruitment from the seaward limit of salt marsh growth to the zone around mean high water spring tides. The Bridgwater Bay marsh gives us an opportunity to see how the performance of this one species varies across the Submergence and Emergence zones. There is some evidence of discontinuity between these zones so far as height of *Spartina anglica* growth is concerned (Fig. 18).

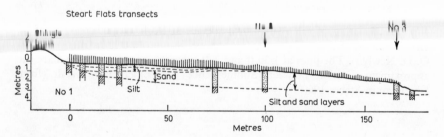

Fig. 18. Vertical height of shoots of *Spartina anglica* from landward (left) to seaward (right) at Bridgwater Bay, Somerset. Note the quite distinct change in height (indicated by closely spaced vertical lines) just to the left of arrow No. 2. Growth in Emergence marsh is much taller than in Submergence marsh (after Braybrooks 1958).

Mechanical effects on Emergence marsh

The incidence of mechanical disturbance from the tide is much reduced on Emergence marsh compared with that affecting establishment and growth on Submergence marsh. It is greatest at higher marsh levels around mean high water spring tides where wave presence often persists, prolonged by onshore winds delaying the ebb. Tidal litter accumulates at this level, crushes weak growths, and temporarily reduces, or cuts off the light supply (Plate 4). This produces the characteristic open ground of the strandline near the landward limit of the marsh favoured by temporary colonists like the annual species of *Atriplex*. Kidson and Carr (1961) recorded disturbance of shingle markers at Bridgwater Bay, Somerset and showed that significant movement was limited to a narrow zone near high water mark. Measurements are needed of mechanical disturbance in different salt marsh zones and fracture devices involving threads of different breaking strains might be employed. It is evident from the gradient of normal tide curves that flood and ebb tides pass relatively swiftly over marsh levels between mean high water neap and mean high water spring tides and mechanical disturbance should be reduced there.

Submergence, or reduced light due to submergence, is unlikely to be a limiting factor for plants of Emergence marsh except at the very lowest levels, because the duration of submergence is too short to seriously impede photosynthesis.

Field Salinity in Relation to Tidal Action

Salinity in Submergence and Emergence marshes

The one common factor that does affect all plants of Emergence salt marsh and precludes the growth of non-halophytic terrestrial species is of course the high level of salinity maintained persistently by the tides. Salinities in Submergence marsh rarely rise above that of the tidal water with which it is regularly and frequently bathed, Emergence marsh however can develop much higher salinities in the soil solution than that of the tidal water as a result of water evaporation during dry inter-tidal periods. Hannon and Bradshaw (1968) have in fact demonstrated that upper marsh populations of *Festuca rubra* are more salt tolerant than those of lower marsh.

Gillham (1957) took advantage of a drought in 1955 to record extreme high salinities in the soil solution of many species regarded as non-halophytes in Emergence marsh on the shores of islands off the west coast of Scotland. Her results (Fig. 19) show that in addition to the normal halophytes, non-

Chlorides as % by weight of soil solution

Range of tolerance of soil salinity

Fig. 19. Distribution of common lochside species in relation to salt-tolerance. Combined data from three west coast lochs, Mull. Samples taken during the drought of August 1955. Note the downshore penetration of moorland plants into soils having as much as 4·0 per cent salt in the soil solution (i.e. full sea strength). Moorland dominants which are apparently intolerant of salt are *Calluna, Erica* spp., *Trichophorum, Juncus acutiflorus* and *Sphagnum* spp. (from Gillham 1957).

halophytes such as *Carex demissa*, *Molinia coerulea* and *Nardus stricta* were surviving chlorinity levels of 2·1 per cent by weight of soil solution (equivalent to full strength sea water salinities), without apparent harm to growth. In addition facultative halophytes like *Agrostis stolonifera*, *Carex distans* and *Juncus articulatus* were surviving hyper-saline conditions of up to 4 per cent chlorinity. Judging from the distribution of these species at the extreme upper limits of Emergence marsh where they are more likely to come under the influence of regular fresh water flushing than these exceptionally high salinities, they would be unlikely to survive the latter for more than brief periods. We need to know much more about the time factor in relation to salinity tolerance than we do at present.

Salinity control of *Phragmites* growth

Field measurements of salinity rarely catch these extreme conditions where levels rise close to a species limit of tolerance. It follows that for much of the time, salinity is not limiting for the growth of many salt marsh plants or facultative halophytes. Only where persistently high levels occur close to a species limit of tolerance does salinity become limiting. Since these conditions occur in quite a narrow sector of the estuarine gradient, where the species may become discontinuous due to other limiting factors, the location of a site where salinity is an operative limiting factor is difficult to find or may not occur at all in particular estuarine marsh systems. If we take the case of *Phragmites communis* in Poole Harbour, the great majority of 87 samples taken in dry summer conditions at the seaward limit of *Phragmites* growth gave salinities well within the tolerance of this species. Limiting values were only found at the point where the seaward limit of growth coincided with the limit of penetration down-estuary of *Phragmites* in salt marsh. The field limit of 1·3 per cent chlorinity of the soil solution at 10 cm depth (Ranwell *et al* 1964) was very close to the experimentally determined limit of 1·25 per cent found by Taylor (1939).

There is little evidence that salinity limits the growth of true halophytes in Cool Temperate zone marshes. It is more likely to do so in Warm Temperate and Sub-Tropical zones where evaporation regularly exceeds precipitation. Purer (1942) records salinities of 17 to 23 per cent on Californian marshes and notes that plant growth is inhibited where salt efflorescence occurs.

However, there is growing evidence that the seaward penetration of facultative halophytes in the Cool Temperate zone is often limited by salinity although other limiting factors such as grazing may prevent a species growing to the limit of its salinity tolerance.

Inversions of zonation

Complexities arise in the highest part of estuaries where inversions of zonation occur (see Gillham 1957 and Beeftink 1966). A similar phenomenon has been observed in the upper parts of the Humber estuary Yorkshire. *Puccinellia maritima* zoned below *Agrostis stolonifera* in the lower estuary retreats to the tops of hummocks above *Agrostis stolonifera* in the upper parts of the estuary where it seems likely that temporarily high salinity or drought in dry weather may exclude *Agrostis*.

Clearly whatever conclusions may be drawn about the relation of species zonation to tidal submergence in the more marine bay marshes or lower estuary marshes, these do not necessarily hold in the special conditions existing in the up-estuary regions.

As marsh levels rise under the influence of tide-borne sediments many factors other than those directly dependent on tidal action control the zonation and growth of the increasing number of species which colonize Emergence marsh. In particular physical soil factors: structure, particle size, aeration and moisture become significant. It is convenient to deal with sedimentation in association with these factors in the next chapter and to discuss biological factors in the two that follow.

5 Salt Marshes: Sedimentation, Drainage and Soil Physical Development

Salt Marsh Precursors

Biological activity on and in tidal mud flats starts off the processes of soil formation from mineral sediments, and salt marsh development accelerates these processes. We have little quantitative information about the role played by tidal flat organisms but there are a number of ways in which these precursors favour salt marsh formation once the flats are formed in sufficiently sheltered conditions, and high enough in relation to tides, for salt marsh plants to grow.

Ginsberg and Lowenstam (1958) review evidence of the stabilizing and silt trapping powers of filamentous algae and marine phanerogams in shallow lagoonal waters. Ginsberg *et al* (1954) also found that a culture of the algae *Phormidium* could re-establish a surface mat through as much as 4 mm of sediment in 24 hours. The burrows of invertebrate animals improve soil aeration, for example those of worms (e.g. *Nereis* sp.) are often lined with a layer of oxidized iron, reddish in colour in contrast to adjoining grey-blackish reduced mud. Colonies of molluscs like the Horse Mussel in San Francisco Bay (Gillham 1957) provide surface roughness which promotes sedimentation. On the sandy-silt flats adjoining Holy Island, Northumberland, *Enteromorpha* first colonizes on loose shells of *Cardium* in more mobile sites. Growth encourages silt deposition. The filament bases of the algae become embedded and ultimately lose their attachment to the now buried shells. Stronger growths of algae on the silt increase stability and accretion for the subsequent establishment of salt marsh species.

Kamps (1962) has shown that molluscs reconstitute clay into faecal pellets which settle quicker than unmodified clay flakes and help to promote accretion. His paper deserves much wider recognition than it has achieved for it gives much valuable quantitative information about the movement of clay in inter-tidal waters and its dependence on wind-induced waves and on the effects of inter-tidal organisms on silt movement in the Dutch Wadden sea.

Sedimentation

Techniques of measurement of salt marsh accretion

Kestner has developed an effective method for measuring changes in surface level of tidal flats using as a marker a creamed suspension of silica flour poured into cored out holes in the mudflats (Inglis and Kestner 1958). Where very high levels of accretion (several cm per year) occur, deeply embedded bamboo canes with about 15 cm sticking out of the surface enable repeated measurements to be made without destruction of the sampling site. They give reliable results when checked against natural markers like depth to previous years rosettes in perennials or successive seed case layers of annual species in the marsh soil profile (Ranwell 1964 a). In marshes with very low accretion rates it is necessary to lay down coloured marker layers (sand, coal dust, brick dust etc.) and record their depth of burial after several years (Jakobsen et al 1955, Steers 1964).

Rates of accretion

True accretion is the depth of sediment deposited in unit time minus the reduction in thickness of the accreted layer due to settlement factors. The latter become increasingly important at the higher levels of Emergence marsh where accretion diminishes, organic matter increases, and drying out occurs more frequently. Stearns and MacCreary (1957) for example found that settlement factors effectively compensated for an annual accretion of 0.04 cm on a high level marsh carrying Scirpus olneyi, Spartina patens and Eleocharis rostellata so that over a 20 year period there was no significant rise in marsh level. However, even over this sort of period, changes in land and sea level can be important and net increase in marsh level has to be considered in relation to them.

Chapman and Ronaldson (1958) found less than 0·2 mm per year accretion on a tropical mangrove marsh where roots and rhizomes are too widely spaced to retain much mud washed between them. In the pioneer zone of temperate marshes *Salicornia* accretion may be as much as 3 cm per year (Oliver 1929) and *Puccinellia maritima* can accrete sandy silt at a rate of 10 cm per year (Jakobsen *et al* 1955). Pioneer *Spartina anglica* can

Table 11. Values of correlation coefficients and their statistical significance for relationships between accretion, topography and vegetation at Bridgwater Bay, Somerset (from Ranwell 1964 a).

* P = 0·05, r = 0·2839
** P = 0·01, r = 0·3676
*** P = 0·001, r = 0·4594
With 46 degrees of freedom

	Dependent variate				Independent variates						
	Mean annual accretion			Mean height of site	Distance seaward	Creek depth	Shoot density	Mean height of vegetation	Air dry weight of vegetation	Dry weight/Density (mean shoot weight)	Dry weight per shoot/Mean height
	1960–61	1961–62	1960–62								
Mean annual vertical accretion (cm) 1960–61		+0·5317 ***	+0·8799 ***	+0·4133 **	−0·4101 **	−0·3316 *	N.S.	+0·5098 ***	+0·5030 ***	+0·3825 **	N.S.
1961–62			+0·8668 ***	+0·4074 **	−0·3955 **	N.S.	−0·3279 *	+0·4372 **	+0·3025 *	+0·3408 *	N.S.
1960–62				+0·4751 ***	−0·4692 ***	−0·3115 *	−0·3277 *	+0·5418 **	+0·4626 ***	+0·4181 **	N.S.
Mean height of site above O.D. (m)					−0·9724 ***	−0·7571 ***	−0·4120 **	+0·6898 ***	+0·5062 ***	+0·7081 ***	N.S.
Distance seaward from landward limit of marsh (m)						+0·6742 ***	+0·4511 **	−0·6474 ***	−0·4866 ***	−0·7006	N.S.
Creek depth (highest minus lowest O.D. level at site) (m)							N.S.	−0·4585 **	−0·3286 *	−0·4118 **	N.S.
Shoot density of vegetation (per m²)								−0·4366 **	N.S.	−0·5143 ***	N.S.
Mean height of vegetation (cm)									+0·7635 ***	+0·8644 ***	N.S.
Total air dry weight of vegetation (g/m²)										+0·7350 ***	N.S.
Dry weight/Density (mean shoot weight)											+0·2992 *
Dry weight per shoot/Mean height											

accrete 5 to 10 cm per year and at higher levels has been recorded as regularly accreting 15 cm of silt per year under exceptionally favourable conditions (Ranwell 1964 a). In general however accretion on temperate European and North-East American marshes in the Emergence zone is between 0·2 and 1 cm per year, and is unlikely to be a limiting factor for survival of salt marsh plants.

Pattern of accretion

In a study of accretion on an exceptionally rapidly accreting marsh at Bridgwater Bay, Somerset it was possible to show how annual accretion varied in different parts of the marsh (Ranwell 1964 a). Maximum accretion occurred in the centre section of the marsh which is not grazed; accretion diminished towards the ends of the marsh which were more exposed and grazed. The seaward to landward pattern (Fig. 20) showed maximum accretion about 50 m seawards of the landward limit of the marsh and minimum accretion at the seaward edge. Richards (1934) found that maximum accretion rates on the Dovey marshes occurred nearer the seaward limit. Now the Bridgwater Bay marsh was young and actively developing at all levels while the Dovey marsh was mature and more or less static at its seaward limit. Flattening out of marsh level occurs just landward of the zone of maximum accretion (evident in Fig. 20). This zone must migrate seawards as the marsh reaches maturity. Analysis of the Bridgwater Bay results suggested that rise in accretion rate was positively correlated with marsh height and the height or weight of the vegetation, and negatively correlated with distance seaward and the density of the vegetation (Table 11). The individual effects of the variables could not be separated and this emphasises the intimate nature of the phytogeomorphological processes at work. The positive correlation of accretion with marsh height only holds for young actively developing marshes. Evidently one significant feature of marsh system development is a change in surface angle from a slope to seaward to a more level surface and consequently a less readily drained one.

Mechanism of accretion

Because of the high rate of accretion at Bridgwater Bay it also proved possible to identify distinct seasonal changes in the pattern of mud supply to the marsh (Fig. 21). It seems that mud builds up at the seaward edge of the marsh during spring and summer, accretion is at a maximum over the whole marsh in the autumn, while in winter there is either no change or a slight trend towards erosion.

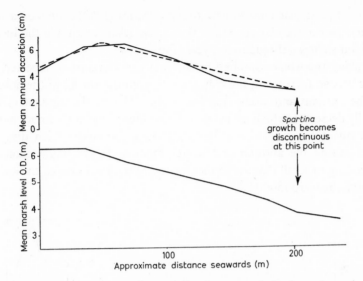

Fig. 20. Annual accretion and marsh-level curves derived as the means of results from five transects combined, Bridgwater Bay, Somerset (from Ranwell 1964 *a*).

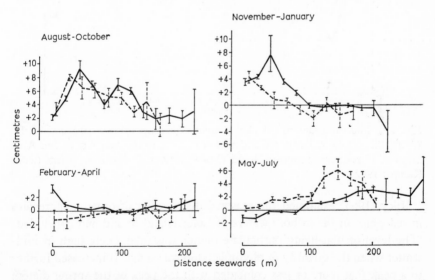

Fig. 21. Seasonal pattern of accretion and erosion on Transects 3 (solid line) and 4 (broken line), 1960–61. Transect 4 results have been slightly offset to the right for clarity. Vertical lines show plus or minus twice the standard error of the mean. *Spartina* growth becomes discontinuous at about 200 m seaward. Bridgwater Bay, Somerset (from Ranwell, 1964 *a*).

It is of particular interest here to note Kamps (1962) results on a study of variations in the clay content of the surface layers of mud in the Eastern Wadden shallows throughout a year (Fig. 22):

'Taking the whole sampling period into consideration it appeared that there was an increase in the clay content from the spring to the autumn. In the autumn and winter months it seemed that the amount of mud rapidly decreases, which means that during the spring and summer months large quantities of mud are deposited along the coast which disappear again during the autumn and winter months. In this connection it is interesting to recall that the former owners of the Banks called the autumn months the warp months.'

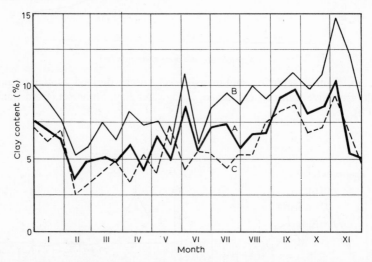

Fig. 22. The variations in the clay content of the upper layer (0·5 cm) of the Westpolder Shallow, Eastern Wadden, Netherlands in the course of a year. A = mean of 15 measuring points; B and C two individual measuring points (from Kamps, 1962.)

Riley (1963) examined the seasonal distribution of organic aggregates in sea-water in the inshore waters of Long Island Sound and concluded: 'The level of non-living particulate matter was moderately high in mid-winter when the quantity of phytoplankton was small. It increased further to a peak that more or less coincided with the peak of the spring diatom flowering and thence declined to the lowest point of the year at about the time of the termination of the flowering. The quantity was relatively small during most of the summer and autumn.'

One further relevant factor is the flocculation effect of salt water on silt which Price and Kendrick (1963) believe may explain seasonal changes in suspended silt in the Thames and other estuarine areas:

'In the summer of 1959 the water became unusually free of silt and visibility increased from 6 in to 2 ft (15 to 60 cm). During the late autumn and early winter the deposits again became muddy. This may be explained as follows: In the dry summer of 1959 fresh water flow was minimal, hence salinity upstream was higher than usual. Charges on the silt particles neutralized by the electrolyte salt water caused flocculation and deposition of silt higher upstream than usual. When the fresh water flow returned to normal it is possible that the charges on the deposited silt could be restored mobilizing it again.'

The pattern of seasonal events in relation to marsh accretion seems to be as follows: In spring and summer large quantities of mud are deposited adjoining seaward edges of sheltered salt marshes as a combined result of flocculation due to high salinity and coagulation of particles through increased biological activity. In autumn the reverse effects occur as salinity declines with increased rainfall and biological activity declines with lowered temperatures. Under the influence of autumn storms mobilized silt arrives over the marsh and settles in maximum amount because the fully grown vegetation is at maximum trapping capacity. In winter fresh supplies of silt are mobilized under conditions of minimal salinity and biological activity, to settle once more against marsh edges in the following spring.

It is worth noting that Jakobsen (1961) using a simple siphon sampler found that under dense salt marsh vegetation not more than half the material suspended in tidal water was deposited.

If the top-most layer of newly accreted autumn silt is analysed for its chemical constituents in samples taken successively from landward to seaward, trends are apparent, at least on a dry weight basis (see Table 7). This suggests that the mud supply to higher marsh zones is derived from those successively lower. In other words the source of silt for accretion seems to be immediately adjacent and to seaward of the site concerned.

If the above interpretation is correct we have here some at least of the elements for a mathematical model of the accretion system. It will not be easy to get measurements of some of the parameters in this complex physico-biological system, but one begins to see the need for continuous monitoring of salinity and temperature and for critical studies on silt coagulation through biological activity in order to understand it.

G

Meanwhile it may be of interest to note that a regression equation has been calculated for the Bridgwater Bay marsh as follows:

Accretion = 0·643 (mean height of site above O.D.) + 0·0462 (mean height of vegetation) + 0·00135 (air dry weight of vegetation) − 1·143.

Stratigraphy and the Age of Marshes

Deep level stratigraphy of marshes is a study more in the province of the physiographer than the ecologist and has little relevance to current ecological processes at the surface which is the concern of this book. But it does have relevance to past land and sea level changes and calculations of the age of marshes.

Rising coastlines

On rising coastlines (e.g. such as parts of the Swedish and Scottish coasts are believed to be) there is little opportunity for salt marsh development to occur and the vertical extent of marsh deposits may be less than the tidal range would permit on a stable coastline. Where the coast is stable, sheltered inlets silt up with marsh deposits to a depth equivalent to that part of the tidal range where salt marsh growth is possible i.e. from about mean high water neaps to extreme high water spring tides.

Falling coastlines

On a subsiding coastline (e.g. south-east England) or one on which the sea level is rising, marsh formation can continue so long as its rate is not exceeded by the isostatic adjustment for so long as this occurs. In this way depths of marsh sediment far in excess of that permissible within the tidal range can accumulate.

The history of the marsh changes can be read from fragments preserved in the marsh soils. The reconstruction of the ontogeny of the Barnstaple marsh, New England by Redfield (1965) is an elegant example, and that of Jacobsen (1960 and 1964) in Denmark another.

Techniques for measuring the age of marshes

Three ways of measuring marsh age have been used: direct records, calculation from existing vertical zonation of plants and accretion rates

Table 12. Minimum rates of development of salt marshes to maturity.

Site	Type of marsh	Method of age estimation	Minimum age to maturity in years	Author
Malltraeth, Anglesey	Part enclosed	Direct observation	10	Ranwell (*pers comm.*)
Bridgwater Bay, Somerset	Open	Accretion rates	40	Ranwell (*pers comm.*)
St. Cyrus, Scotland	Part enclosed	Documentary records	70	Gimingham (1953)
Newport Bay, New England	Part enclosed	D. records	90	Stevenson and Emery (1958)
Fal, Cornwall	Part enclosed	Map records	100	Ranwell (*pers comm.*)
Baltrum Island	Open	Map records	100	Tuxen (1956)
Skallingen, Denmark	Open	Accretion rates	100	Nielsen (1935)
North Bull Island, Eire	Part enclosed	Documentary records	125	Chapman (1960)
Scolt Head Island, Norfolk	Open	Accretion rates	200	Chapman (1960)
Dovey, Wales	Open	Accretion rates	330	Chapman (1960)

corrected for subsidence and settlement, and radio-carbon dating. We need to distinguish between minimum age for reaching maturity and marshes whose life is extended indefinitely by the rejuvenating effect of subsidence at a rate less than that of the accretion rate.

Some minimum ages for marshes reaching maturity (which might be defined as the point where settlement tends to balance accretion) are given in Table 12. In general, part-enclosed marshes develop more rapidly than open coast marshes and the minimum order of time to reach maturity on the majority of marshes is about 100 years. What these estimates do not take into account is the level of the tidal flats when salt marsh formation originally took place. If for example tidal flats are significantly above the submergence limit for the pioneer species to begin with, and salt marsh formation is prevented by too high mobility, they will have a head start on salt marsh formation starting on lower level but less mobile flats if mobility is suddenly reduced by an artificial or natural barrier partly enclosing them. The extremely rapid development of the marsh on the Malltraeth estuary, Anglesey is a case in point. Here high level sand flats suddenly became more stable due to the artificially aided growth of a sand barrier and only 10 years were needed to build from pioneer *Puccinellia maritima* to a mature stage with *Juncus maritimus* (Packham and Liddle 1970). In the case of the Bridgwater Bay marsh, exceptionally silt-laden tidal water combined with the vigorous growth of *Spartina anglica* to speed up marsh development. At Scolt Head Island, Norfolk silt supplies are limited and marsh growth occurs at a much slower rate than normal (Chapman 1960).

Radio-carbon dating of deep level salt marsh deposits has been used by Godwin *et al* (1958) and Newman and Rusnak (1966) to estimate the eustatic rise in sea level and by Redfield and Rubin (1962) in connection with his studies of the Barnstaple marsh.

Supperficial stratigraphic studies are of more immediate concern to the ecologist. They enable comparisons to be made between the vertical zonation of the living plant at the surface and the depth of its organic remains in the soil profile (Fig. 23). Such studies also provide direct evidence of successional relationships that have occurred in the past and that are likely to be occurring at the present time (Fig. 24). Any species present in quantity is likely to leave distinctive remains in the profile. An end can often be put to speculation about successional relationships with the aid of a trowel and a sieve. Subsurface discontinuities in sediments which may profoundly affect soil moisture supplies for growth are also revealed by stratigraphic work.

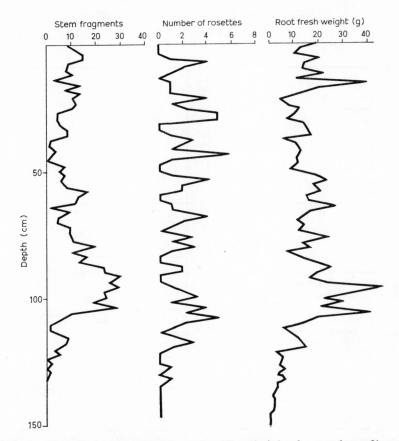

Fig. 23. Distribution of organic remains (*Spartina*) in the marsh profile near the site of the first plantings of *Spartina* in 1929, Bridgwater Bay. Samples were taken every 2 cm down the profile in summer 1962. Note that stem fragments, rosettes and root remains lie progressively deeper at the bottom of the profile as death in the natural position would be expected to leave them. Also, high values obtained near the bottom of the profile and the sudden tailing off of all three items measured near the same general level suggests that the true base level of *Spartina* has been reached and that the results are not significantly affected by loss of material due to decay in the lower half of the profile (from Ranwell 1964 *a*).

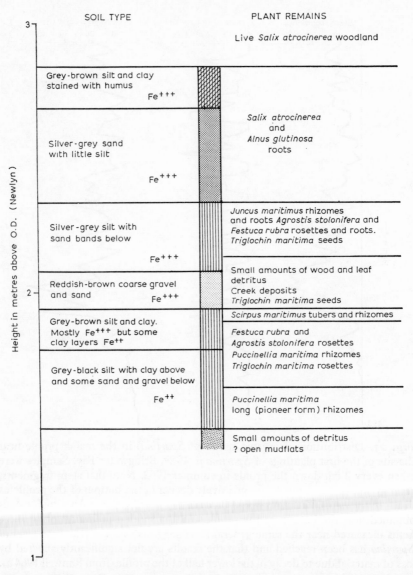

SOIL TYPE

PLANT REMAINS

Live *Salix atrocinerea* woodland

3 —

Height in metres above O.D. (Newlyn)

2 —

1 —

Grey-brown silt and clay
stained with humus
Fe^{+++}

Silver-grey sand
with little silt
Fe^{+++}

Silver-grey silt with
sand bands below
Fe^{+++}

Reddish-brown coarse gravel
and sand Fe^{+++}

Grey-brown silt and clay.
Mostly Fe^{+++} but some
clay layers Fe^{++}

Grey-black silt with clay above
and some sand and gravel below

Fe^{++}

Salix atrocinerea
and
Alnus glutinosa
roots

Juncus maritimus rhizomes
and roots *Agrostis stolonifera* and
Festuca rubra rosettes and roots.
Triglochin maritima seeds

Small amounts of wood and leaf
detritus
Creek deposits
Triglochin maritima seeds

Scirpus maritimus tubers and rhizomes

Festuca rubra and
Agrostis stolonifera rosettes
Puccinellia maritima rhizomes
Triglochin maritima rosettes

Puccinellia maritima
long (pioneer form) rhizomes

Small amounts of detritus
? open mudflats

Fig. 24. Soil profile 150 m to landward of the present seaward limit of tidal
woodland with evidence from plant remains of direct succession from pioneer
salt marsh to tidal woodland. Fal estuary, Cornwall.

Marsh Formation, Drainage and Re-cycling

Marsh relief

Marsh morphology is dominated initially by the surface relief and hydrology of the tidal flats on which it takes place. Localized flood and ebb tide effects in relation to growth form of pioneer species and sedimentation has been studied by Jakobsen (1964) and Møller (1963 and 1964). In general it seems that flood tide effects may dominate under storm conditions while ebb tide effects are dominant in calmer conditions. Flood tide features in higher order creeks with two-way flow are also confined normally to the seaward edge of the marsh, for example the flood bars

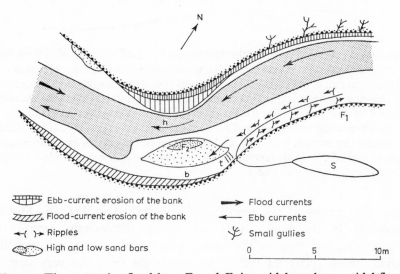

⊞⊞⊞ Ebb-current erosion of the bank	➡ Flood currents
⫽⫽⫽ Flood-current erosion of the bank	⬅ Ebb currents
◂( )▸ Ripples	⍦ Small gullies
⬭ High and low sand bars	0 5 10m

Fig. 25. The successive flood-bars F_1 and F_2 in a tidal creek on a tidal flat at Hojer. The salt marsh plants appear on the tidal flats, and the tidal creek is changing into a salt marsh creek. The flood-bar F_1 was formed in the original wadden gully. The flood-bar has made a barring for the flood-current in the flood-channel which is now a swamp (S). The flood-current now runs round the flood-bar forming ripples and eroding the outside of the bar. In the lower part of the original flood-channel the right side is eroded by the flood-current which forms an isolated flood-bar F_2 to the left. Because of the closing of the original flood-channel and the forming of a new bar the ebb-current is forced to erode the right side of the wadden gully forming a bigger ebb-channel meander. 1. Ebb-current erosion of the bank. 2. Flood-current erosion of the bank. 3. Ripples. 4. High and low sand bars. 5. Flood-currents. 6. Ebb-currents. 7. Small gullies. (from Jakobsen 1964).

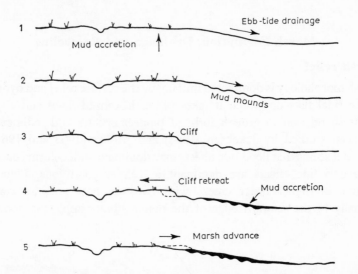

Fig. 26. Theoretical stages in the development of mud-mound and cliff profiles. 1. Accretion of mud on salt marsh due to influence of vegetation. Accretion rate higher than that of adjacent tidal flats. Creation of slope (exaggerated in diagram). 2. Ebb-flow drainage down slope creating mud-mounds. 3. Phase of excessive erosion of salt marsh producing cliffed profile. 4. Retreat of cliff and marsh erosion providing additional mud for deposition on tidal flats. Partial inundation of mounds by mud. 5. Excessive mud deposition on upper tidal flats with inundation of mounds. Possible renewed seaward extension of salt marsh edge. Dengie, Essex (from Greensmith and Tucker 1966).

near the mouths of salt marsh creeks illustrated in Fig. 25. Further landward in the marsh, ebb tide effects increasingly control the topography, and flow in the lower order marsh creeks is essentially unidirectional (Pestrong 1965). However, right from the very start of marsh formation the two opposing processes of accretion and erosion are at work side by side, and one after another, in fashioning the form of the marsh.

Usually one or other of these processes is clearly in the ascendancy. The change from a predominantly accreting situation to one of erosion and vice versa is usually quite rapid. However, Greensmith and Tucker (1966) have made a fascinating study of an Essex marsh where the processes of erosion and accretion are much more neatly balanced than usual (though erosion is believed to be dominant at the present time) and their theoretical conclusions on the cycle of events is summarized in Fig. 26.

Several recent authors (Ragotskie (1959), Redfield (in Ragotskie 1959) and Beeftink (1966)) have described the general changes in relief which accompany marsh genesis as follows:

(1) A change from the convex contours of the open mud flat surface to a concave marsh surface due to better growth at edges and hence levee formation through accretion.
(2) A general levelling of the relief as the marsh approaches maturity and its higher parts receive less and less accretion while the lower parts with more catch up to their level.
(3) A tendency to dissection of large marsh units into small ones, dependent on creek head ramification induced by ebb run-off.

Drainage

Pestrong (1965) has shown that hydraulic velocities and discharge are highest just after the onset of the ebb, and notes that vegetation dominates the hydraulic geometry of the marsh. Using multivariate analysis he concludes that moisture content and particle size exert most control over erodibility.

As studies on loose boundary hydraulics like those of Kestner (1961) become integrated with those on tidal marsh hydraulic geometry (e.g. Myrick and Leopold 1963, Ragotskie 1959 and Pestrong 1965) the approach to mathematical model analogues of the tidal marsh system comes closer. The contributions of physiographer and ecologist still tend to be largely descriptive though much more comprehensive in scope than in the past as shown for example in a study of marsh structure, mud origin, and re-cycling of deposits in Breton estuaries (Guilcher and Berthois 1951). There seems no reason why the various vegetation types and their trapping power for silt and the distinct physiographic units with which they are associated: flats, levees pans, flood bars, slumped blocks and cliff edges should not be analysed (e.g. with the aid of air photographs) separately, quantified, and then re-associated with hydraulic parameters like drainage density to create useful models for predictive purposes.

Re-cycling of sediments

Apart from the small scale re-cycling that accompanies marsh genesis it is a common feature of middle estuary regions that periodic swings of the river channel cause large scale re-cycling of marsh deposits over relatively short periods of time. Studies on a 1,500 acre salt marsh at Caerlaverock, Dumfries led to the conclusion that virtually the whole of it had developed, 'in something less than 140 years, large parts of it in much less' (Marshall

1963). Because of this relatively short period of time, Marshall concludes there would not have been long enough to allow isostatic change to be primarily responsible for the terracing characteristic of these marshes at one time believed to be an indication of a rising coastline.

Soil Composition, Aeration and Water-logging

Soil physical variation and growth

The majority of common salt marsh plants can grow on an extremely wide range of salt marsh soils of highly varied physical structure and composition. For example it is possible to find *Aster tripolium*, *Plantago maritima*, or *Triglochin maritima* equally on the clay-rich muds of south English coast harbours or on almost purely sandy gravel marshes in western Scottish coast sites. Leaving aside for the moment the possibilities of genetically controlled adaptation, it would be wrong to conclude from this that soil physical factors were of minor importance in relation to the salt marsh flora. While each species may have considerable latitude in survival on a wide range of soil types, performance and abundance are very markedly affected by physical factors and their dependent variates such as soil aeration. For this reason, floristic analyses which depend on presence and absence records alone may often give a misleading impression of uniformity in any comparison of marsh vegetation types.

Soil aeration

Adriani (1945) found air contents of 2–4 per cent in *Salicornia – Spartina* marsh and 25–45 per cent in *Salicornia fruticosa – Halimione* marsh. Chapman (1960) found that by poking a hole through the mud surface of submerged salt marsh, gas with significant oxygen trapped below the mud surface was released. His results (Table 13) also show an increase in oxygen content of marsh soils going from pioneer to longer established and higher lying plant communities.

Chapman noted that at root depth soil biological remains were abundant and that the aerated layer was especially associated with them. Green and Askew (1965) have examined soil macropores in reclaimed marshland at Romney marsh in Kent using latex infiltrant techniques. They found fine pores up to 1 mm in diameter were especially associated with roots, *Enchytraeid* worms and *Gammarus* sp. Small cavities and tunnels 2–3 mm or more in diameter were associated with ant activities (*Laesius flavus*). The pore system suggested long periods of activities rather than intensity of current use and the pores and cavities were evidently highly persistent.

Table 13. Composition of salt marsh soil gas (from Chapman 1960).

Region	Marsh	% CO_2*	% O_2	% residual
	Aster marsh a^1	2·99	1·61	95·4
	Aster marsh a^2	2·53	0·82	96·63
Norfolk	Aster marsh a^3	3·26	0·71	96·03
(England)	Aster marsh b	4·22	1·42	94·36
	Limonium marsh 1	1·46	10·5	88·04
	Limonium marsh 2	0·93	17·5	81·57
Romney	Spartina glabra 1	1·79	3·42	94·79
	Spartina glabra 2	3·23	8·28	88·49
(New England)	Spartina patens	0·58	17·3	82·12
	Distichlis	1·17	17·3	81·53
New Zealand	Juncus, Leptocarpus	2·95	17·34	max.
marshes	Juncus, Leptocarpus	0·49	10·05	min.
	Juncus, Leptocarpus	1·75	12·7	av. (12 values)

* The method of analysis (absorption by KOH) also measures any hydrogen sulphide that may be present. This, however, is only likely to be a small percentage.

The mud of pioneer zones of salt marsh contains few large cavities due primarily to activities of *Arenicola* and *Nereid* worms, molluscs (especially *Cardium*), and finer more superficial cavities associated with *Corophium* and *Hydrobia*. A marked increase in finer cavity structure develops as a result of root growth. The persistence of biological effects on soil structure is immediately apparent wherever salt marsh soils show erosion faces.

Air is replenished in these cavities by biological activity (e.g. *Arenicola* air holes) and at higher levels by fissuring of clay soils in dry weather in summer. Air is trapped in these cavities by surface sealing with deposited clay (especially in autumn), and mucilaginous algal growths at the surface in winter and spring.

Clarke and Hannon (1967) have demonstrated with ring infiltrometers just how low the infiltration rate of even highly sandy marsh soils can be (Table 14). They suggest that sodium in the soil may disperse the small amounts of silt and clay so impeding infiltration. However, in a later paper Clarke and Hannon (1969) report that the aerated soil layer is not universal and tends to occur mainly in finer grained, less permeable sediments. Possibly this is because macropores are more abundant and persistent than in sandy soils. Tidal flooding was found to cause water table rise to surface in sandier soils. Penetration of tidal water may be either through solution of crystalline salt, reduction of soil surface salinity, and clay flocculation and/or by lateral seepage due to saturated flow.

Table 14. Infiltration rates in sandy mangrove and salt marsh soils (from Clarke and Hannon 1967).

Species	Infiltration rate 100 cm/hour		% Coarse + fine sand at surface
	Dry period	Wet period	
Avicennia marina	0–8	2–4	79
Arthrocnemum australasicum	25–67	2–42	78
Juncus maritimus var. australis	46–149	14–36	69
Casuarina glauca	240	150	70

Stevenson and Emery (1958) note the large bulk storage of air in shoots of *Spartina* (see also Baker 1970 *a*) and suggest this may account for its success in colonizing frequently submerged zones of fine-particled mud. The same may be true for *Aster tripolium*.

Using Poel's (1960) polarographic apparatus to measure oxygen diffusion rate in sandy salt marsh soils, Brereton (1965) showed that in spite of the increasing water retaining capacity of soils with increasing silt contents associated with rise in altitude, conditions with respect to waterlogging improved. Oxygen diffusion rate rose from $6 \cdot 1$ μA in pioneer *Salicornia* to $8 \cdot 6$ to $13 \cdot 2$ μA in *Puccinellia* zones.

According to Brereton (1965), 'initially population structure is a reflection of the dominant influence of a high water-table which produces a highly plastic marsh surface accompanied by water-logged conditions. Later as the water-table falls population structure is a reflection of point to point variations in soil composition.'

He concludes 'an examination of environmental features show that soil water relations as controlled by drainage (through altitude), and soil physical characters, are primarily responsible for producing differences in species performance between stands and within stands respectively'.

Effects of water-logging

Very little experimental work has been done on the effects of water-logging on salt marsh plants, but Brereton (1971) concludes from his work on *Salicornia* that the main factor affecting *Salicornia* during the succession appears to be aeration. This controlled both germination and growth rates, but there was interaction with salinity. While *Salicornia* shows a preference for soils having high redox levels and shows tolerance of high salt levels, *Puccinellia maritima* shows the opposite. *Puccinellia* performance is improved in water-logged soils of relatively low salt status. *Salicornia* shows the opposite. Field and laboratory culture data confirmed these relationships.

More recently Clarke and Hannon (1970) found that none of the Australian species (*Arthrocnemum australasicum*, *Suaeda australis*, *Triglochin striata*, *Juncus maritimus* var *australiensis* and *Casuarina glauca*) were prevented from germination by submergence in 4 mm of water, but coverage by 5 cm of water retarded and reduced germination. These species and *Sporobolus virginicus* were grown experimentally at three water levels from water-logged to free-drained but damp. All except *Suaeda* and *Casuarina* grew satisfactorily under water-logged conditions, but there is evidence that *Arthrocnemum* and *Aegiceras* seedlings are more intolerant of water-logging than mature plants.

As mentioned in Chapter 4, Goodman and Williams (1961) studying *Spartina* 'die-back' soils found no direct evidence of plant damage due primarily to anaerobiosis. Mineral studies moreover showed no evidence of nutrient unbalance. Since ion accumulation requires oxygen this is further evidence that anaerobiosis is not seriously limiting. They conclude that death is brought about by a toxic reduced ion, but could not definitely establish sulphide as the responsible ion. It might be interesting to compare the tolerance of salt marsh species to different sulphide concentrations side by side with treatments providing a similar level of anaerobiosis, but without sulphide.

While at the present time we seem to be faced again and again with the close interaction of significant factors in the study of causative phenomena in ecology (as illustrated all too apparently in this account of aeration in relation to saltmarsh plant growth) we are at least beginning to understand how the parts of the system are connected even if we do not know exactly how it works.

6 Salt Marshes: Species Strategies

Autecological Limits

Each species on a salt marsh has evolved its own particular strategy for dispersal, establishment and growth; each has its own dimensional limits of age, height and potential clonal size.

Strategies are controlled by the range of environments in which a species can survive and the kinds of change the environments have undergone in the past and are undergoing now acting on the somatic and genetic material of which the species is composed. Perhaps we should remind ourselves right from the start that 'for sexual organisms, it is the local interbreeding population and not the species that is clearly the evolutionary unit of importance' (Ehrlich and Raven 1969).

The salt marsh habitat as a whole imposes certain limits on the kinds of plant that survive in it: all for example must be tolerant of high salinity and some of the ways in which this has been achieved have already been discussed. In addition each sub-habitat of the salt marsh imposes specific additional limits so that certain species survive in them preferentially.

So in this chapter we will see how life in different zones on the salt marsh and in the types of habitats within them has been solved by different species. Autecological studies help us to understand how the various species dovetail into the complex tapestry of populations of which salt marsh plant communities are composed.

Grime (1965) has drawn attention to the necessity of studying and experimenting with events in the field rather than trying to draw nebulous conclusions from data correlations. He also emphasizes the value of looking for susceptibility limits and trying to discover '. . . of what adaptation is the susceptibility a consequence.' This approach is being increasingly adopted with success by workers concerned with the practical application of autecological knowledge and examples are selected for discussion here with this in mind.

Algal Strategies

A small number of red, filamentous green, and dwarf brown algae have become adapted to the salt marsh habitat. Chapman (in Steers 1960) has made a special study of the distribution of some of these in time and space on an English marsh at Scolt Head Island, Norfolk (Fig. 27 and 28).

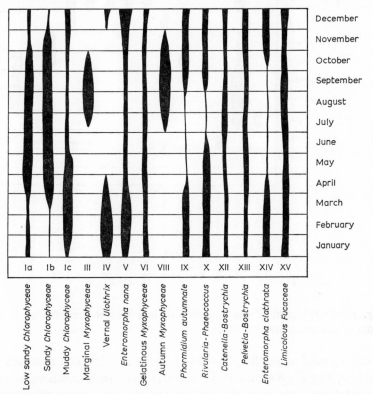

Fig. 27. Distribution of the Norfolk salt marsh algal communities in time (from Chapman in Steers, 1960).

Little is yet known about the autecology of these species and indeed their taxonomic relations are still in some cases little understood. But Chapman's studies reveal clearly some of the distinctive strategies, which enable algae to colonize salt marshes.

Mobile strategies

Certain *Enteromorpha* species (*E. prolifera*) which occur on sandy ground in the pioneer marsh zone have adopted a mobile strategy. They are moved

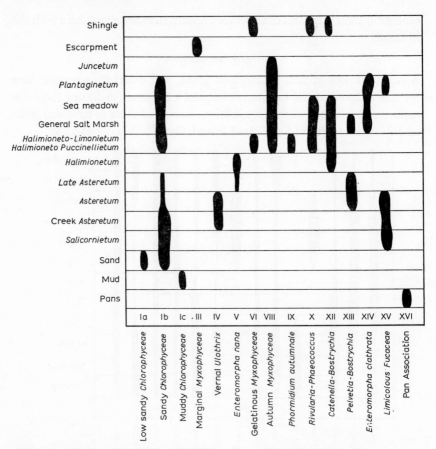

Fig. 28. Distribution of the Norfolk salt marsh algal communities in space (from Chapman in Steers 1960).

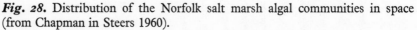

bodily by tidal action from one site to another while still retaining their viability. The fragments may end up in more stable situations entangled around the stem bases of salt marsh plants or as part of the ephemeral algal mixtures stranded in temporarily flooded salt marsh pans. *Pelvetia canaliculata* also produces free-floating forms which accumulate in pans e.g. at Tyninghame marsh, East Lothian, Scotland.

Fixed strategies

Then there are species like *Vaucheria thurettii* and other filamentous bluegreen algae whose gelatinous secretions are sufficiently binding on mud surfaces to enable growth to occur on the steep banks of creeks where no other plants can grow, what one might call an adhesive strategy.

Many algae (e.g. *Ulothrix speciosa* in spring, and *Oscillatoria sancta* in autumn) have developed optimal growth patterns outside the season favourable to the growth of most salt marsh plants. This enables them to take advantage of improved light conditions beneath taller salt marsh plants at the ends of the normal growth season when it is still warm enough for algal metabolism. This is effectively an off-peak seasonal growth strategy.

Yet others adopt a shelter-hold strategy (e.g. *Bostrychia scorpioides*, *Catenella repens*, dwarf *Fucus* species) embedded in mud accreted in the shelter formed by salt marsh plant growth. A few show an epiphyte strategy (e.g. *Catanella repens* or *Enteromorpha nana*), growing on the stems of other plants. This confers advantages of improved light compared with those growing in more shaded conditions at ground level.

Flowering Plant Strategies

Salt marshes are often thought of as an open habitat. If this were true one would expect a high proportion of annuals in the flora, but in fact this is not so. Certainly the pioneer zone is open and is kept open by high incidence of wave break since it is located around mean high water neap tides. Similarly at mean high water spring tides the high incidence of wave break and local smothering of vegetation by tidal litter maintains an open habitat. A few species of annuals (e.g. *Salicornia* sp. in the pioneer zone; *Atriplex* sp. on the strandline) are abundant in these two zones but the zones where annual species are dominant are relatively narrow in width. Between them the bulk of the salt marsh vegetation, whether grazed or ungrazed covers most of the ground when viewed from above and shows little more well-lit bare ground than in an inland grazed pasture for example.

It is not surprising to find therefore that the majority of salt marsh species are perennial and in fact relatively few species of annuals have become adapted to the true salt marsh habitat. Many casual species not specific to the salt marsh flora occur on the strandline and this might account for the relatively high values for Therophytes quoted in Chapman's analyses (Chapman 1960, Table 30). However, he does conclude that 'on the basis of the percentage of total species it is clear that the salt marsh is fundamentally a Hemicryptophyte area'.

Annual Strategies

The majority of salt marsh annuals are members of one family, the Chenopodiaceae. Many of the 500 species comprising this family show a high

H

degree of tolerance to high salinities, but most of them are adapted to relatively stable inland salines: only a few to the very specialized saline *and* tidally-disturbed salt marsh conditions. The genera *Atriplex*, *Suaeda*, and *Salicornia* have all produced annual species adapted to survival on salt marshes.

Salt tolerance

Hunt (1965) has shown that the improvement in salt tolerance of selected seedlings of *Agropyron intermedium* averaged 100 per cent and exceeded 500 per cent in several of the 20 clonal lines examined, indicating it was a highly heritable character. Gutnecht and Dainty (1968) have shown how the appropriate ion systems to utilize high sodium environments could have evolved. In the case of *Salicornia*, selection appears to have run its course to produce species which not only tolerate high salinity, but ones in which the capacity for persistence in fresh water conditions has been either 'bred-out' or is so low that re-invasion of open fresh-water muds is no longer a possibility. It would be interesting to measure any residual capacity for fresh water growth adaptation to see just how low the improvement capacity might be as compared with Hunt's figures for the improvement of salt tolerance as given above.

Resistance to mechanical damage

Boyce (1954) and Oosting (1954) point out the relationship between salt, succulence, and resistance to mechanical damage. It seems there may be a syndrome in which a succulent leaf shape (characteristic of salt marsh Chenopodiaceae and other salt marsh plants) is better resistant to mechanical damage (e.g. by wind and tide on coastal flats) and reduced mechanical damage in turn reduces injury from salt (or in particular the Chloride ion), which stimulates the development of succulence.

The annual strategy in the pioneer zone on a salt marsh demands high resistance to mechanical damage. *Salicornia* shows reduction to a phylloclade form and this presents minimum leaf appendanges for tearing by wave action, but an adequate photosynthetic surface in the high-light open habitats where it occurs.

Tolerance of water-logged conditions

The lowest zones of salt marshes are characteristically water-logged and as Brereton (1965) has shown have low oxygen diffusion rates. But he also points out that *Salicornia* shows a preference for soils having a high redox potential, compared for example with *Puccinellia maritima*. In fact high level tidal flats where *Salicornia* can grow are frequently colonized by algal blooms in spring and summer and it is not uncommon to see a silvery texture on the surface of water-logged mud formed by millions of tiny oxygen bubbles produced by the diatom *Pleurosigma* in early summer. Newly germinating *Salicornia* in April and May may take advantage of this oxygen source and the annual growth strategy in fact takes advantage of the potentially better aerated conditions in summer and passes the unfavourable winter season in seed.

Dispersal

Annual salt marsh species commonly produce seeds of from 1 to 3 mm diameter and not uncommonly the fruit itself (e.g. in *Atriplex*) or even the fruiting head forms the dispersal propagule. Thus Dalby (1963) has shown that the fruiting head with from 4–10 seeds may be dispersed as a whole in *Salicornia pusilla* and can float for up to 3 months in sea water before germination. Stevenson and Emery (1958) found that 10 per cent of seeds of *Salicornia bigelowii* (a Californian species) floated for at least 19 days although Praeger (1913) found that Irish *Salicornia* seeds sank within a minute. Ball and Brown (1970) noted that in *Salicornia europaea* and *S. dolichostachya* some ripe seeds fell out of plants, but in many cases seeds were retained on plants and germinated *in situ*. It seems that dispersal strategy is variable in *Salicornia*. Retention of at least a proportion of propagules occurs in the pioneer zone, some are strewn throughout the marsh by the tide, while a high proportion are carried to the strandline at the upper limits of the marsh. It is of interest here to note that Ball and Brown (1970) found that *Salicornia dolichostachya*, characteristic of the pioneer zone, has larger seeds and a more rapid rate of elongation of the radicle on germination than *S. europaea*, characteristic of more closed marsh habitats (Fig. 29). Moreover *S. dolichostachya* was not capable of maturing seeds in the more shaded sites where *S. europaea* could still achieve maturity.

Phenotypic and genotypic variability

There is a high degree of plasticity within species of *Salicornia* and Ball and Brown (1970) could not find any single character of 14 examined (other than chromosome number) to distinguish the *Salicornia europaea* and *S. dolichostachya*. *Salicornia ramosissima* can survive as isolated depauperate plants beneath tall *Spartina anglica* growth. Extremely vigorous plants of this species developed when the *Spartina* growth was killed in

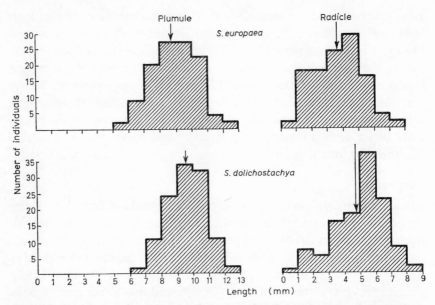

Fig. 29. Frequency distribution of the length of the plumule and radicle of *Salicornia* seedlings 4 days after germination (After Ball and Brown 1970).

herbicide experiments at Bridgwater Bay, Somerset (Ranwell and Downing 1960).

Dalby (1962) has brought together evidence showing that both diploid and tetraploid species occur among British *Salicornia* and that the tetraploids (e.g. *S. dolichostachya*) tend to be heavier seeded than the diploids. There is strong evidence (Fig. 30) that wind-pollination occurs, but plants have been shown to set a high proportion of seed by self-fertilization. This pattern of variation could result in the propagation of micro-species and also segregates from occasional crosses between lines to produce new lines

Short-Lived Perennial Strategies

Flowering behaviour in *Aster* in relation to clines

Aster tripolium is a short-lived perennial widespread on most European and Mediterranean salt marshes. It is also found in inland salines in Europe and Western Asia. Gray (1971) has distinguished geographical and topographical clines in flowering behaviour. In the southern part of its range flowering occurs in the first year; in the northern part of its range flowering may be delayed up to 4 years or more. The topographical cline expressed by flowering behaviour is associated with a tendency for peren-

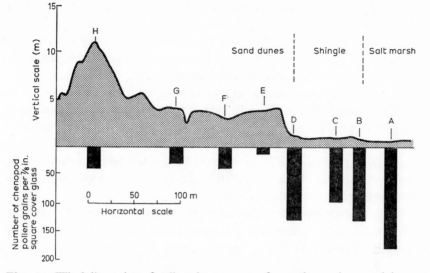

Fig. 30. Wind dispersion of pollen along transect from salt marsh to sand dunes, Blakeney, Norfolk. The lines marking the sampling points, A to H are not drawn to scale vertically (After Dalby 1962).

nial (and therefore earlier-maturing) plants, to occur in Submergence marsh, while annual (and therefore later-maturing) plants, occur more frequently in Emergence marsh.

Perhaps the most striking feature of *Aster* is its remarkable morphological plasticity ranging from tiny depauperate non-flowering plants one or two cm high in grazed salt marsh swards to robust freely flowering plants up to 180 cm high in optimum growing conditions. The latter seem to be associated with lime-rich marshes on soils rich in silt where salinity is generally not above 2 per cent, as in upper estuarine marshes on the Humber estuary, Yorkshire. The early studies of Montfort and Brandrup (1927) and Schratz (1934) indicated that the salinity of the parental habitat influenced seed size and seedling growth rates.

Close environmental 'tracking'

Chapman (1960) found that *Aster* seeds germinated most freely in fresh water, at about half the fresh-water rate in cultures at 2 per cent salinity, and not at all in seawater. However, Chater (in Clapham *et al* 1942) reports plants in inland salines surviving 4·6 per cent salinity and there is evidently genetic adaptation to high salinity in some races of this highly variable species. Indeed Gray (1971) has demonstrated marked physiological and morphological distinctions which are very localized in different *Aster* populations according to their position on a particular marsh.

The short-lived perennial exemplified by *Aster tripolium* illustrates well Ehrlich and Raven's (1969) conception of selection favouring close 'tracking' of the environment and co-adapted genetic combinations related to environmental factors changing with time. Apart from survival selection, its generation time is sufficiently long for environmental modification to interact with the gene complex, but sufficiently short to enable it to adapt more closely to specific environmental conditions at a time and place than longer-lived perennials. The latter must be less specialized to survive the greater vicissitudes of change operating over the longer periods of time they are established at particular locations.

Forms of *Aster* especially adapted to growth on submergence marsh have more numerous air spaces in the rhizome than those adapted to growth on emergence marsh according to Iverson (1936).

Response to grazing

The succulent leaves of *Aster* are attractive to both herbivorous wildfowl like the Brent goose (Ranwell and Downing 1959), and sheep (Ranwell 1961), but plants are capable of surviving in the semi-hemicryptophyte state (normally adopted during the winter), all the year round in grazed pastures. Vegetative propagation by detachable axillary buds still enables plants to reproduce although non-flowering, but continued persistent grazing probably accounts for the absence of this species on some Scottish salting pastures e.g. in some Argyllshire marshes.

Dispersal

Although seeds of *Aster tripolium* are supplied with pappus hairs, they tend to stick together in the capitulum and only some are partially dispersed over relatively short distances by wind; the remainder fall to the ground where they are dispersed by water.

Bearing in mind the limited extent of the salt marsh habitat and the wastage which would occur to unsuitable habitats either side of the shore-line if wind dispersal were not restricted, this compromise seems a very effective adaptation for providing *Aster* with the means of rapidly coloniz-ing open ground within the confines of the salt marsh. Both this and the com-promise between the annual and perennial strategy equip *Aster* to behave like a particularly well-adapted weed species (Gray 1971) and in emergence marsh it is frequently a temporary colonist of gaps created by drought (Fig. 31) or by tidal litter. As with most weeds it seems intolerant of shade

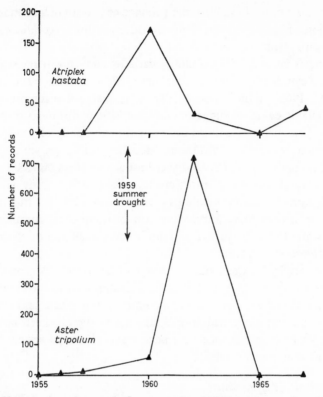

Fig. 31. Changes in salt marsh flora associated with summer drought. Note the peaking of the annual (*Atriplex hastata*) and the short-lived perennial species one year, and two years respectively, after the drought in 1959. Results derived from point quadrat records over a 12 year period in a grazing exclosure at the *Festuca rubra* marsh level, Bridgwater Bay, Somerset.

and is usually sparse in dense or tall communities such as *Spartina* or *Phragmites* marsh. Although an abundant colonist of reclaimed agricultural land temporarily salinized at the time of a sea flood in S.E. England (Hughes 1953), it was unable to persist as a weed element once the salt had leached and the land was again restored to agriculture.

Herbaceous Perennial Strategies

Consequence of longevity

Unlike the more ephemeral strategies discussed above, the herbaceous perennial strategy must cater for persistence at a location on the salt marsh for several decades. During this time the initial conditions operating on the seedling at the time of establishment change as a result of accretion and soil maturation. These produce distinctly different living conditions for the aged mature plant.

Judging from easily visible clonal patterns and known rates of growth individual clones of *Spartina anglica* commonly survive for 50 years or more (Hubbard 1965). While undoubtedly many plants live for much shorter time, available evidence suggests that very little recruitment of perennials by newly established seedlings occurs within the body of the salt marsh. For example, Boorman (1967) found seedlings of *Limonium vulgare* only very occasionally in the field and these usually in areas outside its optimal range, although mature plants were abundant in his study area. Again although *Spartina anglica* seedlings occur scattered beneath mature swards in early spring they do not survive beneath the shade of tall summer growths at Bridgwater Bay in Somerset, and rarely occur at all in the denser growths of Poole Harbour, Dorset.

Grasses are by far the commonest type of herbaceous perennial in most salt marshes. The relatively few species found such as *Spartina anglica*, *Puccinellia maritima*, *Festuca rubra*, *Agrostis stolonifera* and *Phragmites communis* are extremely widespread, at least in the northern hemisphere. In spite of their importance they have received comparatively little autecological study until recently.

Adaptations of *Spartina*

Very few species have succeeded in spanning survival from the absolute seaward limit of salt marsh growth on open high level mudflats to the landward limit of salt marsh growth at high water equinoctial tides, and from fully saline to brackish water conditions. The recently evolved *Spartina anglica* has achieved this. Longer established species of *Spartina* on American marshes (Mobberly 1956) have become specialized for growth in specific zones within this range but only *Spartina anglica* has the capacity to span the whole range. It has achieved this through a type of polyploidy (see Marchant 1967) which confers vigorous growth, large size, and high fertility, enabling it to dominate other species and reproduce extremely rapidly. At the same time it has developed unusually high phenotypic plasticity. This enables it to elongate stems as much as 10 or 15 cm a year to grow up through accreting mud in pioneer marsh and at a later stage in its life to adjust to accretion between one tenth and one twentieth of this rate in fully mature marsh. As Bradshaw (1965) has pointed out, 'where changes in environment occur over very short distances, adaptation by the formation of genetically different populations may be precluded. In these conditions very spectacular types of plasticity may be evolved'. The salt marsh habitat and *Spartina anglica* exemplify this.

Adaptations to survival at the seaward limit of submergence marsh include: a relatively large seed with considerable food reserves; rapid rate of shoot and root growth; development of deep, stout, anchor roots, and shoots well supplied with air spaces.

Taylor and Burrows (1968) have shown that some establishment does occur by fragments, but this seems to be of minor importance compared with seedling establishment except perhaps in long distance establishment via the tide-line to new sites. One of the putative parent species, *Spartina maritima*, sets little or no fertile seed (Marchant 1968). Even in favoured sites (e.g. Foulness, Essex), only widely scattered isolated clones develop from the occasional established fragment. *Spartina anglica* by contrast, rapidly fills in gaps with seedlings once pioneer clones have established. This enables it to develop a continuous sward over large areas in about 20 years.

Experimental studies have shown that *Spartina anglica* plants are tolerant of salinities up to 9 per cent in culture. Even in Emergence marsh where higher salinities than sea water develop salinity is unlikely to limit growth. Summer drought probably limits seedling establishment at higher levels, but it is often the density of its own tidal litter which kills out plants near the strandline and finally defeats its growth (Ranwell 1964 *b*). Grazing reduces flowering, but increases tillering to produce short dense swards (Ranwell 1961).

Adaptation of *Puccinellia*

Puccinellia maritima also spans a very wide range of the salt marsh habitat, but it is distinguished from *Spartina anglica* by much smaller size and much greater reliance on vegetative, as opposed to sexual reproduction. In common with *Spartina anglica* it is tolerant (but to a lesser extent), of water-logging, high salinity and high accretion rates of up to 5 cm per year. It too exhibits considerable phenotypic plasticity and pioneer forms are charac-terized by stolons up to 50 cm long, while under intense sheep grazing a tight mat-like growth little more than 1 cm high develops.

A vegetative propagation strategy is favoured in this species by tendencies to apomictic seed development (Hubbard 1968) and by sheep grazing which produces quantities of discarded fragments (much in evidence on the strandline of salting pastures), which root readily when heeled into damp marsh surfaces by sheep treading. In an experimental study of sheep grazing at Bridgwater Bay, Somerset, tread-planting was particularly noticeable where a period of grazing was followed by a big tide flooding the plots so irrigating the newly 'planted' *Puccinellia* and aiding its establishment.

A distinctive growth of narrow-leaved, widely spaced, upright shoots of *Puccinellia maritima* is characteristic of ungrazed marsh at Dengie, Essex, a marsh which is subject to surface scour erosion. This and other distinctive forms are in cultivation at the Coastal Ecology Research Station, Norwich to discover their phenotypic and genotypic relationships. *Puccinellia maritima* is not entirely apomictic and some sexual reproduction occurs, so one would expect greater variation in genotype on ungrazed marshes where seed propagation is likely to occur and greater uniformity on grazed marshes where vegetative reproduction would result in propagation of the few initially established types.

Adaptations in *Agrostis* and *Phragmites*

Spartina anglica and *Puccinellia maritima* have adapted to pioneer growth on water-logged saline silt liable to accretion, in ungrazed and grazed conditions respectively. Their counterparts in the brackish zone, *Phragmites communis* in ungrazed, and *Agrostis stolonifera* in grazed salt marsh, play a similar role and show similar adaptations related to tolerance of water-logging, rapid powers of horizontal spread, and capacity for vertical adjustment. They might be expected to differ principally from the first two species in their tolerance of saline conditions, and this proves to be so. Field measurements (Ranwell 1964) and culture experiments (Taylor 1939 and Gray 1971) indicate that both *Agrostis stolonifera* and *Phragmites communis*, in temperate zones at least, are restricted to estuarine marshes where chlorinity of the soil solution does not rise much above 1 per cent. This does not necessarily mean that chlorinity is the limiting factor at the seaward limit for these species and Hannon and Bradshaw (1968) give evidence suggesting that it is not in the case of *Agrostis stolonifera*.

All four species are likely to be limited to landward by competition for soil moisture with more drought tolerant species or by shade in the case of the shorter species. Experimental studies are needed to determine these tolerance limits and in the case of drought, with and without association with other species.

Woody Perennial Strategies

Adaptations in *Limonium*

We can take *Limonium* species as representative of the woody perennial strategy as recent studies by Boorman (1967, 1968) have added considerably to knowledge of the autecology of *Limonium vulgare* and *L. humile*. They both possess a stout woody rootstock and deep tap root and are tolerant of salinities in excess of sea water. In fact pre-treatment with sea-water followed by fresh water may actually enhance germination in *Limonium humile* compared with that in fresh water alone, (Fig. 32). Boorman suggests that sea water pre-conditions the embryo for germination and has an osmotic shock effect which weakens the seed coat and stimulates subsequent germination in fresh water. As in the case of *Aster*, seed size and early environmental history play a part (in addition to genetic control), in variations in germination response to different treatments. Germination is reduced by low oxygen levels and the seaward limit of *Limonium vulgare* is related to tidal flooding frequency, while the landward limit of both species seems to be controlled by competition for light or soil moisture with other species.

Both species are very susceptible to trampling damage by grazing animals, and sheep bite young buds off *L. vulgare* in spring. This rapidly leads to its disappearance. Both species are insect-pollinated and clearly likely to

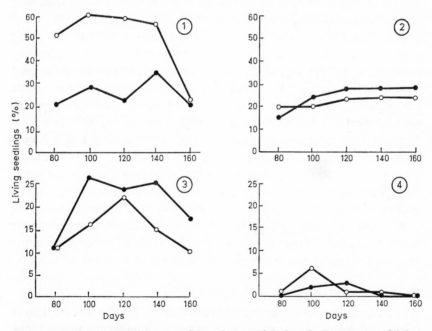

Fig. 32. Seedling establishment of *L. vulgare* and *L. humile*. Percentage of living seedlings after 160 days in an unheated greenhouse. 1. Fresh water and sand. 2. Fresh water and mud. Sea water/fresh water and sand. 4. Sea water/fresh water and mud. *L. vulgare* ○, *L. humile* ● (from Boorman 1968).

be left unpollinated if populations are so reduced that bees and other insects are no longer attracted to them. It may be a combination of intense sheep grazing and depressed insect activity in the cooler climate of Scotland, rather than a simple direct climatic factor alone, which has prevented both species from penetrating into more northerly Scottish marshes.

Advantages of high density growth in Emergence marsh

Boorman (1967) found that the vertical range of *L. humile* was restricted to one third of its potential range when in competition with *L. vulgare* and to one half its potential range when other species were present in high density. Rhizomes are little more than 5 cm long and it is evident that in contrast to Submergence marsh, where long rhizomatous species or ephemeral species occur, Emergence marsh favours short rhizome plants and dense or tufted growths. Most Emergence marsh species have dense woody rootstocks (e.g. *Armeria maritima, Halimione portulacoides, Inula crithmoides, Limonium* sp. and *Plantago maritima*). Others while not woody, tend to have compact short rhizomatous growth (e.g. *Festuca rubra, Juncus gerardii, Juncus maritimus* and *Triglochin maritima*). The latter are less sensitive to trampling than the brittle woody perennials and persist better in grazed marsh.

There is obviously selective advantage in relatively impenetrable dense growth in Emergence marsh. This is presumably related to the increasing competition that develops as the marsh vegetation becomes diversified and closes up. It is clearly shown in air photographs of *Spartina anglica* where the original rounded clone structure becomes compressed into polygonal clonal boundaries in more mature marsh. Marchant (1967) notes that *Spartina anglica* derivatives thought to be of polyhaploid origin have a much higher tiller density, about double that of the parent. It is noteworthy that these high density *Spartina* forms are particularly found in the upper Emergence marsh levels in Poole Harbour, Dorset and elsewhere. There is little vertical root layering in salt marsh soils because of the limits on respiration imposed by water-logging not far below the surface. Competition for moisture and nutrients at the 5 to 10 cm level is likely to be keen at the upper limits of Emergence marsh especially on more coarse particled substrata.

Problems of distinguishing limiting factors

Autecological studies of the type described above help to sort out master factors controlling the strategies appropriate to different salt marsh zones. Within the major zones, limiting factors may sometimes be too closely confounded for statistical approaches like the partial component analysis employed by Dalby 1970, to distinguish them. The solution of these problems must lie in laboratory study and field experimental study at critical seasons of growth and at both actual and potential limits of growth.

Limited knowledge of animal autecology on salt marshes

It should not be assumed that animals are of negligible importance in salt marshes because they receive so little mention here. This is due mainly to lack of knowledge.

The dominant influence of animals on salt marshes is vertebrate grazing but very little is known about animal behavioural patterns influencing this. Invertebrate influences tend to be localized to particular sub-habitats of limited area such as creeks, pans, tidal litter and the rather limited epifauna associated with certain plant species. With some exceptions such as Dahl's (1959) outstanding autecological studies on Scandinavian Ephydridae (Diptera), much of the work on salt marsh invertebrates remains at the taxonomic and distribution stage of study. There is great scope for autecological study of invertebrate adaptations to life on salt marshes and speciation arising from this.

Some attempt to balance the largely plant ecological emphasis of this chapter, by reference to animal population studies, is made in the next chapter concerning synecology.

7 Salt Marshes: Structure and Function of Communities

The primary constraint on the types and numbers of organisms found on a salt marsh is the availability of the organisms themselves, that is the composition of evolved biological material at any particular place at any particular time.

The next constraint is the energy level imposed particularly by the climatic factors temperature and light. As we have seen in Chapter 1 these are primarily responsible for determining the regional type of marsh vegetation found.

Subordinate to these higher orders of restraint are water and particularly water quality (especially salinity) and oxygen availability. In other words this amounts to position on landward to seaward gradients and degree of submergence or emergence in relation to that position.

The ultimate level in the hierarchy of environmental constraints is nutritional and dependent not only on physical and chemical factors but also on the biological material which is itself energetic and can in turn generate the evolution of new biologic material.

This chapter concerns the accumulation of biological material, its movement, and the energy flowing through it in the salt marsh ecosystem. It is not concerned with the floristic or faunistic composition of different salt marsh communities except so far as they illustrate relation between structure and function. The presence or absence of most species in a habitat is irrelevant to the great majority of other species (including man) in the habitat. The dimensions, population size, and behaviour of a few species, and the degree of diversity of the remaining species (rather than their particular type), seem to be the more significant biological elements of the ecosystem. It is worth keeping in mind in the approach to the complexities of community study that, as Odum (1961) points out, 'basic work which is functional in approach is almost immediately practical . . . description alone, no matter how detailed, does not bring understanding.'

Plant Populations

Haline zones and plant distributions

Beeftink (1962) has produced a conspectus of phanerogamic salt plant communities in the Netherlands and considers that their zonation coincides very well with the classification of saline waters known as the Venice system (Final Resolution of the Symposium on the Classification of Brackish Waters, 1959) i.e.:

Zone	% Chlorinity (mean values at limits)
Euhaline	1·65 – 2·2
Polyhaline	1·0 – 1·65
Mesohaline	0·3 – 1·0
α - mesohaline	0·55 – 1·0
β - mesohaline	0·3 – 0·55
Oligohaline	0·03 – 0·3
Fresh water	0·03 – or less

To the extent that some of these limits coincide approximately with boundaries of some of the more abundant species controlling the character of certain communities these divisions seem of practical value in relation to British habitats also.

In particular there is a small group of highly salt tolerant species (e.g. *Halimione portulacoides, Limonium vulgare*) which do not normally penetrate beyond the up-estuary limit of the polyhaline zone. There are others which penetrate seaward just so far as the down estuary limit of the Polyhaline zone (e.g. *Agrostis stolonifera* and *Phragmites communis*). The limit of tidal woodland growth (e.g. *Alnus glutinosa, Salix cinerea* spp. *atrocinerea*) lies close to the down estuary limit of the oligohaline zone. Too many other considerations affect distribution to press these relationships too hard, but a competent ecologist should be able to deduce the halinity zone from the spectrum of species or vice versa quite reliably.

Sub-habitats of the salt marsh ecosystem

There are 10 quite distinctive sub-habitats (Fig. 33) found in most salt marshes and each provides distinctive growing conditions for the communities that occupy them. Teal (1962) has attempted to sum the proportions of sub-habitats on a complete marsh and find out how they equate with the total populations of the more abundant species occupying them. High quality air photographs which are now available should enable this type of analysis to be carried out quite readily, and it seems a useful basis for rapid survey of wildlife resources over large areas comparable to that developed by Poore and Robertson (1964).

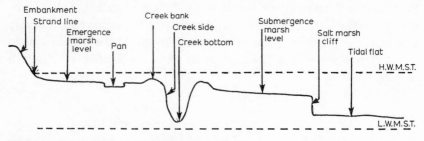

Fig. 33. Sub-habitats of the salt marsh ecosystem.

While it is true that a sizeable area of a salt marsh consists of level marsh, the other component sub-habitats may together make up an even greater area on much dissected marshlands. Yet the distinctive communities of these sub-habitats have been subject to very little individual study. Much of what follows therefore concerns level marsh communities. However, as Odum (1961) points out, because of the importance of tidal action in nutrient cycling and production, the entire estuarine system must eventually be considered as one ecosystem or productive unit. This means that the sub-systems based on plankton, benthos, and marsh-detritus food econo- mies and the sub-habitats with which they are associated, must be analysed separately and ultimately related, before the system as a whole can be understood.

Transitional habitats

Salt marshes normally develop as relatively narrow belts adjoining sheltered coasts. Consequently they have extensive boundaries adjoining other sys- tems where transitional habitats between the two are developed. In smaller marsh systems, transitional habitats may be more extensive in area than the pure salt marsh system itself.

Transitions to wet land, dry land, shingle and cliff tend to be relatively sharp with fairly steep salinity gradients near the top of the marsh in which many of the less common and more locally distributed species find a home. Transitions to sand dune may be much less sharp owing to the mobility of sand in wind and water.

In coastal sectors which have been reworked by wave action, horizontal and vertical mixtures of contrasting particle size; clay, silt, sand or shingle, impose patterns of transitional habitat type on the more typical salt marsh habitat.

Formation of the plant communities

The threshold level for salt marsh plant growth on a tidal flat often develops quite suddenly, and new colonization over a comparatively large surface area may occur very rapidly. West (1956) also finds that 'colonization of a mud flat (by mangrove) is not gradual but sudden and this results in stepwise bands of even age growth adjoining the coast'.

This threshold level varies in height in relation to the tidal regime and in accordance with stability, turbidity, and the light climate as we have seen. If this threshold happens to be low in level there is likely to be rapid colonization by a very pure community of the lowest growing pioneer species (e.g. *Salicornia* or *Spartina*); if it is higher then the amount of emergence may be sufficient for most of the main marsh species to colonize almost simultaneously and a mixed marsh community develops. In the intermediate case it depends very much on the proportions of annuals and perennials as pioneers whether diversification takes place early or late in marsh development, for the entry of new species depends very much on available space.

The subsequent vegetational history of the marsh is a product of interacting physical and biological boundaries. These are developed in horizontal and vertical planes and become diversified in time. Consequently it is of vital importance, to measure the rate at which the various interfaces and boundaries are changing to understand the plant and animal community transformations which both accompany, and at the same time, modify them.

Types of population change

What is becoming evident is that whether a pure dominant marsh community (like *Spartina anglica* marsh) or a mixed marsh community (e.g. *Triglochin, Plantago, Limonium, Puccinellia* marsh) develops initially, it may be relatively stable in composition for decades. Changes occur either in the vicinity of significant vertical changes in level (e.g. cliffs, creeks, pan edges or accretion to some new critical threshold level) or, where vertical changes in height of the vegetation are imposed by grazing, cutting or the invasion of taller species which can over-shade shorter ones.

Minor population changes are associated with physiographic development

I

of creeks, pans and cliffing. More far-reaching ones are associated with management interferences with the surface growths. The primary population changes which are perhaps of more fundamental interest will depend on the pioneer species growing and accreting silt to a level at which their reproductive performance is sub-optimal, and a new threshold for change in the flora has been reached.

There are surprisingly few studies of population changes on salt marsh though there are many assumptions in the literature implying that zonation can be equated with succession. Chapman (1959) has provided a valuable series of maps showing plant community changes over a period of 25 years at Scolt Head Island, Norfolk. But one has only to look at the slumped clods of main marsh level communities doomed to die in the bottom of a creek to realize that the probabilities of any particular square metre of salt marsh turf taking part in uninterrupted text-book succession may be very low indeed. Just what these probabilities are from site to site remains to be worked out.

Successional processes

Studies of population changes in mature *Spartina* marshes have helped to illustrate some of the general points made above and perhaps at the same time throw a little light on the successional processes.

In the Bridgwater Bay marsh it was found that at least three processes were involved in replacement of *Spartina* marsh by other species in mesohaline zones near the landward limit of *Spartina*, (1) suppression of *Spartina* growth by accumulation of its litter, (2) accretion towards a less saline and drier zone which favoured reproduction and growth of such invading species as *Agropyron pungens, Scirpus maritimus* and *Phragmites communis* and depressed reproduction and growth of the *Spartina* and, (3) shading out of *Spartina* beneath vegetatively expanding taller growths (Ranwell 1964 *b*). It was found that *Spartina* retained dominance for about 20 years, but in the subsequent 12 years about 50 per cent of the *Spartina* had been replaced by the invading species along the 2 mile (1·6 km) landward edge of the marsh. It was noted also that the build-up of levels suitable for growth of the invading species occurred more rapidly than they could be utilized. This was demonstrated by experimental transplants of the invading species well beyond their natural limits within *Spartina* marsh where they survived in competition with *Spartina*.

Yet another successional process, involving frost damage to *Spartina* growth near its upper limit, became apparent after the 1962–1963 cold winter in the Keysworth marsh in Poole Harbour. Patches of

Spartina killed back by frost together with suppression of growth locally by patches of litter, opened up the marsh surface for colonization by invaders similar to those at Bridgwater Bay (Hubbard and Stebbings 1968).

The younger marsh at Bridgwater Bay is still relatively lower in relation to tidal flooding than that at Keysworth and invasion is still largely linear in association with litter along the landward boundary. By contrast at Keysworth, litter is more widely scattered over an older and relatively higher marsh and *Spartina* is being invaded in irregular patches over the whole surface because it has all reached the new threshold level for such a transformation. It looks as though succession occurs in sudden jumps after long periods of relative stability and that it is the loss of vigour of the original species in sub-optimal growth conditions that results in its withdrawal to make room for the next phase.

Invasion boundaries

Fig. 34 shows a typical profile of one of many linear invasion boundaries subsequently mapped over a number of years by plane table mapping. The profile shows a distinctive pattern in which the *invading* species (*Phragmites*) grades quite gradually from high to low in height or biomass from landward to seaward i.e. from near optimal to sub-optimal growth conditions. By contrast the *invaded* species (*Spartina*) shows a characteristic

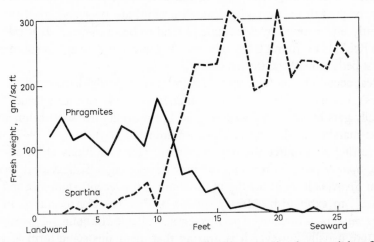

Fig. 34. Invasion boundary. Note the gradual increase in shoot weight of the invading species (*Phragmites*) and the sudden decrease in shoot weight of the invaded species (*Spartina*) from seaward to landward across the boundary. Poole Harbour, Dorset.

sudden decline and eventual extinction, within the taller growths of the invading species. This pattern was similar in boundaries between *Spartina* and other invaders such as *Scirpus maritimus* or *Agropyron pungens*.

It was found that if shoots were removed reciprocally at points across a mixed boundary of *Spartina* and *Phragmites*, *Spartina* maintains, but does not increase, its density in the absence of *Phragmites*, but can be extinguished by *Phragmites* growths of density 150 shoots per metre or more. By contrast, the removal of *Spartina* had no significant effect on *Phragmites* at the mid-point of the boundary.

Crude as this experiment is, it illustrates the susceptibility of *Spartina* near its landward survival limit. It is of interest that reciprocal shoot removal experiments in main marsh communities recently carried out at Scolt Head Island (Woodall *pers comm.*) show very little adjustment between species which implies much greater stability in these populations, at present in the middle rather than near the limit of their vertical range of growth.

Influence of grazing and fire

Grazing and exclosure experiments (Ranwell 1961 and 1968) show that very rapid readjustments in population balances can be induced by such wholesale alterations of the habitat. Recent studies in oligohaline marshes on the Fal estuary have demonstrated that it is possible for ungrazed salt marsh to succeed to tidal woodland without major isostatic change, but conditions for tree growth in the badly drained ground are poor and trees are frequently undermined by flooding and tend to be short-lived. It is relevant that Reid (1913) found trees to be mostly quite young in age in submerged forest beds around the British coast.

Peat accumulation (e.g. up to 2 ft (60 cm) of slowly decaying litter in 8 years), occurs in *Spartina patens* marsh in south east Louisiana. This usually gets burnt in dry weather and fire prevents [...] on these marshes so they remain grass-dominated (Lynch *et al* 1947). It is interesting that under the highly nutrient-rich conditions at Bridgwater Bay, *Spartina anglica* marshes are now developing a distinct peat formed from *Spartina* litter at the top of the shore. This recently took fire and was difficult to extinguish (Morley (*in litt.*)). Fire has also occurred in the *Phragmites* beds invading *Spartina* marsh in Poole Harbour.

More usually however it is grazing that maintains some form of grass marsh whether it be by sheep and cattle in Europe; cattle in North America; camels in the Red Sea marshes (Kassas 1957), or marsupials and rabbits in Australia or New Zealand.

Truncated development

Polyhaline marshes tend to form abrupt saline to non-saline boundaries with adjoining coasts since by their nature they are remote from ameliorating influences of fresh-water. They are more prone to disturbance from wave action and tend to be coarse-particled as they are also remote from river-borne silt sources. There is some evidence (Guilcher and Berthois (1957)) that their more readily erodable sandy-silt may tend to re-cycle and plant communities on them may not undergo significant directional succession. Human activities of course frequently truncate the development of marshland before it can reach its final stages.

Animal Populations

Numbers and biomass

Apart from vertebrate grazers there seems to have arisen a general belief that animals are of minor significance in the salt marsh habitat. Chapman (1960) for instance devotes less than two pages to them in a 350-page book on salt marshes and salt deserts. In fact it is only in the last decade or so since Chapman wrote that the abundance and significance of animals in salt marshes has come to be realized.

Paviour-Smith (1956) obtained the astounding figure of 7,631,460 animals per m^2 from a closely rabbit-grazed salt marsh turf in New Zealand with a soil (admittedly highly organic in character) only 20 cm deep over almost pure sand. Her figures for biomass show that animals represent only about 2 per cent of the value for plant biomass:

	mg/m^2 dry wt.
Total zoomass (max.)	32,436
Phytomass (bacteria)	10
(higher plants)	1,680,000
	1,712,446

Of particular interest also are her figures for organic matter. They immediately suggest the importance of detritus and hence of detritus feeders in the salt marsh economy:

	g/m^2 organic matter dry wt
Dead	17,374·4
Live plants	760·9
Live animals	25·6
	18,160·9

Origins of animal groups

Teal (1962) examined the terrestrial and aquatic macro-invertebrate fauna of a salt marsh in Georgia, U.S.A. (Fig. 35) and found it was distributed as follows:

(a) Terrestrial species	(1) General marsh levels
	(2) Upper limits of marsh
(b) Aquatic species	(1) Seaward edge of marsh
	(2) Creek sides
	(3) General marsh levels
(c) Marsh species (aquatic derived origin)	(1) Planktonic in larval stage
	(2) Marsh-living throughout the life cycle

Terrestrial groups formed nearly 50 per cent of the marsh fauna, but aquatic groups were found to be more important in the energetics of the system. He also found there was only slight adaptation to marsh conditions

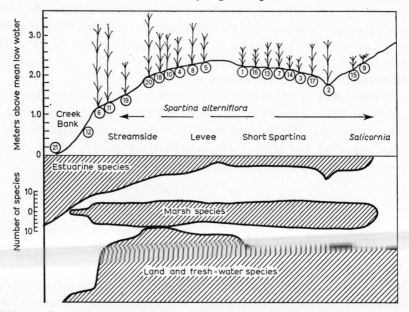

Fig. 35. Representative section of a Georgia salt marsh with horizontal scale distorted non-uniformly. Sample sites indicated by circled numbers. Site 2 represents the beginning of a drainage channel, not an isolated low spot. Symbols for grass are drawn to correct height for average maximum growth at those sites. The number of species of animals of 3 groups listed in Table 1* are plotted against sample sites. Names of marsh types used herein are also indicated (from Teal, 1962, by permission of the Duke University Press).

* Not given here.

Table 15. Ordinal composition of sets of ten samples taken in five types of salt marsh vegetation in the summer of 1960. Newport river estuary, North Carolina, U.S.A. From Davis and Gray, 1966, by permission of Duke University Press).

Stations	Mean percentage composition							
	Homoptera	Diptera	Hemiptera	Orthoptera	Coleoptera	Hymenoptera	Other orders	Average number of insects per sample
Spartina alterniflora								
Bogue Banks*	75·15	9·27	12·31	2·05	0·46	0·61	0·08	1,316
Piver's Island	53·47	40·28	0·70	0·70	2·78	2·08		288
Beaufort Channel	55·09	30·94	5·28	3·02	3·02	2·26	0·38	265
Bell Creek*	87·74	10·20	0·16	1·22	0·26	0·37	0·05	1,893
Harlowe Creek**	95·73	3·07	0·68	0·13	0·21	0·16	0·02	11,095
Lennoxville Point	31·65	52·23	3·16	7·91	2·22	2·53	0·32	316
All stations	90·11	6·72	1·76	0·66	0·38	0·37	0·04	2,529
Spartina-Salicornia-Limonium								
Bogue Banks	78·10	13·41	3·89	2·67	0·98	0·73	0·24	411
Juncus roemerianus								
Bogue Banks	85·61	5·30	1·52	5·30		2·27		132
Core Creek	30·00	15·00	20·00	20·00		10·00	2·27	20
Nelson Bay	73·17	7·32	1·22	15·85	1·22	1·22		82
Bell Creek	16·66	50·00		22·22	11·11	11·11		18
All stations	72·22	9·92	2·78	11·11	0·79	2·78	0·40	63
Distichlis spicata								
Lennoxville Point	60·83	13·64	21·83	2·35	0·51	0·78	0·06	1,782
Core Creek	72·29	14·13	9·45	0·39	3·04	0·62	0·08	1,281
Nelson Bay	38·41	40·71	14·60	1·50	3·54	1·15	0·09	1,130
Harlowe Creek	54·32	10·12	30·19	2·36	1·85	1·18	0·08	1,186
All stations	57·32	18·66	19·18	1·17	2·04	0·91	0·07	1,345
Spartina patens								
Bogue Banks	41·06	25·17	17·22	2·65	9·27	3·31	1·32	115
Piver's Island	19·90	61·22	4·59	2·04	3·07	7·65	1·53	196
Beaufort Channel	28·65	40·00	10·81	3·24	5·41	10·81	1·08	185
Harlowe Creek	43·90	31·22	6·83	4·39	1·95	11·22	0·49	205
Lennoxville Point	22·04	54·69	6·94	2·45	3·67	9·39	0·80	245
All stations	30·41	43·88	8·78	2·96	4·39	8·78	1·02	196

* *Prokelisia marginata* (Homoptera) estimated in two samples.
** *P. marginata* estimated in four samples.

under flood, most climbing to escape (e.g. spiders) or trapping air (e.g. ants). Certainly one of the most dramatic and enlightening experiences the author has had was in watching the mass escape of terrestrial animals by flying, crawling up stems, swimming, or walking over the water surface supported by surface tension, one quiet evening on the equinoctial flood of the Fal marshes in Cornwall.

The basically terrestrial nature of the fauna of these marshes was confirmed by Stebbing's (1971) findings that, 'in general the faunal species recorded were representative of any marshland ecosystem in southern Britain and were not indicative of saline or brackish conditions'.

Distribution of insects on marshes

Davis and Gray (1966) found some 250 species of insects on North Carolina salt marshes and concluded they were abundant in both variety and quantity. They studied the distribution of insect groups above ground with respect to plant zones of increasing elevation (Table 15). Most of the insect species spend the winter in the egg state either in dead *Spartina* stems or in the ground. They found that shelter and food are factors that affect the size of insect groups more than tidal influences. For example the grass *Distichalis spicata* was rich in insects as it provided much cover and food, while the slender tough stems of the rush *Juncus roemarianus* attracted *Orthoptera* which are characteristic of open stands of coarse vegetation and can utilize tough plant tissues for food better than most insects. *Homoptera* decreased with increasing elevation, but ants, common in *Spartina patens*, were excluded by the tide at lower levels.

Dahl (1959) has made a special study of the distribution of species and numbers within species of Diptera Brachycera in salt marsh and dune habitats on the coasts of Norway and Sweden. Six sample surfaces of each sub-habitat were recorded and proportions of the more abundant species compared to determine in which sub habitat particular species were dominant. Studies on the biology of the different species reveal their preferences and adaptations. Work on the species – habitat relationships of wide ranging groups of closely related species of this type are of particular value because they show how the capacity for dominance may be altered by climate or other environmental factors.

It will be of absorbing interest to watch the build up of the marsh fauna on the relatively new *Spartina anglica* marshes in Europe. Preliminary studies on one of the oldest of these new marshes in Poole Harbour, Dorset show that the principal species at present include a herbivorous bug (*Euscelis obovata*), an omnivorous grasshopper (*Conocephalus dorsalis*) and a carnivore (*Dolichonabis lineatus*), a rather nice illustration of the balanced way in which this new animal community seems to be developing. *Euscelis* feeds on *Spartina*, *Conocephalus* on *Euscelis* and *Spartina*, and *Dolichonabis* on *Euscelis* (Payne 1972).

Trophic Levels and Relationships

Paviour-Smith (1956) first outlined some basic trophic relationships on a salt marsh (Fig. 36).

Marples (1966) has recently utilized radio-isotopes to clarify the food

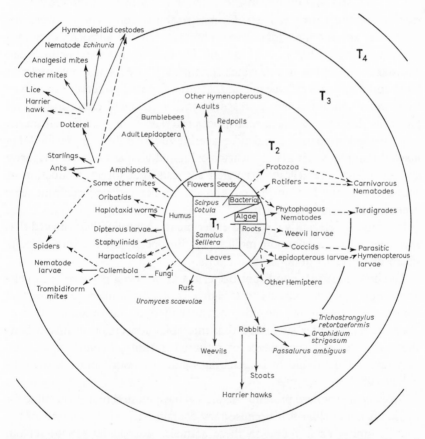

Fig. 36. Foodweb of the salt meadow community showing trophic (T_1, T_2 etc.) levels. The producer organisms are enclosed in boxes, and succeeding trophic levels are enclosed in succeeding concentric circles. Solid lines represent known relationships and broken lines assumed relationships. Hooper's Inlet, Otago Peninsula, New Zealand. (After Paviour-Smith 1956.)

chains of Arthropods. He labelled *Spartina* and detritus-rich sediment surfaces with the Phosphorus isotope P^{32}. He sampled standing crops and used
sweep netting to capture insects to record their distribution and changes in
their radioactivity with time (Fig. 37).

Results showed that four species of insects were dominant grazing
organisms (one *Orthoptera*, two *Hemiptera* and one *Homoptera*). Species in
two families of Diptera (*Dolichopodidae* and *Ephydridae*) and *Littorina*
snails were dominantly detritus feeders. Spiders were the important carni-
vores and obtained their energy from both the detritus and the grazing
food chains.

Luxton (1964) has examined the zonation of *Acarina* on the grazed salt
marshes of the Burry estuary, Glamorganshire. Some species were restricted to specific intertidal zones, others occurred in all zones, even into
the seawardmost *Spartina anglica* zone. He showed that these animals can
withstand immersion in sea water for up to 12 weeks without apparent
harm and that neither larvae nor adults showed special preference for salt or
fresh water conditions when presented with a choice of either in culture.
However these mites did have distinct preferences for specific salt marsh
fungi as food, so salinity could affect acarine zonation through the food. He
noticed that many salt marsh Acarina exhibited viviparity or ovoviviparity
and since eggs are readily dislodged suggests that direct production of
active larvae may help to prevent the species being dislodged from their
preferred habitats by tidal action.

In a series of elegantly designed experiments, Newell (1965) showed that
Hydrobia ulvae (a common mollusc on European salt marshes) digests
micro-organisms, but not organic debris.

Taschdjian (1954) found that bacteria and protozoa participate in conversion of *Spartina* extracts to a higher content of mixed vegetable and
animal protein. Studies on composition and bacterial decomposition of
Spartina marsh litter suggested that microbial conversion in marsh function was a key to maintenance of estuarine fertility, notably production
of Vitamin B 12 found in invertebrates and fish (Burkholder and Burkholder 1956).

Spartina alterniflora proteins (Table 16) have limited biological value for
marine fish and shell-fish because they contain only small amounts of the
specific amino acids found in these animals. Burkholder (1956) set out
cages of *Spartina* marsh litter in creeks and found that about 50 per cent of
the dry matter disappeared after a period of about 6 months. About 11 per
cent (dry wt. basis) of the annual crop of marsh grass may be rapidly converted to bacteria, but microbial utilization of crude fibre takes place more

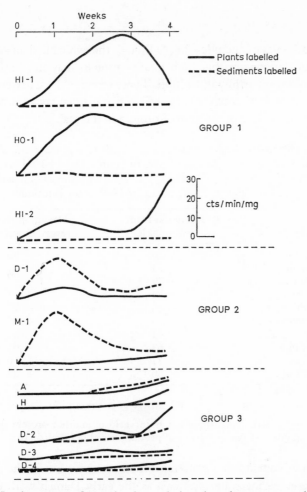

Fig. 37. Uptake curves of 10 animal populations based on mean weekly activity density for 4 weeks following the labelling of plants. (*Spartina alterniflora*) and sediments with P^{32}.

Group 1 includes three species (in descending order, *Trigonotylus* sp., *Prokelisia marginata* and *Ischnodemus badius*) which became highly labelled within 1 or 2 weeks after the grass was labelled. These species were judged to be primarily grazing herbivores.

Group 2 includes the group of highly related Dolichopodid flies and the *Littorina* snails which became highly labelled when the sediments were labelled, but less so when the grass was labelled.

Group 3 includes those Anthropods (Arachnida, Hymenoptera: Ichneumonidae, Braconidae, Chalcidae and Scelionidae, *Oscinella insularis*, *Chaetopsis apicalis* and *C. aenea* and *Hoplodicta*) which did not become highly labelled in either quadrant or became labelled only after 3 to 4 weeks. These groups were judged not to be actively feeding on either the growing grass or the detritus, or to be predators, in the case of delayed uptake. Sapelo Island marshes, Georgia (from Marples, 1966, by permission of the Duke University Press).

slowly. Burkholder concludes that 'although the available data are too few, still the indications are that high quality protein may not be formed by either marsh grass or phytoplankton. There remains the unexplored possibility that microbial conversion may act like a huge transformer to step up the potential value of the pool of protein in the sea'.

Table 16. Deviation* in per cent of amino acids of mature terminal leaf stalks of *Spartina alterniflora* (collected in August from Sapelo Island area, Georgia, U.S.A.), above (+) or below (−) the amino acids in proteins of fish and average *Graminae*. Data from Block, 1945 and Lugg 1949 (after Burkholder 1965).

Amino acids	Deviation from fish muscle	Deviation from average Gramineae
Arginine	− 78	− 90
Leucine	− 73	} − 56
Isoleucine	− 79	
Lysine	− 24	+ 7
Methionine	− 90	− 76
Phenylalanine	− 75	− 55
Tryptophane	− 41	− 60
Histidine	− 63	− 93
Valine	− 77	− 60
Threonine	− 50	− 24

* Per cent deviation $= \dfrac{x-y}{y}$. 100, where x is the amino acid of one protein (*Spartina*) and y is the corresponding amino acid of another protein the values of x and y being given in gm. per 100 g of protein, based upon N = 16%.

The sea of course has a plankton-based economy but in the marsh and near-shore estuarine water systems, as the early Danish work on *Zostera* (Petersen 1915, 1918) suggested, detrital food chains are likely to be of greater importance. These unlike the direct plant/herbivore/carnivore food chain are much more complex. Both of these food chains are operative in most ecosystems, but often in widely different proportions (Odum 1963). It is largely thanks to Odum and his co-workers that we are at last beginning to understand how a salt marsh nutritional system really works, largely through the concept of energy flow.

Energy Flow

Odum and Smalley (1959) showed how numbers tend to overemphasize, and biomass to underemphasize, the importance of small organisms in the community (see Paviour-Smith's figures above), while the reverse tends to be true of large organisms. Numbers and biomass can be integrated by a consideration of energy flow. These relationships were compared in two species (*a*) a herbivore and (*b*) an omnivore in *Spartina* marsh.

These workers obtained data by seasonal sampling, respirometry and calorimetry, of *Spartina alterniflora*, the herbivorous grasshopper *Orchelimum fidicinium*, and the omnivorous mollusc *Littorina irrorata*. They found that energy flow fluctuated only two-fold while numbers and biomass fluctuated five- or six-fold (Fig. 38). They noted that there was synchronization of the energy flow peak with medium numbers of median sizes (i.e. stages of active growth) of the secondary producers rather than with maximum numbers or maximum biomass. Food availability was related to periods of high energy flow and operated over a longer period for the mollusc than the grasshopper (Fig. 39).

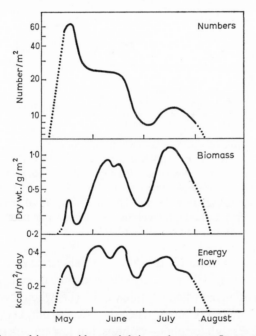

Fig. 38. Numbers, biomass (dry weight), and energy flow per square metre (1 kcal. = 4186 J) in a population of salt marsh grasshoppers (*Orchelimum fidicinium*) living in low-level *Spartina alterniflora* marsh, Sapelo Island, Georgia, U.S.A. (from Odum and Smalley 1959).

Role of benthic algae

Now benthic algae have a high production all the year round in Georgia, U.S.A. at least and these and detritus were considered to be the principal food of the mollusc *Littorina*. Pomeroy (1959) found that net production of

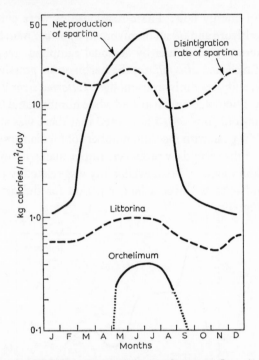

Fig. 39. Comparison of the annual pattern of energy flow (1 kcal = 4186 J) in *Littorina* and *Orchelimum* populations in relation to certain potential food sources. Net production of *Spartina alterniflora* in low level marsh is the sole source of food energy for *Orchelimum* while the disintegration of dead *Spartina* through the entire marsh and the subsequent transport of detritus (including associated microflora) to the high level marsh provides one potential food source for *Littorina* (from Odum and Smalley 1959).

'mud-algae' makes a major contribution to total primary production of the salt marsh ecosystem. His work also showed that in summer, maximum photosynthesis ~~~~~~~~~~~~~~~~~~~~~ when the tide was in, (i.e. when the marsh was not desiccated); in winter it occurred when the tide was out, i.e. when temperatures were high enough for photosynthesis, but low enough not to desiccate the algae.

It is of interest to note here in relation to the above that the herbivorous Brent Goose was found to synchronize its feeding at Scolt Head Island, Norfolk on tidal flat algae in winter (where temperatures even at these latitudes favour active growth of algae) and on the salt marshes in spring (Ranwell and Downing 1959). We begin to see why the tidal flats are so productive for waders and wildfowl during winter months in the northern hemisphere.

On a larger scale of course, productivity is also related to regional climate. One study on the mollusc faunas of *Spartina-Salicornia* marshes illustrates this. The local, seasonal and latitudinal variations in their faunas were analysed quantitatively in 11 marshes ranging over 20° of latitude on the North American Pacific Coast by Macdonald (1969). He found that the standing crop of the living animals increases considerably from north to south, suggesting that available resources increase at lower latitudes.

Grazing and detrital pathways

Odum (1962) and Teal (1962) found that major energy flow between autotrophic and heterotrophic levels on a marsh is by way of the detritus food chain rather than the grazing food chain. In Georgia estuaries dominated by *Spartina alterniflora*, organic detritus (more than 90 per cent of *Spartina* origin) is the chief link between primary and secondary produc-

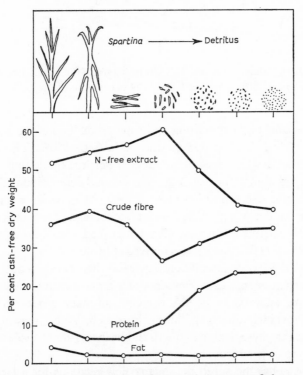

Fig. 40. The nutritive composition of successive stages of decomposition of *Spartina alterniflora* marsh grass, showing increase in protein and decrease in carbohydrate with increasing age and decreasing size of detritus particles. Sapelo Island, Georgia, U.S.A. (from Odum and Cruz 1967).

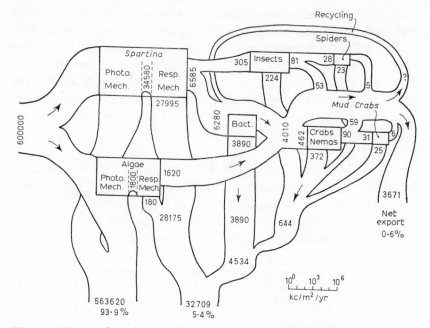

Fig. 41. Energy flow (1 K cal = 4186 J) diagram for a salt marsh. Sapelo Island, Georgia, U.S.A. (from Teal 1962, by permission of the Duke University Press).

tivity because only a small portion of the net production of the marsh grass is grazed while it is alive (Odum and de la Cruz 1967). These authors studied the seasonal changes in amounts of detritus by netting at a creek mouth, they examined the distribution of size and composition of particles, their origin, the decomposition rates of litter, its nutritive value and the metabolism of detritus particles under incubation. They conclude that bacteria-rich detritus is nutritionally a better food source for animals than the fresh *Spartina* from which it is derived (Fig. 40).

Pomeroy (1959) concludes that in water less than 2 m deep benthos is the more important energy converter; in water greater than 2 m deep phytoplankton are believed to be the principal primary producers. In fact, increasing turbidity due to pollution in inshore waters may reduce the possibilities for phytoplankton growth and be increasing the role of benthos in inshore water productivity.

Teal (1962) has measured the energy flow relations for a Georgia salt marsh (Fig. 41) and these are summarized in Table 17 which shows that 45 per cent of the net production of the marshes is exported to the estuarine waters where it is believed to largely support harvestable shrimps and crabs in waters too turbid for significant phytoplankton production. Clearly increasing turbidity may not merely modify the lower limit of salt marsh growth but also affect profoundly the balance in energy paths at critical junctions between ecosystems.

Table 17. Summary of salt marsh energetics derived from studies at Sapelo Island, Georgia, U.S.A. One kc = 4186 J (from Teal 1962 by permission of the Duke University Press).

Input as light	600,000 kcal/m^2/year
Loss in photosynthesis	563,620 or 93·9%
Gross production	36,380 or 6·1% of light
Producer Respiration	28,175 or 77% of gross production
Net Production	8205 kcal/m^2/year
Bacterial respiration	3,890 or 47% of net production
1° consumer respiration	596 or 7% of net production
2° consumer respiration	48 or 0·6% of net production
Total energy dissipation by consumers	4,534 or 55% of net production
Export	3,671 or 45% of net production

K

PART THREE   Sand Dunes

8 Sand Dunes: Formation and Differentiation of the Habitat

One thing that salt marsh and sand dune plants have in common, in spite of the striking differences between these two habitats, is the problem of establishing in a soil which is initially unstable. Foreshore sand washed daily by the tides on an open shore is in fact so unstable that no flowering plants or even macro-algae have yet succeeded in colonizing it. Even when sand is exposed for days at a time, it soon dries out in the wind and may still be blown about too frequently for plants to establish. Moreover, unlike silt on which salt marsh plants grow, sand is very deficient in plant nutrients and moisture (at least in the surface layers). Without nutrient income from the tide, sand would be unlikely to support much plant growth for long even if it were stable.

All three of these deficiencies; instability, lack of nutrients, and lack of soil moisture, are ameliorated by tidal litter, deposited at the top of the fore-shore in strandlines, and it is here that the process of dune formation can start.

The Strandline

Sand feeding to the strandline

Krumbein and Slack (1956) recognize four zones on sandy shores as shown in Table 18. To the extent that each zone feeds sand to the zone above, adequate sand supply in all of them is essential to the continued long term growth of dunes. But width, height and orientation of the backshore zone is of more immediate concern, as it is from this zone that the bulk of the sand is derived by wind action for dune building (Plate 9).

Coastal physiographers have carried out intensive studies of the sweep zone of open shores (see King 1972), but so far there has been little attempt to link these changes with rates of supply to dune systems, though studies on this are now in progress in Northern Ireland.

Sandy shores bordering estuaries or sounds are usually narrow, and being well protected from strong wave action tend to accumulate considerable quantities of tidal litter. This enables strandline plants to establish but there is usually insufficient sand supply to lead to significant dune formation.

In contrast sandy shores on the open coast are often wide and what tidal litter there is forms temporary surface accumulations above mean high water spring tide level. Litter sticking up from the sand reduces windflow near the sand surface and wind blown sand is deposited until the litter is buried. No further sand is likely to accumulate once a smooth surface is restored again, and the deposit is likely to be re-worked by the next tide to reach it.

Table 18. Sand shore zones (Krumbein & Slack 1956)

Shore Zone	Limits	Tidal relations	Agents of sand movement
1. Nearshore bottom	Mean low water to minus 9 m	Nearly always submerged	Currents and breaking waves
2. Foreshore	Mean low water to high tide line	Alternately submerged and exposed	Currents, breaking waves, occasional wind action
3. Backshore	High tide line to dunes	Nearly always exposed but occasionally submerged during storms or exceptionally high water	Breaking waves, wind action
4. Dunes	Above highest tide limit	Always exposed	Wind action

Colonization of the strandline

Hulme (1957) has shown (Fig. 42) how after the high tides of the spring equinox, falling high water levels leave a zone up to 11·5 m wide seaward of maximum high spring tide level at Longniddry, East Lothian. Annual strandline plants can colonize in this zone. The tidal litter contains or traps varying quantities of viable seeds. Tidal litter reduces daily temperature fluctuations in summer at the sand surface from 25°C in open sand to 7°C

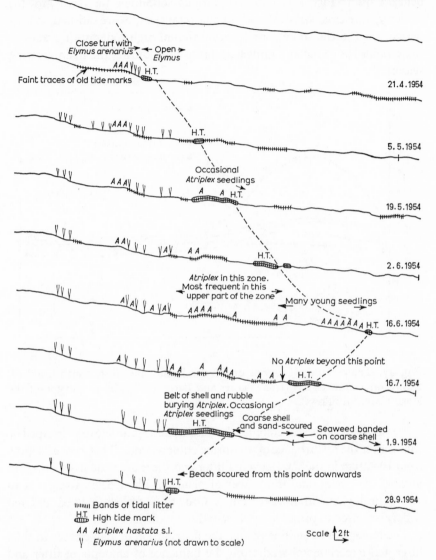

Profile of transect 16.7.1954

Close turf with
Elymus arenarius ← Open → Elymus

Faint traces of old tide marks

AAAVVV H.T.

21.4.1954

VVV V V VAAAVV V VV H.T.

5.5.1954

AAAV VV VV

Occasional
Atriplex seedlings

A A H.T.

19.5.1954

VVV AAVVVVAV AA

H.T.

2.6.1954

Atriplex in this zone.
← Most frequent in this
upper part of the zone →

VV AVAVAVAV AAAA A AA

Many young seedlings →

AAAAAAA H.T. 16.6.1954

VV VV

No Atriplex beyond this point

AVVVVAA A AAA AA H.T.

16.7.1954

Belt of shell and rubble
burying Atriplex. Occasional
Atriplex seedlings

VVVVVVV H.T.

Coarse shell
and sand-scoured
→ ←

Seaweed banded
on coarse shell →

1.9.1954

VVV

← Beach scoured from this point downwards

VVVVV H.T.

28.9.1954

ιιιιιιιι Bands of tidal litter
H.T. High tide mark
AA   Atriplex hastata s.l.
V   Elymus arenarius (not drawn to scale)

Scale ↑2ft
       →

Fig. 42. A permanent transect across the foreshore at Longniddry, East Lothian, charted at intervals throughout the summer. Note the downward extension of colonization by *Atriplex*, as the zone free from tidal scour (to left of dotted line) increases during the early part of the summer. (After Hulme, 1957).

beneath litter (Fig. 43). Thus the various conditions for plant growth; stability, nutrients, moisture and suitable temperatures are satisfied, at least temporarily, in the shore zone from maximum high water spring tides to some point above mean high water spring tides during the main growing season.

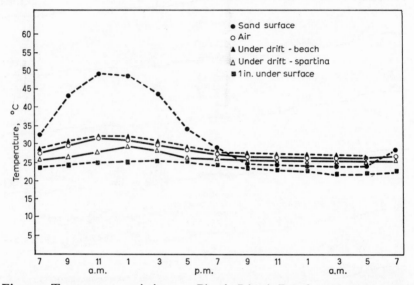

Fig. 43. Temperature variations on Piver's Island, Beaufort, North Carolina, U.S.A. on a summer day (from Barnes and Barnes, 1954, by permission of the Duke University Press).

The annual plants that colonize the strandline appear late (e.g. in April or May), after the disturbance of the spring equinox tides. They root at depths from 10–40 cm in the sand-covered litter and there are wide fluctuations in number of species, and in number of plants within species, from year to year (Cunningham in Darwen 1964). Growth is too short-lived and too widely scattered to promote significant dune growth.

The biology of strandline plants, the distribution of viable seeds in tidal litter and experimental studies on the influence of amounts of litter and seeds on the thresholds for embryo dune formation, all deserve further study.

The Embryo Dune

Perennial grass pioneers and accretion

Tidal litter and strandline plants accumulate sand to a level just above H.W.M.O.S.T. This is sufficient for perennial grasses like *Agropyron junceiforme* and *Elymus arenarius* to establish, and their growth laterally and vertically is sufficiently persistent to raise a dune a metre or two high. Bond (1952) found evidence of continued vegetative growth in *Elymus arenarius* in all months of the year except January at Aberdeen, but Nicholson (1952) found that *Agropyron junceiforme* was dormant during winter at the same latitude. Nevertheless even in winter the dead shoots of *Agropyron* are persistent and help to retain sand trapped in summer.

The inherent capacity of these plants and others like them elsewhere in the world (e.g. *Uniola paniculata*, North Carolina, U.S.A.) to bind sand lies in the ability to perennate and to develop extensive horizontal and vertical rhizome systems. Bond (1952) recorded vertical rhizomes 150 cm long in *E. arenarius* and noted that viable buds survived at depths of 60 cm. Viable buds of *Agropyron junceiforme* occur at depths of 60 cm but this species is not tolerant of accretion rates of more than 60 cm per year (Nicholson 1952). This is probably about the limit for both species, but it needs to be determined experimentally.

Agropyron junceiforme propagates readily by seed and within 10 days the seedling root has elongated 7 cm to more or less permanently humid sand. Rhizome fragments are also important in reproduction and according to Nicholson (1952) propagation from broken rhizomes is common. *Elymus arenarius* propagates rather less freely from seed in the field than *Agropyron* according to Bond (1952).

Seedling regeneration only becomes significant in *Elymus* when plants are abundant. Germination tends to be delayed by the presence in seeds and glumes of a water soluble germination inhibitor until spring, when seedlings have a better chance of survival. Seedlings can not withstand more than about 7·6 cm of sand burial (Clarke 1965).

Growth of *Agropyron* embryo dune

Gimingham (in Burnett 1964) gives a good account of the way in which *Agropyron junceiforme* forms a fore dune from a newly established seedling:

'The single primary root quickly extends to a depth of about 15 cm where a level of moisture content rather higher than that of surface layers is often maintained. The first lateral roots, however, extend horizontally closely below the sand surface. After a rosette of tillers has been established, short rhizomes are formed extending obliquely for distances of between 5 and 30 cm from the original plant giving rise to new groups of tillers (Fig. 44 A to C). This type of growth may continue for two seasons, but in time long horizontal rhizomes are produced greatly increasing the vegetative spread of the plant (Fig. 44 D). Their tips normally turn upwards in autumn, first breaking the surface, ready to produce a new group of shoots in spring. Development may continue indefinitely in this way if sand accumulation is only slight, for elongation of the shoots can bring them to the surface through layers not exceeding about 23 cm in depth. Where however, burial is more rapid, shoots are killed and rhizomes instead of extending laterally assume a vertical direction until the new surface is reached, when again tillering takes place. This sympodial development may keep pace with repeated sand deposition, often up to heights of 1·8 m and considerably more.'

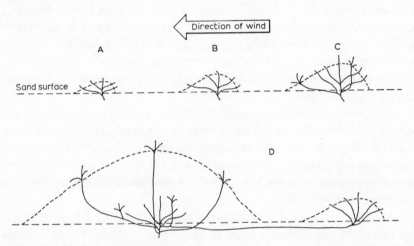

Fig. 44. Stages in colony development and formation of 'embryonic dunes' by *Agropyron junceiforme*. The upper broken line represents the surface of the dune. (from Nicholson, 1952).

Plant growth habit and dune formation

Although the occasional find at depths of 60 cm in *Agropyron junceiforme* and *Elymus arenarius* may produce vertical growth to reach the surface, continuous accretion of this order per year would result in such sparse surface growth that plants would be unlikely to survive. Effectively they are limited to annual accretion zones of about 30 cm a year, and are incapable of building the really high dunes produced by *Ammophila* growth, and certain other species.

Cowles (1899) recognized two contrasting growth habits among dune-forming plants which are of fundamental importance in understanding their capacities and limitations. *Ammophila* species and *Agropyron junceiforme* both produce horizontal rhizomes of potentially unlimited growth. Others like *Elymus arenarius, Salix repens* and *Populus* species seem to lack the capacity for rapid horizontal spread, but do readjust to sand burial with oblique or vertical rhizome growth. In the case of the two shrub species the vertical rhizome growth may be virtually unlimited at acceptable accretion rates. Their tight growth form tends to produce rather steep-sided hummock dunes in contrast to the much broader dune units formed by the more widely spreading growth of *Ammophila*.

Limitations of the pioneer grasses

It is not clear whether or not *Agropyron junceiforme* and *Elymus arenarius* are simply overwhelmed by high accretion rates and/or shading (see Nicholson 1952) which *Ammophila* induces, or whether their moisture or nutrient requirements cannot be satisfied in high dunes. Gimingham (in Burnett 1964) concludes that since *Agropyron junceiforme* seldom has active roots below 60 cm and the water table may be over 1·2 m below the surface the roots are independent of it. However, they may be more dependent on organic matter and spray-borne nutrients than *Ammophila*. It may be significant also that *Elymus arenarius* does survive in high *Ammophila* dune at Durness, Sutherland where rainfall and spray are high compared with more southerly dunes. Clearly there is scope for experimental transplant studies and studies of moisture and nutrient requirements to help solve this problem.

We are now in a position to appreciate the special advantages which *Ammophila* species possess in dune building, namely potentially unlimited horizontal *and* vertical rhizome growth. No other species combine these two vital attributes and throughout the world it is either *Ammophila arenaria* or *Ammophila breviligulata* which have created the really high dune landscapes.

Establishment and Growth Patterns of *Ammophila*

Pioneer studies by Gemmell, Greig-Smith and Gimingham (1953) showed how *Ammophila arenaria* initiates dune building. They found that establishment by seedlings on the higher parts of the backshore at Luskentyre in the Outer Hebrides was sporadic. At Ainsdale, Lancashire establishment from rhizome fragments from the eroded coast dune occurred more commonly than seedling establishment.

Shoot tufts from rhizome fragments or seedlings were initially unbranched and created smooth dunes parallel with the upper shore like those formed by *Agropyron*. These leafy shoots were capable of growth through moderate accretion by leaf elongation. If leaves were buried, axillary buds developed to form vertical shoots with long internodes which produced new leafy shoots at the surface. Adventitious roots formed on the vertical rhizomes just below the surface and deeper horizontal rhizome connections gradually died. As the leafy shoots occasionally produced more than one vertical rhizome branching increased and dome-shaped tussocks developed.

Laing (1954) confirmed and amplified this picture with detailed studies of the American species *Ammophila breviligulata* on the inland dunes around Lake Michigan. He found this species regenerating mainly from eroded rhizome fragments on the beach. Seedling regeneration was confined to damp hollows or protected sites on the lee slopes of eroding dunes.

The evidence suggests that seedling establishment on shore or dunes depends on periods of heavy rainfall which gives both moisture and temporary stability and that where coastal dunes are eroding, rhizome fragments from toppled clumps are the principal means of re-establishment of a new embryo dune. Where erosion of a coast dune cuts back to forested dunes beneath which *Ammophila* has been shaded out, such regeneration may be prevented as at Holkham, Norfolk.

Laing (1954) found that shoot elongation occurs in spring, especially from buried vertical stems which at the onset of dormancy in the previous autumn had a fully formed blade but an incompletely elongated sheath and internode. Newly formed internodes of the current spring also develop and elongate. Buds of the continuous development type form only on vigorous shoots from depositing surfaces and only on those internodes which mature from late April to early June. Dormant buds form elsewhere and may be dormant for months or years. Branching of the vertical shoots creates a cluster of shoots around the parent shoot; loose open clumps in accreting surfaces, compact tufts on stable areas.

Dune stratigraphy

Both Laing (1954) and Olson (1958 c) have shown how past depositional patterns can be determined through measurement of internodal lengths which occur in response to burial (Fig. 45). Olson (1958 c) found that fore-dunes accrete only about 30 cm a year probably because shoot burial removes their power to hold more sand until new growth appears in the following year. He notes how the appearance of a new foredune effectively cuts off sand supply to the one to landward where dead growths persist, clumping becomes more compact and flowering diminishes markedly within 3 or 4 years of stabilization. These very swift reactions of *Ammophila* to changes in sand accretion indicate how greatly its vigour depends upon them. Both *Ammophila breviligulata* and *A. arenaria* have been shown (Laing 1954 and Ranwell 1958) to just tolerate an absolute limit of sand burial of 1 m per year, but density diminishes rapidly if these conditions persist. These high rates of accretion are especially characteristic of the higher lee slopes of dunes.

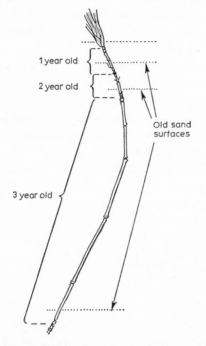

Fig. 45. Three annual growth cycles of a buried marram grass stem. Wide spacing of internodes occur in years following rapid deposition of sand in winter. Stabilization of the dune shown by sudden decrease in annual growth elongation (from Olsen 1958 *c*).

In order to understand the mechanics of dune building and development of the dune landscape it is necessary at this point to consider some fundamental principles relating to the effect of surface roughness in the form of vegetation on wind flow and sand movement.

Windflow, Sand Movement and Dune Vegetation

Bagnold (1941) has shown that sand moves by saltation, a process whereby the first grains moved by a sufficiently strong wind fall under gravity to the loose sand surface and bounce back into the wind at the same time setting other grains in motion by their impact. He showed that the impact gradient threshold varies approximately as the square root of the grain diameter. Above the impact velocity, about 10 miles per hour (4·5 m/s), rate of sand flow varies as the cube of the wind velocity. It follows that really substantial sand movement is only accomplished by high wind velocities.

Much remains to be learned about the frequency of movement of shore sand in relation to the incidence of rainfall and the special conditions operating on drying out sandflats with or without variously spaced pioneer growths of algae or higher plants.

Air flow over a smooth level surface decreases in velocity in a regular manner near to the surface. Over a curved smooth surface, the rate of velocity decrease increases near the surface especially at the point of maximum curvative. Surface roughness interferes with the smooth laminar flow of air and creates turbulence. As a result the profile of mean velocity ($\overline{V}$) as a function of height (Z) is not linear, as it is in laminar flow, but logarithmic. The logarithmic relationship implies that velocity decreases to zero at some height greater than zero (Z_0).

Bagnold (1941) showed that Z_0 can be related to height and spacing of

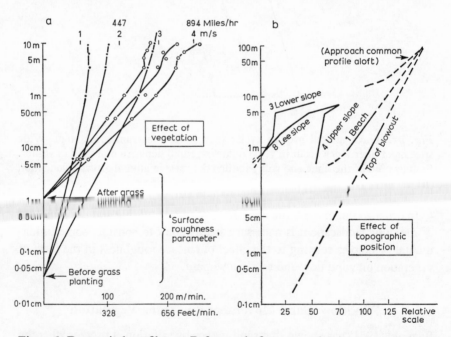

Fig. 46. Dune wind profiles. *a*, Before and after grass planting on an Indiana dune; *b*, comparable plotting of key profiles for a bare Michigan dune, after Landsberg and Riley 1943 (from Olsen 1958 *b*).

surface irregularities and he called it 'the surface roughness parameter'. For a given roughness (Z_0), the slope of velocity with respect to $\log Z$ increases as velocities aloft increase. This slope is proportional to the 'drag velocity' (V_*) which equals the square root of shear stress over air density. The proportionality constant is 5·75 when $\log Z$ is to base 10. Hence the relationship:

$$\overline{V} = 5\cdot75\ V_* (\log Z - \log Z_0)$$
$$= 5\cdot75\ V_* \log \frac{Z}{Z_0}$$

Using this relationship on anemometer measurements of wind velocity at series of heights above dune surfaces, Olson (1958 b) showed that the upper level of calm air near the surface (i.e. Z_0) was raised approximately thirty-fold from the bare sand value to the new value after the sand was planted with *Ammophila breviligulata* (Fig. 46).

A fairly low surface roughness (Z_0) around 0·03 cm seems to be a general characteristic of bare dune surfaces (Bagnold 1941, Landsberg and Riley 1943 and Olson 1958 b).

Now the threshold velocity for sand movement, 4·5 m/s must be exceeded at the 1 cm Z_0 level for sand to move from a vegetated surface. In fact Olson's results show that most dune-building vegetation reduces wind velocity at the sand surface well below this value, indeed to zero in an *Ammophila* plantation. As Olson points out we can see why most sand is trapped within a few metres of a vegetated edge. The effect is maintained by the fact that unlike other obstacles, dune-building vegetation regenerates surface roughness by growth.

Wind profiles over a dune

Ammophila keeps pace with sand accretion in the building phase as we have seen, but changes in dune shape themselves modify the overall air flow patterns. It is known from aerodynamics that laminar flow over an aerofoil crowds the streamlines and accelerates flow near the point of curvature. This produces the well-known half Venturi effect on which the lift factor of an aerofoil depends. Now an *Ammophila* dunelet or a mature coast dune, especially in regions where the prevailing and dominant wind is on shore, approximates an aerofoil shape and measurements over the profile show that wind profiles (Fig. 47) behave somewhat similarly to those over the aerofoil. The anatomy of a dune system with dunes and intervening slacks (Plate 12) is explicable in terms of these relationships.

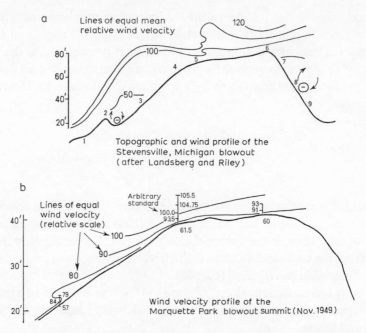

Fig. 47. Effects of topography on wind profiles over dunes. *a*, Michigan profile shows negative velocities behind small foredune ridge and large blowout dune, and crowding of high velocities very near dune surface at the upper slope (position 5); *b*, Indiana profile of present study (see table 1) shows similar crowding of high velocity near surface on windward slope. Velocities here are given relative to 3·34+ meter anemometer on the main tower, labelled 'arbitrary standard' (from Olson 1958 *b*).

Critical zones

Critical zones to bear in mind are (1) Protection in front of a big dune due to a 'stalling' effect (suggested by the spreading of the streamlines in Fig. 47); (2) Maximum wind velocity near the surface leading to maximum erosion near the crest of the windward face of the dune which according to exposure, wind and rain climate controls the height to which dunes can grow in any particular region; (3) the vortex behind the lee slope which creates calm for deposition in relation to winds flowing over the dune (and where non-prevailing winds have greater influence); (4) the extended shelter to leeward of the dune where a dune slack may be developed and (because the wind has deposited most of its sand load already on the lee slope) accretion is minimal and (5) the point beyond the shelter of the dune to landward (which is a function of the dune height) where higher wind velocities approach the sand surface carving down to non-erodable damp

1   *Arthrocnemum* marsh (sansouire) in the Camargue (Rhone delta). France. Note the open nature of the vegetation in this fully mature marsh in a climate where evapo-transpiration exceeds precipitation.

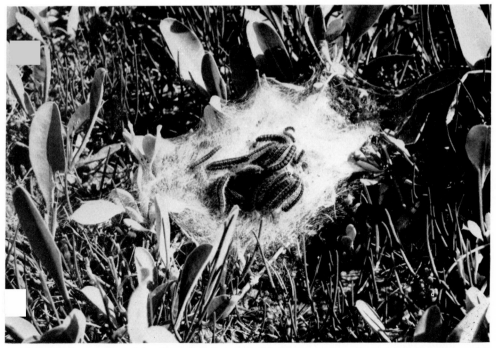

2   A 'nest' of caterpillars of the Ground Lackey moth (*Malacosoma castrensis*), one of the larger terrestrial invertebrates specifically adapted to living on salt marsh vegetation at the higher Emergence marsh level. This species has a very restricted distribution in Britain and is confined to ungrazed *Halimione* and *Limonium* marsh in south-east England. Havergate Island, Suffolk.

3 Pioneer growth form of *Puccinellia maritima* with stolons radiating onto open silt at Morecambe Bay, Lancashire. Sheep-grazing prevents flowering over most of these marshes and it is only in the more remote pioneer zones to seaward that sexual reproduction becomes important, and plants are more inherently variable. Note also the hummock form of growth which right at the start of marsh formation imposes local topographic point to point variation, later expressed as soil, moisture, and plant species variation in the fully colonized marsh.

4 Tidal litter (foreground on right) from *Spartina* marsh accumulates at the upper limit of the marsh and open up the dense *Spartina anglica* sward (foreground on left) allowing invaders like *Typha latifolia* (centre) to colonize. Bridgwater Bay, Somerset.

5 Oil pollution experiments on *Puccinellia maritima* marsh in the Burry estuary, Glamorganshire, South Wales. The plot shows the effect of chronic pollution with persistent applications of oil. Occasional pollution with oil has much less dramatic effects on the growth of salt marsh plants.

6 Sheep grazing experiments in progress at the upper limits of *Spartina anglica* marsh, Bridgwater Bay, Somerset. This is a critical transition zone where the *Spartina* marsh has reached maturity. Grazing favoured invasion by *Puccinellia maritima*, a short grass palatable to both sheep and wildfowl. The ungrazed marsh became invaded by tall growths of *Scirpus maritimus* and *Phragmites communis*.

7 Cattle walkway and flooded borrow pits in Gulf Coast marshland, Louisiana, U.S.A. These walkways are built so that man and animals can get in and out of marshes when they are flooded at high tide. The borrow pits from which silt has been dug to build the walkway provide habitat for wildfowl. (*Photograph by R. E. Williams.*)

8 Turf cutting experiment in *Festuca rubra* salting pasture at Bridgwater Bay, Somerset. This marsh has been undergrazed and sheep and wildfowl tend to avoid the tussocky *Festuca*. Turf has been cut to see if the succession can be put back to the earlier *Puccinellia* stage, as this grass is more palatable. Small amounts of *Puccinellia* are still present in the *Festuca* marsh, and in addition to the complete turf-cutting treatment, strips of marsh from which regeneration can take place are left in another treatment. The uncut control plots are also clearly visible. (*Photograph by P. G. Ainsworth.*)

9 Backshore zone of a sandy shore with abundant tidal litter. Unlike the foreshore (top left) which remains damp, the backshore sand readily dries out and it is from this zone that most shore sand is blown by the wind to feed dune vegetation (right). The tidal litter supplies nutrients for the growth of pioneer species *Agropyron junceiforme* and *Elymus arenarius*. Holy Island, Northumberland.

10 Coast dunes exposed to the maximum onslaught of prevailing and dominant winds at Morfa Dyffryn, Merionethshire, Wales. Once the dunes have grown to their maximum height they erode back from the shore. In the gaps so formed, strandline vegetation and embryo dunes start the cycle of dune building again. This shore is much trampled by tourists, but prickly Saltwort (*Salsola kali*) is avoided and scattered patches are developing in spite of the trampling.

11 *Salix repens* hummocks ('hedgehogs') at Newborough Warren, Anglesey. These very characteristic bio-topographic units are a common sub-habitat type in dunes in many parts of the world, although formed by different plant species. They are produced by alternating periods of accretion and erosion.

12 Dune slack colonized by *Salix repens* formed in the wake of a landward-migrating parabola dune (background) at Newborough Warren, Anglesey. Low-lying hollows like that in the foreground flood with fresh water in the winter.

13 Vigorous and free-flowering *Ammophila arenaria* among mobile dunes at Newborough Warren, Anglesey. This grass and the related *Ammophila breviligulata* are responsible for the build-up of dunes in many parts of the world.

14 De-pauperate growths of non-flowering *Ammophila arenaria* on stabilized dunes at Ross Links, Northumberland. The upright habit of growth persists but sand accretion has stopped, shoots topple and are very susceptible to damage from trampling at this stage.

15 A plantation of *Ammophila arenaria* protected by fishing netting pegged about 30 cm above the ground surface at Gullane dunes, East Lothian, Scotland. Sand movement at the surface is instantly stilled in the plantation. Nets prevent people trampling on sites planted to heal erosion scars and are visually unobtrusive.

16 A graded and hydraulically seeded dune at Camber, Sussex, showing good growth of introduced turf grasses. Hydraulic seeding is carried out by machine spray. Chopped straw is sprayed dry onto the bare sand to still the sand surface and provide a mulch. Seed and fertilizer are then sprayed on in a water mix. In this way a compensated environment for germination and growth is provided. Chestnut pale fencing protects the plantations and is an ideal permeable barrier for catching blown sand and helping to heal erosion gaps at the coast.

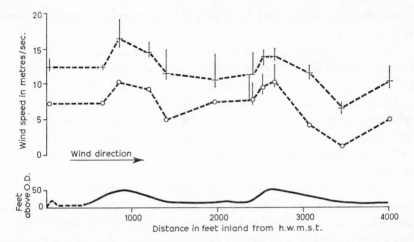

Fig. 48. Wind speeds recorded at 5 cm. (0—0) and 1m. (+—+) above the ground surface on T1 - T4 during a south-west gale of 40 knots (20 m/sec.) at Newborough Warren. The verticals on the curves show the range of speeds recorded at individual sites. The point where the dotted lines cut the verticals is the estimated average speed at the site (from Ranwell 1958).

sand just above the water table. The wind profile in Fig. 48 illustrates these relationships well.

Formation of the Dune and Slack System

Displacement of the coast dune

As we saw in Chapter 2, sand supply, orientation in relation to prevailing wind, and local topography, all greatly influence the type and extent of any particular dune system. But whatever type is considered, growth of the coast dune is initially in a linear or curvi-linear manner parallel with the strandline.

Here it may either stabilize at a low level, erode and re-cycle as in a small bay, or continue to accumulate in open coast sites where sand supply is abundant. One of two things can then happen to the coastal dune, either (1) a new coast dune forms to seaward e.g. where there are broad and high backshore levels and moderate onshore winds or (2) the coast dune grows to its maximum height and then erodes moving landwards e.g. where there are narrow backshore levels and prevailing and dominant winds are on shore.

The first or prograding type of system may simply add ridge on ridge which become stable *in situ* or, if there is more than one backshore

L

zone, alternate ridges and hollows which may again become stabilized *in situ*.

The second or eroding type of system (which of course may also develop from the first if the vegetation is destroyed in any way) may undergo centuries of instability before the sand is fixed permanently by vegetation.

Much of the earlier work on dune ecology in this country was concerned with the first type of system. Special emphasis is given here to the second or more plastic system because it has been the subject of more recent study and has much to teach us about problems of combating instability in dune landscapes.

As the coast dune builds up to the wind limit it takes on the characteristic form in relation to the prevailing wind which as we have seen approximates the streamline form of half an aerofoil section. In effect the vegetated dune has a relatively short and steeply sloping windward slope and a relatively long and gently sloping leeward slope. Now the non-vegetated barchan dune common in deserts has exactly the opposite. Taken together these facts imply that the natural tendency of a sand mound as big as a dune is to develop a shallow windward slope, but vegetation, and the growth of *Ammophila* in particular, modifies this tendency in the direction of a dune with a steep windward slope. Bearing in mind that the windward face of a vegetated coastal dune is rarely completely closed by vegetation it is clear that the vegetated coastal dune form is inherently unstable. This of course has been tacitly recognized in classical techniques of dune restoration where the aim is to create a more stable gently sloping windward face (see Steers 1964 p. 513 Fig. 108).

Seaward growth of the coast dune is restricted by the height of storm tides which can undercut the dune to form a near vertical seaward face. Once this condition develops in regions where there are strong onshore winds the coast dune windward face continues to erode sand which accumulates on the grass-covered leeward slopes. Thus the dune effectively moves back from the shoreline while still continuing to build to its maximum height. Ultimately the crest of the dune may reach a critical height in exposed areas where *Ammophila* can no longer hold the sand and the entire seaward face and crest becomes bare eroding sand. Whole coastal dune ridges may move landward in this way (Plate 10) and on the western coast of Britain where prevailing Atlantic winds are on shore this is a natural phenomenon which occurs quite independently of human disturbance.

The highest dunes are usually found some way inland in sites where prevailing winds are directly onshore (Oosting 1954; Willis *et al* 1959). On the Atlantic coast of France or Spain the inland dunes may reach 70 or

80 m in height. On coasts where the prevailing wind is offshore maximum heights are likely to occur at the coast dune (e.g. on the east coast of the British Isles at Strathbeg, Aberdeen).

Rates of dune building and travel

In seeking to understand complex phenomena it is especially valuable to study situations in which particular effects are maximized. For example the seasonal mechanics of salt marsh accretion (see Chapter 5), only became readily apparent from the studies at Bridgwater Bay where accretion was at a maximum. In just the same way, the mechanics of mobile dune system development can be more readily understood by studying a maximal erosion situation where the prevailing and dominant wind has uninterrupted flow to a coastline exactly normal to its direction. Such a situation occurs at Newborough Warren, Anglesey. Landsberg (1956) found perfect correlation at this site between a calculated wind resultant and the orientation of parabola or U-shaped dunes (Plate 12) of which many parts of it are composed. Subsequently the rate of dune building and dune travel in a region where entire dune ridges were moving landward successively were measured by means of repeatedly levelled transects at this site (Ranwell 1958).

The theoretical point of maximum erosion was confirmed and in this case occurred about 18 m to windward of the crest of 15 m high dunes. Zones of maximum accretion varied from 0 to 18 m behind the crest in low stable dune sections to as much as 164 to 183 m to leeward of the crest in high unstable sections.

It was calculated that the coastal dune must take at least 50 years to build

Table 19. Some recorded rates of dune movement (from Ranwell 1958).

Place	Rate m/annum	Authority
Inland		
Indiana	1–2	Cowles (1911)
Lake Michigan	2–4	Gates (1950)
Coastal		
Kurische Nehrung	5·5–6·1	Care & Oliver (1918)
Gascony	9·1 (mean)	
Wales, Morfa Harlech	3·7 (max.)	Steers (1939)
Morfa Dyffryn	6·1 (max.)	
South Lancashire		
Great Crosby	1·1	Salisbury (1952)
Freshfield	5·5–7·3	
Norfolk coast	1·5	

to maximum height and its mean rate of travel inland near the coast was estimated at 6·7 m per year. It would therefore take at least another 20 years or so for the coast dune to travel landwards sufficiently for a new embryo dune system to develop. So the cycle could take some 70 or 80 years to complete. Failure to understand such time factors may result in costly, unnecessary and undesirable attempts to stabilize a system which ultimately achieves its own stabilization.

Some recorded rates of dune movement are given in Table 19.

The water table and slack differentiation

The wind ceases to erode a bare dune surface when some underlying non-erodable surface such as shingle, rock, clay or wet sand is reached. Most usually, dune slacks have either a freely-drained shingle base or a damp sand base.

As Willis *et al* (1959) have pointed out, a big dune system perched on low lying ground acts itself as an isolated catchment. They showed that water percolated through the dunes at Braunton Burrows, Devon and accumulated over impermeable sub-surface deposits to form a dome-shaped water table (Fig. 49).

They point out that steeper water gradients at the margins of the system

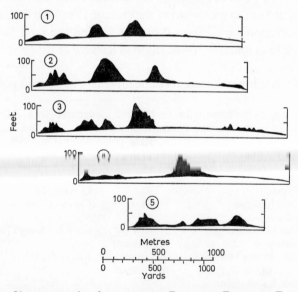

Fig. 49. Profiles across the dune system, Braunton Burrows, Devon. Heights obtained by survey are given in feet above O.D. (Newlyn). The sand above the water table of June 1952 is shown in black (from Willis *et al* 1959).

result from the fact that greater volumes of water (dependent on the greater catchment involved) percolate through the margins of the system compared with the centre of the system. They note the close correspondence of slack ground level with water table level and similar results were obtained at Newborough Warren, Anglesey (Ranwell 1959).

Parabolic dune units and cyclic alternation between dune and slack

It is rare for whole ridges to erode uniformly in the way described earlier for Newborough. Even on this system, ideally orientated for maximum uniform erosion, parts of the coast dune reach maximum height more rapidly than adjoining parts locally and this produces irregular erosion of ridges in the form of parabolic or U-shaped dune units (Fig. 50).

From the direct measurements of dune movement and studies of the growth and age patterns of *Salix repens* either side of mobile dunes, it was possible to demonstrate that there must have been cyclic alternation of dune

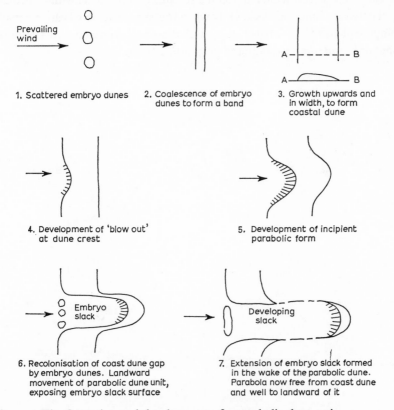

Fig. 50. The formation and development of a parabolic dune unit.

and slack at many points among the more mobile parts of the system. The period of this cycle was estimated at about 80 years and clearly corresponds to the period of the dune building cycle at the coastline (Ranwell 1960 *a*).

There is similar *a priori* evidence in N. American dunes as Oosting's (1954) graphic account testifies: 'When a dune moves over a forest the trees are buried as they stand and are preserved in the dune. Again and again "ghost" or "grave-yard" forests are reported where such long-dead trees have again been exposed as a dune moves on.' However there seems to have been no critical study of the dune and slack relationships in these American sites.

It is not implied of course that any particular point will alternate regularly, because once the dune ridge structure has become broken up complex local shelter effects play a part, and development becomes irregular.

Ultimately dunes are worn down and are sufficiently remote from coastal exposure and strong winds to become stabilized, often at some intermediate level between dune and slack. Only when this stage is reached can one really compare plant successional changes with those found on dunes that stabilize more or less *in situ* on a sheltered prograding coast.

9 Sand Dunes:
Sand, Water Relations and
Processes of Soil Formation

If initially the problem for growth of plants on salt marshes is too much water, for dune plant growth it is the reverse. Dune sand is not only remote from the permanent water table but also very low compared with silt, for example, in water-holding capacity. Plants and their dead remains increase the water-holding capacity of sand. Increasing organic matter increases the capacity of the soil to retain nutrients. This chapter concerns the properties of sand and especially its water relations. It is also concerned with the way sand is transformed into soil capable of supporting the many hundreds of plant and animal species found on dunes. The basic ideas on these subjects are still largely derived from the pioneer work of Salisbury (1952) and his results are quoted extensively. However, it is evident that on some of the more controversial points more data and more critical work with modern techniques is badly needed in both the study of water and nutrient relations on dune systems.

Properties of Sand

Particle size in dune sands

Salisbury (1952) concluded that the average particle size of dune sand has a general relationship to the average strength of the prevailing onshore winds, but this conclusion was derived from very limited data.

Subsequent studies (Cooper 1958 and Ritchie and Mather 1969) show that there is as much variation in either average or median particle size from site to site within a particular climatic region, or even within a dune system (Fig. 51), as there is from one major climatic region to another. The original source and sedimentation history of the shore sand of any particular dune system is probably of far greater significance in relation to particle size, than the wind strengths in the area. Ritchie and Mather (1969) define sand sizes in general terms as follows:

	Median particle diameter in microns
Coarse sand	> 600 to < 1100
Medium sand	< 600 to > 200
Fine sand	< 200

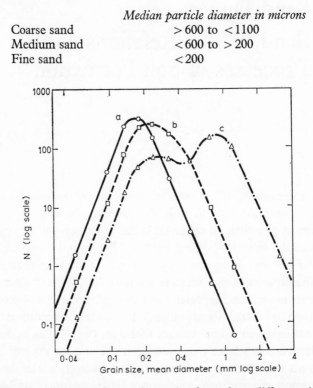

Fig. 51. Grading diagrams for sand samples from three different situations at Braunton Burrows. For each of the three samples the graphs show the proportion of sand having a particular grain size. This proportion is expressed by the parameter N, which is the percentage of the total sample which falls in a given fraction, divided by the difference between the logarithms of the maximum and minimum particle sizes in that fraction (*see* Bagnold 1941, p. 113 et seq.). The ~~complete distribution and in millimetre (a) Fine sand from among juniper shrubs~~ on the lee slope of the main line of dunes. (*b*) Medium sand from the shore above high water mark. (*c*) Sand from the erosion face of a blow-out and containing two components, a coarse fraction left on the surface by wind sorting and a medium sand from below (from Willis *et al* 1959).

In their study of 16 dune sites in N.W. Scotland they found the median ranged from 192 to 496 microns and other studies confirm that most dune systems are composed of medium grade sand. At Newborough Warren, Anglesey particles of less than 20 microns (clay/ silt fraction) only contributed two per cent to the total. Particulate air pollution may well be augmenting this finer fraction on some of our dune systems now and this could well have far reaching effects on their water and nutrient holding capacity and consequently their flora.

Pore space

Measurements on dune soils at Braunton Burrows, Devon and Harlech, Merionethshire indicated a pore space around 40 per cent of the soil volume (Salisbury 1952). In the closest packing array the pore space between spherical particles would be 26 per cent of the volume. The difference is a measure of sand particle angularity and the extent to which particles are held apart by interstitial live and dead organic material. It is this organic matter which plays such a vital part in improving the water-holding capacity of sand.

Water Relations in the Dune

Field moisture capacity and availability

It is essential to keep in mind the changing weight to volume ratios which occur with soil maturation on a dune system. Old dune soils weigh only about half as much per unit volume as young dune soils.

Field moisture capacity may vary from 7 per cent (by volume) in young dune sand to 33 per cent in old dune sand (Salisbury 1952). In dry slack sand the field moisture capacity was between 25 and 30 per cent and in surface humus horizons of wet slacks as high as 50 per cent (by volume) at Newborough Warren, Angelsey (Fig. 52). Salisbury (1952) records minimum water contents of 1 per cent or less in dune sand and notes that water is no longer available to plants when it falls to values of 0·5 per cent, when wilting ensues. However, this does not necessarily mean the death of plants, for wilting cuts down the surface for evapo-transpiration and at least some dune plants can survive daily wilting (Oosting 1954).

Water content and plant requirements

The water content (by weight) to loss on ignition (corrected for carbon dioxide loss from carbonate) ratio is rather constant; usually from 1 to 2·5 (full range 0·15 to 3·48) Salisbury (1952). In general the water content of old dune soils is about twice that of young dune soils when the soils are at field capacity. This is clearly another indication of the changing weight to volume ratio referred to above and evidence that the water content is closely dependent on the organic matter content of dune soil.

The water content of the soil exploited by a plant of *Trifolium arvense*

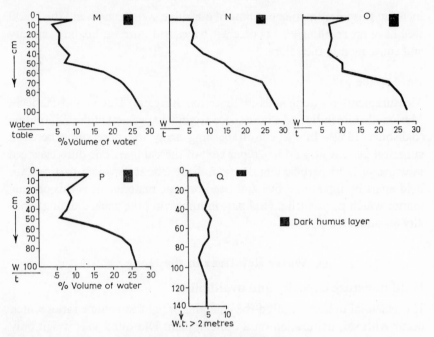

Fig. 52. Soil moisture profiles, Newborough Warren.
M & N beneath fixed dry slack *Agrostis tenuis – Festuca rubra* turf associes.
O & P beneath fixed dry slack *Salix repens* associes.
Q beneath semi-fixed dune *Salix repens* associes (Ranwell 1959).

would be used up in less than 4 days by evapo-transpiration in dry weather but the species can survive apparently unharmed on dunes up to 6 weeks without rain (Salisbury 1952). In general the water content at any one time in young dune soils is only enough for plants growing in it to survive for 2 to 5 days.

To resolve this apparent anomaly we must consider the distribution of soil moisture within the dune and the range in which this moisture can be augmented other than by rainfall.

Soil moisture distribution within the dune

Several studies in open dune communities have shown that soil moisture augments to depths of about 60 cm below the dune surface and then tends to fall off to a more constant level (Salisbury 1952, Ranwell 1959 and Willis *et al* 1959). This is usually at about 1 m below the surface (Fig. 52). Live roots of plants characteristic of the open dune such as those of *Euphorbia portlandica* or *Ammophila* penetrate to depths of about 1 m, but not significantly below this.

In closed dune communities light rainfall is absorbed and held near the surface by organic matter to give a reversal of the soil moisture gradient characteristic of open dune soils. The water content of sand at depths between 60 to 90 cm in dry seasons is lower beneath dry dune pasture than beneath *Ammophila* on a high dune. In August 1955 at Braunton Burrows for example the values were 1 per cent and 4·9 per cent respectively (Willis *et al* 1959). However, it is still true that the establishment of seedlings in the surface layers of an open dune is very much dependent on the incidence of rainfall because the top few centimetres heat up and dry out daily in hot dry weather. In artificially stabilized mobile dunes where there has not been time for organic matter to build up it seems likely that serious moisture deficiencies might occur limiting the establishment of other species, and this would be worth investigating.

Sources of water for dune plants

Olsson-Seffer (1909) showed that the capillary rise of water from a free water surface even in very fine sand 30 to 50 microns particle size was not more than about 40 cm. The water table in a dune only 3 or 4 m high can therefore make no direct contribution to the moisture requirements of plants rooting to depths of only 1 m. In really high dunes the water table lies many metres below the surface and has no significance for plant growth at the dune surface.

The primary source of water for dune plants comes from rainfall, and in particular that proportion of it held as pendular water dependent on the moisture-holding capacity of the sand. But as Salisbury's studies have shown there must be some other source of water to carry plants through long periods of dry weather. Olsson-Seffer (1909) was the first to suggest a possible source: 'It must be remembered that the diurnal and nocturnal temperature variations are considerable on an open sand formation, on which the radiation factor is one of considerable moment. Such fluctuations in soil temperature . . . are sufficient to cause periodical condensation of water vapour in the soil.'

Salisbury (1952) demonstrated that the average water increment from dew was 0·9 ml per 100 ml soil per night in cloudless conditions, and transpiration measurements showed that this was sufficient to maintain plants exploiting that soil volume in rainless periods. Salisbury believed that warm moisture-laden air from above the adjacent sea after sunny days was drawn into the pore spaces of the sand 'as a concomitant of the upward convection currents maintained especially on the southern face and crest of the dune after dusk', where it was deposited on cold grains as internal dew.

Willis *et al* (1959) point out that at night the temperature gradient in the soil (Fig. 53) is favourable for an *upward* movement of water vapour from the warm and wetter layers of the sand below and this is so even when the upper layers do not fall below the dew point of the external air. The actual moisture contents found by Salisbury (Table 20) seem to preclude the possibility of drainage of dew from surface condensation. But as Willis *et al* (1959) point out, the greatest increase of moisture content after dew formation recorded by Salisbury (Table 20) occurred at a depth of 36 in (0·9 m) where the temperature is very unlikely to fall below the dew point. The problem clearly requires further study, perhaps with the aid of tracers, and one would like to know more about the distribution of moisture in the various components of the soil including that imbibed by micro-organisms which possibly undergo diurnal/nocturnal migration in the soil.

Table 20. Water content of sand after and before dew formation. Blakeney Point, Norfolk (from Salisbury 1952).

	Sample depth (cm)	Water contents by weight		
		27/7/38 Night samples %	27/7/38 Day samples %	Gain night-day
Single samples from the side of a pit	7	0·59	0·18	+ 0·41
	30	0·99	0·35	+ 0·64
	90	3·80	1·94	+ 1·86
Composite samples	7	0·71	0·53	+ 0·18
	30	1·31	1·18	+ 0·13

Water Relations in the Slack

Very little work has been published on the ecology of dune slacks or low lying flat areas where growth is influenced by the proximity of the water table although they may occupy up to half the area of some dune systems.

Shape of the water table and drainage

As we have seen, the overall shape of the water table in a large isolated dune system is dome-shaped (Fig. 49). This means that peripheral slack communities are particularly likely to have nutrient enriched ground water derived from lateral seepage outwards from the centre of the dune system. It also explains why permanent dune lakes often occur at the landward side of the dune system where hinterland and dune system drainage meets.

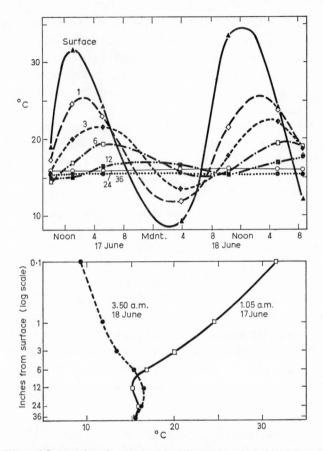

Fig. 53. Diurnal fluctuations in temperature down a sand profile. An undisturbed profile about 40 in (1 m) deep was exposed by digging a pit in the top of a bare dune. Resistance thermometers were inserted without delay into the profile at 36, 24, 12, 6, 3 and 1 in from the surface, and the excavated sand was restored as far as possible in its original position. After 2 days, periodic measurements of temperature were made, and are shown in the upper diagram. The temperature at the surface was recorded by means of a mercury-in-glass thermometer. The lower diagram shows the maximum extent of the fluctuation against a logarithmic scale of depth. Times are given in G.M.T. Braunton Burrows, Devon (from Willis *et al* 1959).

The ground surface closely follows the shape of the water table from slack to slack indicating the limit to which wind deflation of the dunes can occur. At the edge of a slack, the water table rises slightly, but does not follow the steep contours of the dune. Any one slack therefore has a saucer-shaped water table unit tilted slightly downwards towards the periphery of the dune system.

In most dune systems with well developed wet slacks impermeable clay or rock underlies the sand and holds the water up. Where they are built on permeable shingle slacks tend to be dry.

Tidal effects on the water table

Sea water does not readily penetrate into the ground water zone through a coastal dune (unless a reverse gradient is created by ground water extraction). The positive drainage gradient out from the dune system normally prevents this. Consequently, no fluctuation of the water table with respect to tide is found within the larger hindshore dune systems like Braunton Burrows, Devon or Newborough Warren, Anglesey (Willis *et al* 1959, Ranwell, 1959). Where a large part of the dune system is surrounded by sea water and dunes are built on shingle, tidal fluctuations of the fresh water table floating on salt water among the permeable shingle can occur (Hill and Hanley 1914). Brown (1925) showed that the fresh water body beneath small pervious islands capped with dunes is lens-shaped, and floats upon the convex salt ground water surface.

Seasonal fluctuations of the water table

In a wet year there may be widespread flooding in dune slacks at Newborough Warren, Anglesey from November to April. The water table falls from April to August and recovers the high winter levels during autumn rains. As Fig. 54 shows there is close correlation in this seasonal pattern with the distribution of rainfall. The rapid fall of the water table in April and May coincides with the leafing of deciduous plants like *Salix repens* (dominant in the slacks) and the autumn rise with the leaf fall in mid-October.

A ten year study of water level and rainfall fluctuations at Braunton Burrows, Devon enabled Willis *et al* (1959) to estimate the extent and duration of recent flooding at any point on the site from a knowledge of its land height and water level. They found that the slopes of lines for the regression of water level on rainfall were nearly proportional to the mean heights of the water table at each sampling point. They also calculated an index of flooding which could be related to different plant communities.

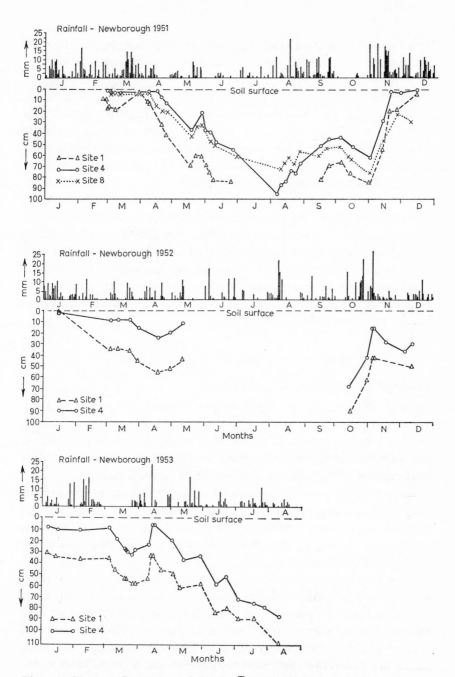

Fig. 54. Seasonal fluctuation of the free water table at selected sites in wet slacks with *Salix repens* associes, and daily rainfall 1951–1953 at Newborough Warren, Anglesey (from Ranwell 1959).

This was defined as the average numbers of months in a year for which the site is under water, from 0, free of flooding, to 12, permanently flooded.

Water table range

Willis *et al* (1959) concluded from their study that maximum annual range of the water table occurred near the flatter centre of the dome-shaped water table and smaller ranges occurred at the more steeply sloping water table of the peripheral sites. This relationship was not confirmed at Newborough Warren where a rock ridge running through the centre of the system may complicate the pattern of water movements. In both studies the annual range of the water table was of the order of 1 m and this probably depends on the total annual rainfall which was similar in both areas. In drier climates as at Winterton, Norfolk the annual range of the water table is reduced to about 0·5 m and the possible vertical range of communities dependent on the water table must be telescoped accordingly. Clearly there is an analogy here with the vertical range of salt marsh communities in relation to the vertical range of the tide.

Soil Development in Dunes and Slacks

Changes in soil properties with time

Striking differences in soil properties of young dunes compared with those of increasing age were detected by Salisbury (1925). He recorded an increase in organic matter paralleled by a decrease in pH value of the soil solution and a decrease in the calcium carbonate content of dunes with increasing age at Blakeney Point, Norfolk and Southport dunes, Lancashire.

These trends depend upon decrease in mobility of dunes as they become fully vegetated and accumulate organic matter and the time they are exposed to the leaching effects of rainfall. This dissolves carbonate in the soluble bicarbonate form and carries it downwards to the water table where it may flow out of the system.

The opposing agencies favouring nutrient accumulation and nutrient depletion interact with the changing soil properties in a rather complicated way as we shall see. Also the trends may be obscured in systems with high initial carbonate content (Gimingham in Burnett 1964), or persistent mobility (Ranwell 1959, and Willis *et al* 1959). Nevertheless, Salisbury's conception of this basic pattern of soil development is generally applicable to dune systems wherever they occur.

Differences in soil moisture in young and old dune and slack soils have already been discussed. Right from the start this effectively controls the oxidation of organic matter so that young slack soils start with twice the amount of organic matter that comparable aged dune soils contain (Ranwell 1959). In addition, gravity favours the accumulation of nutrients in the slacks at the expense of the bank of nutrients in dunes. As Olson (1958 a) succinctly puts it, 'the rich system gets richer and the poor system poorer', at least until wind deflation brings the two systems together so closely at the dry slack level that the systems interact as in a chalk heath situation where shallow-rooted plants live in an acid soil side by side with deeper rooted plants tapping base rich soil below (Fig. 55 Profile EF).

Particle size changes

Perhaps because the initial silt and clay contents of dune sand are so low as to be almost unmeasurable, little attention has been given to changes in the finest fractions of dune and slack soil. However Olson's (1958 a) work on the ancient inland dune systems of Indiana, U.S.A., has shown that these finer particle fractions do accumulate with time as a result of weathering *in situ* and accumulation of airborne dust. The exchange capacity of the sand will be increased by clay accumulation but is of course decreased by hydrogen ion replacement as leaching proceeds with age.

Rates of change in carbonate content

The evidence from a number of dune systems with an initial carbonate content of not more than 5 per cent (by weight) shows that most free carbonate is lost from the first decimetre of surface dune soil within 300 to 400 years (Salisbury 1952, Olson 1958 a, Ranwell 1959). Under the prevailing weather conditions, Olson (1958 a) found that it takes about 1,000 years for carbonate to leach out of the first 2 metres of dune soil in the Indiana dunes. The rate of carbonate loss was found to be proportional to the amount of cabonate left at any point in time. Salisbury (1952) points out that calcium may be replenished at the surface in three ways: by wind blow of shell fragments from mobile dunes, by re-cycling via plant roots and leaves, and by the burrowing activity of rabbits. Ultimately however it seems from Olson's studies that leaching wins in the end, even where forest cover is developed as on the Indiana dunes. Similarly Ovington (1950) found in studies of the afforested Culbin dunes that nutrients are lost from the soil at a greater rate than they are being made available. He points out that if an allowance were made for the nutrients in the trees there would be an overall increase of nutrients in the afforested areas, but these of course will be removed at felling.

M

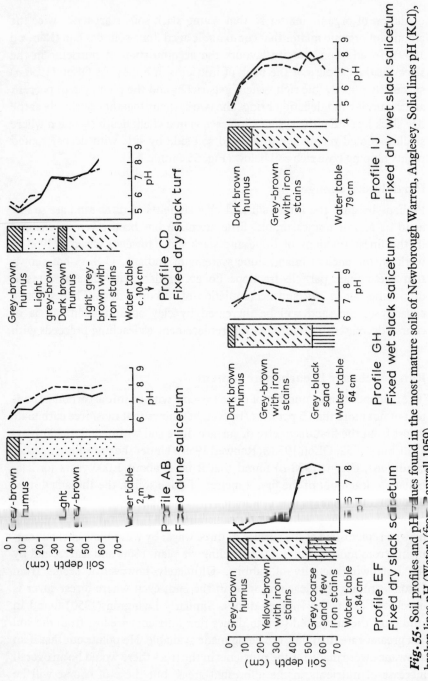

Fig. 55. Soil profiles and pH values found in the most mature soils of Newborough Warren, Anglesey. Solid lines pH (KCl), broken lines pH (Water) (from Ranwell 1959).

Profile AB
Fixed dune salicetum

Profile CD
Fixed dry slack turf

Profile EF
Fixed dry slack salicetum

Profile GH
Fixed wet slack salicetum

Profile IJ
Fixed dry wet slack salicetum

Soil depth (cm)

Grey-brown humus
Light grey-brown
Water table 2 m

Grey-brown humus
Light grey-brown
Dark brown humus
Light grey-brown with iron stains
Water table c.104 cm

Grey-brown humus
Yellow-brown with iron stains
Grey, coarse sand few iron stains
Water table c.84 cm

Dark brown humus
Grey-brown with iron stains
Grey-black sand
Water table 64 cm

Dark brown humus
Grey-brown with iron stains
Water table 79 cm

Rates of organic matter and nitrogen changes

Salisbury (1925) found that organic matter augments slowly at first, but appreciably faster after about 200 years in the dunes especially in the higher rainfall climate at Southport, Lancashire.

In contrast Wilson (1960) found very rapid increase in organic matter in the very lime-deficient dunes at Studland, Dorset. This he attributes to early invasion by *Calluna* which is largely responsible for the rapid litter accumulation, and possibly also accelerated leaching of what little carbonate there is present initially, by means of humic acids as well as carbonic acid. Under the rapidly developing acid conditions litter breakdown is inhibited and organic matter accumulation promoted (Fig. 56). Optimum organic matter accumulation was found at the limit of winter flooding at Newborough Warren. Olson (1958 *a*) found that organic carbon increases about three times faster at the surface compared with 10 cm depth on the Indiana dunes. Even in soils believed to be about 500 years old not more than 2 per cent organic matter accumulated at depths of 20 to 25 cm at Newborough Warren (Ranwell 1959).

Carbon to nitrogen ratios were found to vary from 10:1 in young dune

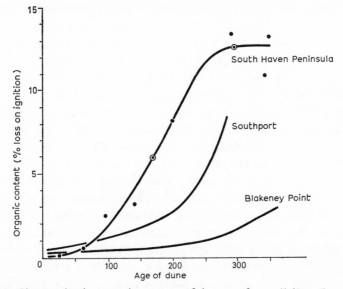

Fig. 56. Changes in the organic content of dune surface soil (0 to 5 cm depth) with age at South Haven Peninsula, Dorset. The ringed points represent overall means for the second and third dune ridges from the coast. Salisbury's (1925) curves for the Southport, Lancashire and Blakeney Point, Norfolk dune systems have been inserted for comparison (from Wilson 1960).

grassland soils, to 20:1 in old forest dune soils in the Indiana dunes (Olson 1958 *a*). A balance between gain and loss of nitrogen seems to be reached at about 1 000 years following stabilization of the dune surface.

Cation exchange capacities

The cation exchange capacity of the slack soils at Newborough rose from 2–3 m E per cent in young dry slack soils to 15 to 20 m E per cent in older wet slack soils (Ranwell 1959). Olson (1958 *a*) found low values in very ancient dunes at Indiana: 5·3 m E per cent in 8,000 year old dunes and 6·5 to 8 m E per cent in 10,000-year-old dunes. In contrast Ovington (1950) found quite high values in the humus layers at Tentsmuir, Fife up to 25–30 m E per cent and these were probably due to the presence of *Calluna* litter, the dominant species in the area examined.

Biological influences on soil formation

The initial organic matter supplied to the shore in tidal litter forms a relatively rich nutrient medium for the growth of strandline plants. It is processed by temporary faunas including abundant amphipods and mites (McGrorty *pers comm.*). Brown (1958) found little evidence of fungi in tide-washed sand, but Gunkel (1968) has recently demonstrated that oil-decomposing bacteria are present in shore sand and pollutant products decomposed by bacteria may well be enriching not only the shore, but also the sand being blown onto coastal dunes at the present time.

Prior to the advent of serious shore pollution, the switch from the relatively rich tidal litter-based nutrient economy of the shore to the nutrient deficient high level *Ammophila* dune sand must clearly have presented serious nutritional problems for the inhabitants of the open dune community. Webley *et al* (1952) developed a technique whereby the microfloras of the open sand, the rhizosphere, and the root surface of *Agropyron* and *Ammophila* could be compared. They showed that the rhizosphere of these sand dune plants contains abundant bacteria which are present only in very low numbers in intervening sand areas. Hassouna and Wareing (1964) have demonstrated by experimental cultures that nitrogen is limiting for the growth of plants of the open dune and that the growth of root-surface sterilized *Ammophila* seedlings exhibited much poorer growth than those inoculated with bacteria capable of fixing nitrogen (providing carbon sources, possibly derived from exudates, are adequate). The regular association of fungi e.g. *Inocybe* species with *Ammophila* suggests that mycorrhizal symbiosis may also be important in the supply of nitrogen.

Webley *et al* (1952) also demonstrated that the bacterial flora of the early stages of dune fixation increased to the dune pasture stage, but decreased markedly where dune heath was developed. At this stage the fungal flora, which like the bacterial flora augmented with increasing fixation, became more abundant than the bacterial flora (Table 21). However, it should be borne in mind that the values are given on a weight basis.

Table 21. Microbiological analyses of dune soils on a transect through the Newburgh dunes, Aberdeenshire, 8 September 1948 (from Webley *et al* 1952).

Sample (depth 5–15 cm)	Moisture content (% of dry wt. of sample)	pH	Bacteria per g oven-dried material	Fungi per g oven-dried material
(1) Open sand	3·5	6·80	18,000	270
(2) Yellow dunes, *Ammophila arenaria*	3·7	6·68	1,630,000	1,700
(3) Early fixed dunes *Ammophila arenaria* with grasses, etc.	1·5	5·14	1,700,000*	69,470
(4) Dune pasture	7·1	4·80	2,230,000	109,780
(5) Dune heath	16·8	4·27	127,000	148,190

* Just over 50% were actinomycetes.

Gimingham (in Burnett 1964) notes that legumes increase in the later stages of stabilization and shrubs like *Hippophaë rhamnoides* also develop root nodules with bacteria which have been shown to be capable of nitrogen fixation (Bond *et al* 1956).

We are still very ignorant of the nutrient pathways in sand dune habitats, but it does seem evident that there is a distinct switch from the bacterial-based economy of the younger or more base-rich dune soils to a fungal-based economy on the older or more base-deficient soils dominated by *Calluna* or conifer plantations where litter accumulates. No information seems to be available on the biological influences on soil formation in dune slacks, but those that flood late into spring have an additional source of production from algal blooms contributing to their enrichment. Shields (1957) has demonstrated high levels of amino nitrogen in algal lichen surface crusts compared with sand at 15 cm depth in New Mexico desert soils. Similar crusts formed by congeneric species occur in young lime-rich dune slacks and probably engender a continually renewable supply of soil nitrogen. In fact it has been demonstrated with the use of labelled nitrogen that blue-green algae in dune slacks fix atmospheric nitrogen and that such labelled nitrogen is taken up by mosses and higher plants from the soil and assimilated (Stewart 1967).

10 Sand Dunes: Structure and Function of Dune Communities

Dunes are immensely rich in species of plants and animals in contrast to salt marshes. Unlike a salt marsh with exacting constraints imposed by salt-dominated relatively level ground, dune habitats are highly variable. They range from mobile to fixed dunes of varying aspects and from ground-water dependent, to ground-water independent levels. This complex mosaic of habitats is further diversified at the surface by the plant and animal components which both inhabit and help to create the environment in which they live.

Ecologists were rather mesmerized by this wealth of diversity and, until recently devoted much of their time to lengthy descriptive studies and rather little to behavioural study and experiment. As Elton (1966) puts it, 'One wishes that some of the very elaborate European investigations of dune faunas had given less time to statistical abstractions and cryptic classical terminologies, and more to finding out what the animals do and where they do it, in relation to the rather obvious patterns of habitat structure and climate.' This is equally true of the study of dune floras and diatoms limits to the accounts of the dune and slack communities given in this and the next chapter. The emphasis is therefore primarily on structure and rather less on function, but it is hoped that the accounts will encourage future study on function of the component parts of the dune system, such as the ecology of the *Ammophila* tussock, the *Salix repens* hummock, or *Hippophaë* scrub.

The Dune Flora and Fauna

Species diversity

Taking British dune systems as a whole, i.e. dune and slack complexes, Salisbury (1952) notes there are about 400 species of vascular plants. It is clear that this represents only the truly native flora, for a recent tally of native and introduced vascular plants on 43 of the more important dune systems in Great Britain shows that over 900 species occur on them. Many of these additional species are associated with the forestry plantations developed on dunes over the past 100 years. More than half the species of vascular plants growing on British dunes at the present time were probably introduced there directly or indirectly by man or by birds (especially gulls, see below). It has always been accepted of course that the dune flora contains a large element derived from the weed flora of agricultural land. This element of heterogeneity from site to site in the dune flora presents classification problems for classical phytosociologists. Floristic assemblages are often as unstable as those on a rubbish dump. Bearing out Darwin's conclusion that the indigenous plants of a district are not necessarily those best suited to it, Westhoff (1952) points out that no less than 31 species in the *Hippophaë – Ligustrum* community on Dutch dunes are exotics.

There are in addition several hundred species of lichens, bryophytes, fungi and algae on our dune systems and no doubt an equally rich microflora. It would be a formidable task to develop floristic classification of the dune floras of the world let alone the fact that species have not even been listed for such major European dune systems as the Coto Doñana in Spain for example.

No figures are available for the animal species found on a whole sand dune system. Heerdt and Morzer Bruyns (1960) found 368 species of arthropods in the open dune communities on the island of Terschelling off the Dutch coast. Hincks *et al* (1951–1954) recorded over 2,000 species of invertebrates (between one fifth and one quarter of the British fauna) on the sand dune and salt marsh complex at Spurn Head, Yorkshire in an area of less than 1 square mile (less than 200 ha). Duffey (1968) found no less than 188 species of spiders alone in systematic sampling on the lime-rich dunes of Whiteford Burrows, Glamorgan and the more lime-deficient dunes at Tentsmuir, Fife.

He points out that the relatively low total of only 54 species of spiders found on Terschelling by Heerdt and Morzer Bruyns (1960) is partly due to the fact that the collections were limited to a particular time of the year (August) and partly to the limited area within each vegetation type sampled. The sampling intensity is particularly important, because even with spring and summer sampling at Whiteford Burrows, Cotton (1967) found only 25 per cent of Duffey's total of spider species for that site.

Coleoptera, Hymenoptera and Diptera seem to be the best represented insect groups in the dune habitat.

Communities

Biological spectra

Raunkiaer's system of life form groups as modified by Braun-Blanquet (1932) is based on the position of the perennating organs during the unfavourable season, i.e. during cold winter or hot dry summer, and it is a useful way of analysing complex floras.

Böcher (1952) gives results for a series of sand ridges on shingle at Isefjord, Denmark (Table 22). The flora of dunes and slacks were analysed separately at Newborough (Table 23).

Both analyses clearly emphasize the dominance of the hemicryptophyte habit i.e. plants with perennial shoots and buds close to the earth's surface, and this is reinforced by the fact that the abundant cryptogams of dune systems also are to be classified as hemicryptophytes. Also notable is the importance of therophytes (annual species) in the open habitats of the early stages of succession in Böcher's figures and the high preponderance of this group in both dunes and slacks at Newborough, a west coast dune system with a high degree of mobility and hence extensive areas of open ground.

Nobuhara (1967) has studied the way in which proportions of life form types change zonally and seasonally in the Japanese strand flora.

Analytical studies

Much of the European literature on sand dune ecology is dominated by subjective classification of vegetation types which appear relatively homogeneous to the observer. Often they are accompanied by somewhat arbitrarily chosen measurements of habitat factors, but the information contained in them is not readily applicable to functional aspects of the vegetation groups or usable in relation to modern management requirements. More recently their value as a basis for vegetation mapping, which as Westhoff (1952) points out is of value to the dune landscape architect in enabling him to see what will grow where and maintain itself in competition with existing species, has been demonstrated by such studies as those of Martin (1959) in America and Boerboom (1960) and Maarel and Westhoff (1964) in Holland. At the same time attempts are being made to draw together classifications of dune associes and selected environmental factors for dune systems in several European countries (Wiemann and Domke 1967).

More objective methods of purely floristic analysis such as the association analysis developed by Williams and Lambert (1960) have been applied to dune floras in Holland (Maarel 1966), in Australia (Welbourn and Lange

Table 22. Biological spectra of dune ridges at Isefjord, Denmark.
Figures refer to numbers of species in each group (from Böcher 1952)

	Phanerophyte	Chamaephyte	Hemicryptophyte	Geophyte	Therophyte
Strandline	0	0	33	18	48
Coast ridge	3	0	56	19	22
2nd ridge	8	0	68	11	13
3rd ridge	12	2	65	12	9
4th ridge	10	9	70	5	5
5th ridge	17	5	63	5	9
Landward dune	11	7	64	7	11
Heath	13	13	70	4	0

Table 23. Biological spectra of dunes and slacks at Newborough Warren, Anglesey.
Figures refer to numbers of species in each group (from Ranwell 1959).

	Phanerophytes	Chamaephytes	Hemicryptophytes	Geophytes	Helophytes	Therophytes	Total species
Dunes	4	11	40	5	0	40	122
Slacks	0	9	57	9	9	16	109

1969) and in England (Moore 1971). In addition Maarel (1966) has sought to combine classification and ordination techniques and to correlate directly vegetation and environmental types (analysed separately) in a unified system.

Study of the Island beach dune spit in New Jersey led Martin (1959) to conclude that the dune system consisted of a zoned mosaic dominated by topographically determined environmental features. Topography and vegetation were interrelated and interacting. Most community types could occur on more than one topographic facet and topographic facets could support more than one community type.

The hummock is a good example of a biotopographic unit which maintains integrity as a habitat unit in dune systems in many parts of the world. Thus Osborn and Robertson (1939) writing of New South Wales dunes, Australia note 'that mat plants (*Mesembryanthemum aequilaterale, Scaveola suaveolens* and *Stackhausia spathulata*) may persist, building the sand into rounded hummocks a metre or more in height, long after wind erosion has removed the low dune on which they had been growing'. Ramaley (1918) describing San Francisco dunes in California, U.S.A. notes that, 'Distributed throughout the dune area are many small mounds 2 to 4 m high capped with willow (*Salix lasiolepis*).' Yano (1962) in Japan speaks of clonal hummocks in unfixed dune, and Duffey (1968) notes that at Whiteford Burrows, South Wales *Salix repens* hummocks 2 to 3 m high form small steep-sided dunes which have earned the local name 'hedgehogs' (Plate 11).

The point to be made here is that clonally based pattern is of such universal significance as a module of plant and animal community structure that it must become more widely utilized in the study of dune ecology if functional aspects are to be successfully unravelled.

Duffey (1968) points out that 'phytosociological concepts are of limited value in the zoologist studying animal associations on dunes and habitat classification is proposed based mainly on structural characteristics of the vegetation cover' (Fig. 57). He finds that the more distinctive spider faunas

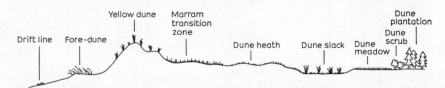

Fig. 57. Diagrammatic representation of habitats on a dune system (from Duffey 1968).

are associated with the more specialized open dune and dune heath habitats compared with other dune habitat types and notes close similarity in dune heath and inland heath spider faunas.

Ardö (1957) found that the dipterous fauna of sand dunes was 'overwhelmingly rich'. He distinguished a eurytope group of species and a stenotope group. In the latter a close relationship was demonstrated between thermal preference and choice of zone. Drought resistance and light preference were also important.

The main factors affecting distribution of invertebrates include: mechanical damage by flying sand particles; physical injury by desiccation and salt content of onshore wind; shelter; and food according to Heerdt and Morzer Bruyns (1960). They note that few species can survive seaward of the main coast dune ridge and that this is therefore a principal boundary for invertebrates of the open dune areas they studied.

Primary biotopographic units of the dunes

The primary biotopographic units of dunes are those associated with orientation, particularly in regard to incidence of direct insolation and incidence of dominant winds. Boerboom (1964) as we saw in Chapter 1, has recorded the microclimatic differences due to aspect of dune slopes. In many continental studies plant community analyses are related to aspect in a general way. However, we are a long way from understanding precisely how *Empetrum nigrum* becomes dominant on a shade slope and how its establishment seems to be prevented completely on a sun slope as on Terschelling, for example. Primary topographic units include:

(1) Dune plateaux
(2) Solar slopes
(3) Shade slopes
(4) Windward slopes

(5) Leeward slopes
(6) Intermediate slopes
(7) Dune hollows

The ecology of any one of these major units would be worth studying on its own in relation to the zonal gradients of a dune system.

Secondary biotopographic units of dunes

Superimposed on the plateaux or orientated slopes of dunes are secondary units ranging from physiographically dominated units like blow-outs, through biotopographic units like tussocks, and hummocks, gulleries, warrens, burrow mouths, ant hills and pathways to patterned plant shape and height arrangements which themselves create diverse topography on otherwise level ground.

Once again one would like to see studies orientated more specifically on these individual secondary biotopographic units of the dune system and already the trend towards this type of study is starting. For example, Ardö (1957) studied the microclimate of *Elymus* dunes in Scandinavia in relation to Diptera, Heerdt and Morzer Bruyns (1960) the microclimate of *Ammophila* tussocks in Holland in relation to the fauna, while Elton (1966) gives us a fascinating insight into the oasis-like character of this habitat from observations on the Daymer dunes, Cornwall.

The clonal hummock habitat is of particular interest because the plants that create it frequently can only originate in a slack where there is adequate moisture for germination. Subsequently they keep pace with accretion from the advancing dune and ultimately come to lie at the dune summit (e.g. *Salix repens* at Newborough Warren, *Populus alba* in the Coto Doñana, Spain). This fundamental form has received very little specialized study and offers particularly attractive opportunities for comparative study in discrete units in a great variety of orientations, vertical heights, and horizontal zones from seaward to landward.

Animal-controlled biotopographic units are just beginning to receive detailed study. Work is in progress for example on the South Walney Island dunes, Lancashire where the largest Lesser Black-backed Gull colony in Europe has transformed the dune vegetation over considerable areas from open *Ammophila* dune to a distinctive lush carpeting growth of annual weed species such as *Stellaria media*. Trampling by gulls has been observed to destroy robust *Ammophila* tussock growth at Newborough Warren, Anglesey but to so enrich the dune sand with guano locally that *Dactylorchis* species (normally confined to slacks), grow in lush turf among the high level dunes. Gillham (1970) records that the commonest means of arrival of viable weed seeds in off-shore island sites with gulleries was in the pellets which gulls eject from their crops. Single plants of weed species such as *Brassica sinapis*, *Plantago lanceolata* and *Stellaria media* were found on perching hummocks where regurgitation pellets also occurred at Newborough Warren.

The activities of grazing animals (especially rabbits) on dunes have not yet received the systematic study they deserve. We are aware in a general way of the profound effects that rabbit grazing has had on the dune flora, especially following the striking changes that have occurred since myxomatosis. But we do not have any critical experimental data and nor has there been any serious attempt to relate specific population densities of rabbits to plant community types. Rabbit population density and grazing intensity varied enormously from site to site on any particular dune system prior to myxomatosis. Intensively warrened areas were particularly associated with the better vegetated more landward parts of the dune system which are frequently worn down to a level intermediate between the dune and dry slack level. On larger dune systems with extensive areas of highly mobile dunes to seaward, rabbit density and grazing intensity was much reduced in these seaward parts. On smaller more stable systems such as that at Blakeney, Norfolk, rabbit grazing evidently did occur extensively at the coast and White (1961) records much improved growth and flowering of *Agropyron junceiforme* in embryo dunes following loss of rabbits from myxomatosis. The general changes he recorded on transect studies at Blakeney are similar to those found in dry slack transect studies at Newborough Warren, Anglesey described in the next chapter.

Both grazing and wind exposure have profound effects on the structure of vegetation of dunes and it is useful at this point to consider the vertical layering of vegetation.

The Vegetation Layers

Boerboom (1960) points out that deviations in the correlated occurrence of the respective vegetation layers may lead to anomalies in classification and suggests that more attention should be given to their separate analysis. It is interesting here to note that no correlation was found between the distribution of species of filamentous algae on a salt marsh and the species of higher plants in a recent (unpublished) study of a Norfolk coast marsh. Stewart and Pugh (1963) found a similar lack of correlation between blue-green algae and the dominant flora at Gibraltar Point, Lincolnshire. Similarly one would expect that shade tolerant bryophytes with wide edaphic tolerance might well prove to be indifferent to what species of plant provides the shade so long as it has the right structure. Experimental work with artificial structures could soon clear up this point. Such studies are incidentally of direct relevance to the colonization of erosion scars after their treatment with dead brushwood.

The ground carpet layer

One of the most noticeable features of dune vegetation in the later stages of stabilization is the abundance of bryophytes and lichens. There has been very little study of the growth of dune lichens, but interesting work has been carried out on bryophytes. Richards (1929), and Ducker (in Steers 1960), demonstrated their zonation at Blakeney Point, and Scolt Head Island, Norfolk respectively, and Birse and Gimingham (1955) have studied growth form in relation to increasing stability. Pioneer species like *Tortula ruraliformis* on open sand are of the acrocarpous type with an upright growth habit capable of growing through small amounts of accreting sand. In more stable areas pleurocarpous mosses with a spreading habit of growth like *Hypnum cupressiforme* are found.

In moss transplant experiments (Birse *et al* 1957) there was no emergence of 8 species transplanted into *Ammophila* zones subject to 4 to 5 cm sand accretion in 10 months. In more stable *Ammophila*, 3 species emerged through 3 cm accretion and only where accretion was less than 1 cm in 10 months did all 8 species survive. In pot burial experiments several species emerged through 4 cm burial and none from deeper burial. The ability to produce rhizoids in overlying sand and the rapidity of upward growth were important in the ability to survive burial.

Robertson (1955) demonstrated the importance of shade by transplant experiments and found, with the exception of two species which were indifferent, the order in which transplants to a sunny site died out was in the same order as the level of shading in which they normally grew. North-field (1968) found that pioneer bryophytes at Studland, Dorset were always in well protected sites associated with other plants and only began to move out into open sand with the invasion of *Calluna* which occurs at an early stage on this lime-deficient dune system. Lichens tend to become more abundant in dry rabbit-disturbed ground than bryophytes. With the general growth of grasses since myxomatosis, bryophytes at first increased in the formerly lichen-rich areas, but are now decreasing as shade increases and litter isolates them from the sand surface.

Alvin (1960) has recorded the lichen zonation on Studland dunes (Fig. 58) and compares his results with Böcher's (1952) study of lichen zonation on the island dunes at Lacsø, Denmark. Differences were believed to be primarily due to climatic factors as both are lime-deficient dune systems. Brown and Brown (1969) found that lichens at Blakeney, Norfolk were well represented in arid areas less favourable to higher plant growth and Robertson (1955) found that on dry eminences at Ross Links, Northumberland, lichen mats break into polygons especially where turf death attributed to drought due to rabbit burrows close to the surface occurs. Such areas were especially prone to erosion.

Dune annuals are a very characteristic element of the dune flora occurring on the ground layer among lichens and especially in the sheltered mouths of old rabbit burrows. Salisbury (1952) has shown that these are

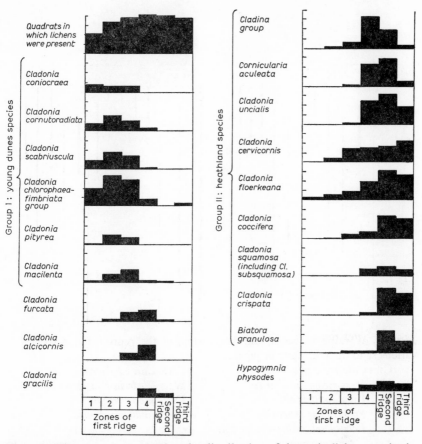

Fig. 58. Histograms representing the distribution of the main lichen species in six zones of the dunes as determined by their occurrence in 100 random quadrats in each zone. One division of the vertical scale represents 25 occurrences. The top left histogram shows the number of quadrats in which any lichens occurred. South Haven Peninsula, Dorset (from Alvin, 1960).

shallow-rooted plants which mostly germinate in autumn and are able to grow in the warmer days of winter at a season when moisture is adequate. Lichen rich sites are 'hot-spots' and winter temperatures are adequate for growth. In summer the winter annuals pass the unfavourable season in seed.

The grass/herb layer

It is of particular interest that in addition to many of the hummock species, such dominant plants of the dunes as *Carex arenaria* can also only establish from seed in damp hollows. Unlike the hummock formers which

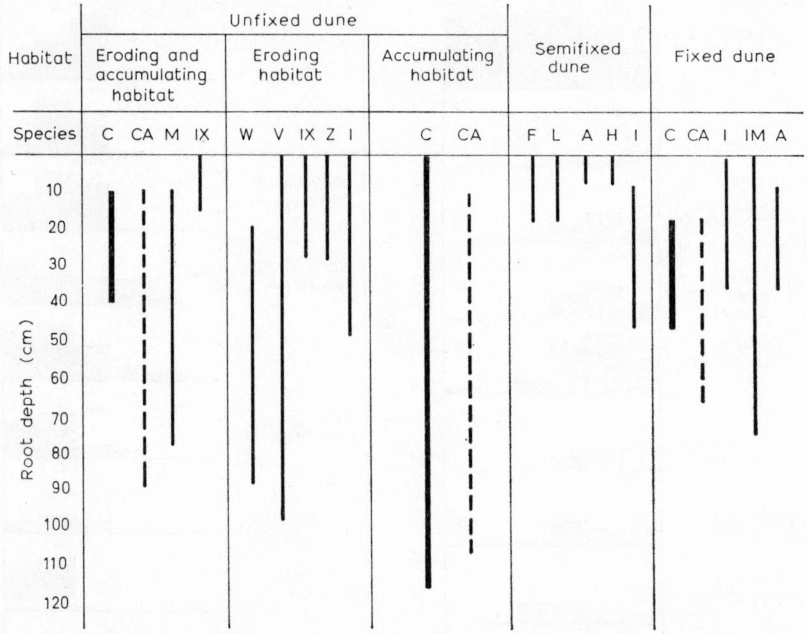

Fig. 59. Working ranges of the root system of the representative species in various sand dune habitats in Japan.

C: *Calystegia soldanella*
M: *Messerschmidia sibirica*
V: *Vitex rotundifolia*
F: *Fimbristylis sericea*
I: *Ischaemum anthephroides* var.
     eriostachyum
IM: *Imperata cylindrica* var. *koenigii*
A: *Artemisia capillaris*

CA: *Carex kobomugi*
W: *Wederia prostrata*
IX: *Ixeris repens*
L: *Linaria japonica*

Z: *Zoysia macrostachya*
H: *Heteropappus arenarius*

(from Yano 1962)

have rather limited horizontal, as opposed to vertical powers of growth, this species spreads widely onto dunes by means of rapidly extending horizontal growth. In relatively dry systems like that at Holkham or Blakeney, Norfolk, *Carex arenaria* may well be of uniform clonal origin over very large areas. It would be interesting to apply Harberd's (1961) technique of clonal analysis to see if this can be demonstrated. Certainly White's (1961) observation that *Carex arenaria* is holding its own, but not spreading to new areas at Blakeney Point since myxomatosis implies problems of establishment.

Those biennial or perennial species which do regenerate at the dune level to become part of the herb layer like *Euphorbia paralias* or *Cyno-*

glossum officinalis tend to be large seeded and capable of very rapid root extension down to moist layers at 15 cm depth within a week of germination. Thus their occupancy as seedlings of the tricky arid ground layer is cut down to a minimum. Yano (1962) has studied root formation of Japanese dune plants in relation to depth, root area, morphology, and propagation across the dune zones. He found that plants with well developed rhizomes rooting deeply over a wide area, formed large clones on mobile dunes. On fixed dunes plants had poorly-developed rhizome systems, were generally shallow-rooted over more limited areas, and formed small clones (Fig. 59).

The striking change in the growth form of *Ammophila* species from the vigorous close tussock habit of mobile dunes (Plate 13) to the sparse depauperate isolated shoots of fixed dunes (Plate 14) has been variously interpreted as due to drought, mineral deficiency, toxicity or senescence (Marshall 1965). Olson (1958 *c*) was the first to suggest that normal internodal elongation in *Ammophila breviligulata* on a stable surface raises the meristem into surface dry sand which prevents normal development of adventitious roots. However Laing (1954) produced experimental evidence that mineral deficiency and toxicity were not associated with decline in vigour of *Ammophila breviligulata* and found that sand burial alone was sufficient to restore vigour. Marshall (1965) reached similar conclusions (see also Hope-Simpson and Jefferies 1966) with regard to decline of both *Ammophila arenaria* and *Corynephorus canescens* (Fig. 60). In a nice demonstration using split root-culture technique he found that new adventitious roots in *Corynephorus canescens* were more efficient in water and nutrient uptake than nine-month-old roots. The interest of these studies lies in the emphasis they give to inherent morphological, growth, and senescence characteristics of dune dominants in relation to successional changes of plant pattern. This tendency for *Ammophila* to literally grow out of the ground in stable dune surfaces is well illustrated in the toppling of *Ammophila* shoot tufts in response to trampling (Plate 14).

With the development of really fine, detailed studies of the types just mentioned one is forcibly reminded of Watt's (1947) vision in his classical paper on 'Pattern and process in the plant community'. We begin to see the possibilities of, as he puts it, 'fusing the shattered fragments into the original unity.' But we have a long way to go in understanding the complex interacting patterns of the dune grass/herb layer. As Olson (1958 *a*) points out, 'successions in the dunes are going off in different directions and have different destinations according to the many possible combinations of independent variables which determine the original site and subsequent

N

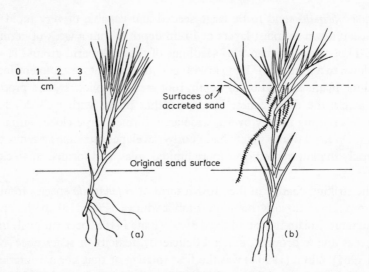

Fig. 60. Tillers from two plants of *Corynephorus canescens* growing approximately 20 cm apart. In plant (a) the site of adventitious root production was above the sand surface and the roots failed to develop. Plant (b) was partially covered with sand by rabbits. The site of adventitious root production was below the sand surface and the new roots, which have not been drawn to their full extent, had developed. Note the difference in diameter of the new roots in comparison with the older roots and also the presence of root hairs on the former (from Marshall, 1965).

conditions for development.' He emphasizes the value of multivariate techniques of analysis such as Maarel (1966) has recently applied to the Voorne dune environments in Holland, in helping us to understand these complex relationships.

The shrub and woodland layers

Partly for reasons of space and partly the lack of detailed study it is not possible here to deal adequately with the woody components of the dune flora. In Europe at the present time we are witnessing a resurgence of scrub on dune systems as a result of myxomatosis. In many areas these developing communities have not yet achieved a stable equilibrium with the environment, and especially with the human part of it.

An attempt to analyse some of the problems associated with the development of a particular type of dune scrub, *Hippophaë rhamnoides*, which is transforming many areas of dune grassland in Europe has recently been made by a group of Nature Conservancy biologists (Ranwell (ed.) 1972).

Some discussion of the dwarf shrub community formed by *Salix repens* in dune slacks is given in the next chapter, and of afforestation in the last chapter. Dwarf shrub communities anyway tend to be associated with dune slacks and those landward parts of the dune system where erosive and accumulative processes draw together the dune and slack levels to a plateau level somewhat intermediate between the two. Native woodland is a rather rare phenomenon on dunes and the accounts that do exist are primarily of a general descriptive character (e.g. Osborn and Robertson 1939; Westhoff 1947 and 1952; Lambinon 1956; Olson 1958; Boerboom (1960)). If the study of the ecology of dune scrub is in its infancy, that of the afforested dunes has scarcely yet begun and it offers challenging opportunities for work relating to the changing communities associated with fire and felling-recovery sequences of considerable practical interest.

Perhaps one might end this chapter with a plea that instead of directing attention to the generalized zonal trends that are more or less universal and fairly well known in dunes throughout the world but which tend to obscure what goes on in time at a particular spot in a particular dune system, we should turn our attention to the more detailed study of the unit 'fragments' of the ecosystem, the better to eventually understand the whole.

11 Sand Dunes:
Structure and function of
slack communities

Surprisingly little work has been carried out on the ecology of dune slacks
outside the British Isles and Holland. This may be because these damp or
wet hollows among the dunes are much more restricted in distribution than
dunes and are sparsely represented in the more arid parts of the Mediterranean climatic zone for example. Slacks are however a very characteristic
feature of large dune systems underlain by impervious deposits in the
more humid Temperate zones, and it would be valuable to have fuller
accounts than we have at present of slack systems in American and Austral-
asian sites to say nothing of the still largely undescribed magnificent slack
communities of the Coto Doñana in Spain.

Apart from their intrinsic interest as floristically and faunistically
rich sites, their study is vital to an understanding of dune communities
because many species of the dunes regenerate either more freely or
solely at damp slack levels. The study of plant growth in the vicinity of
the water table is also of considerable significance to both agriculturalists
and water engineers concerned with cropping water-logged land, or water
extraction

In many ways a dune slack with its level surface; often influenced by salt
in the early stages of formation; generally influenced by moderate accretion; and subject to the opposing influences of submergence or drought
seasonally or at different stages of its development over longer periods of
time, has much in common with a salt marsh. Certainly in transitional zones
between the two, the sandy salt marsh and the saline dune slack merge so
completely that they become indistinguishable.

It is not possible with the present state of knowledge to give a balanced
account of dune slack ecology for we know little about the biology of
most dune slack plants and have scarcely begun to study their animal

communities. It is hoped that the somewhat fragmentary account given here will nevertheless stimulate further study of this neglected habitat.

Species Diversity

The biological spectrum given in Table 23 shows that in a site where slacks form nearly half the area of the dune system, they are almost as rich in vascular plants as the dunes. When we take into account the cryptogamic flora, and especially bryophytes which are particularly abundant, there is little doubt that in some sites the dune slack flora is the richer of the two. This forms a striking contrast with the relative poverty of the salt marsh flora and indicates optimum conditions in the dune slack for plant establishment, though not necessarily as we shall see, for plant growth.

We have no data on the relative species diversities of dunes and slacks so far as animals are concerned, but from general observations, the cooler climate of slacks, and the unpredictable tendencies towards flooding or surface desiccation from season to season it seems likely that fewer species of animals will have become adapted to them than to the dunes. Arthropods and molluscs (on lime-rich systems) are the most abundantly represented groups of the larger invertebrates, and annelids form a small but important section of the soil fauna in older slacks as at Newborough Warren. On machair, annelids are especially found in association with dung pats (Boyd 1957). The soil macrofauna of fully vegetated slacks at Newborough is sufficient to attract moles in quite large numbers in winter (e.g. 80 fresh mole hills noted in an area of less than $350\,m^2$ in December 1953 at Newborough.

Prior to myxomatosis, rabbits exerted a controlling influence on the vegetation of dry slacks and a more indirect influence on that of wet slacks (see section on grazing below).

Analytical Studies of Slack Vegetation Gradients

Much of what has already been said about the analysis of the dune flora in Chapter 10 is applicable also to the flora of slacks, but there is one important series of papers (Crawford and Wishart 1966, 1967 and 1968), devoted to the analysis of the dune slack flora of Tentsmuir, Fife. This provides an objective analysis which is enlightening. A grid of quadrats were examined for floristic cover and abundance, analysed by association analysis, and the groupings compared for similarity (Crawford and Wishart 1966). Results gave a spatially orientated series which was meaningful in relation to the

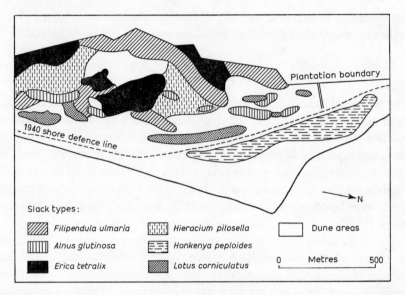

Fig. 61. Distribution of slack types determined by association analysis. Data from Tentsmuir, Fife (from Crawford and Wishart 1966).

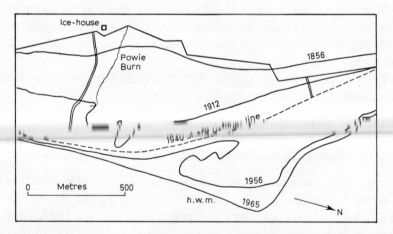

Fig. 62. Coastal changes at Tentsmuir from 1856 to 1965. All the coastlines except the most recent are taken from the unpublished report of Grove, A.T. (1953) Tentsmuir, Fife; soil blowing and coastal changes. Nature Conservancy, Edinburgh (from Crawford and Wishart 1966).

temporal development of this prograding dune system (Fig. 61 and 62). It was found that seasonally high salinity was correlated with the floristic groups associated with seawardmost slacks, while water level and soil activity were correlated with distinctive groupings in landwardmost slacks.

In a further treatment of this data (Crawford and Wishart 1967), a multivariate technique based on coincidence of occurrence and species interaction distinguished fewer groups than the original analysis and showed that many were ecotonal in character (Fig. 63) as might be expected in rapidly changing vegetation of this type. In their final paper (Crawford and Wishart 1968), an agglomerative method is used following the original divisive process to check for misclassification and secondly a means of representing the variance both within and between the terminal groups of an ordination procedure. It is then shown how the potential of any quadrat for membership of any classified type can be used to give computer maps of varying group potential, rather than discrete vegetation boundaries. Significantly the authors point out that, 'While it is always possible to draw a boundary marking the distribution of one particular species . . . no boundary can be drawn with any precision for any vegetation type that is defined on the basis of the probable occurrence of a number of species.' Objective studies of this type provide valuable confirmation of the

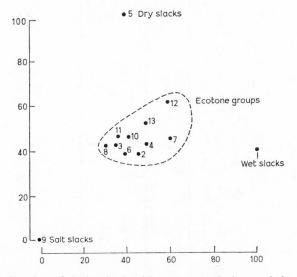

Fig. 63. Ordination of slacks obtained by group analysis; x axis based on types 9 and 1, y axis on types 9 and 5. Data from Tentsmuir, Fife (from Crawford and Wishart 1967).

Table 24. Soil analyses of samples from five different stands in the transition from sand dune to salt marsh. Each value represents the mean of five samples as expressed as g/100g oven dry weight. Mairiut District, Egypt (after Rezk 1970).

Soil type	Hygroscopic moisture	Loss on ignition	Org. C	Loss on acid treatment	Exchangeable Ca	Total soluble salts	Soluble chlorides	Soluble sulphates
Dune sand	0·4	2·7	0·033	99·0	20·29	0·11	0·004	0·001
Partly stabilized dune	0·4	2·8	0·080	98·1	18·31	0·10	0·004	0·001
Stabilized dune	0·6	5·0	0·156	95·3	15·71	0·14	0·004	0·007
Transition to salt marsh	1·1	5·7	0·138	86·1	16·29	0·23	0·015	0·009
Salt marsh	1·6	15·1	0·306	76·5	23·14	1·31	0·424	0·351

significance of trends hitherto distinguished primarily by more sub-jective approaches.

Westhoff *et al* (1961), Freijsen (1967) and Rezk, M. R. (1970) have studied dune slack to salt marsh transitions including relationships between plant associes and physico-chemical soil properties (Table 24).

On the dune to slack gradient most of the environmental changes are dependent solely on the change in water relations, and the gradient contains a mixture of species from each habitat, but none confined to the gradient zone. In contrast, at the salt marsh to sand dune slack gradient environ-mental changes are much more profound and involve changes in soil type, in salinity, *and* in water relations. Many species are more or less confined to the intermediate gradient zone (e.g. *Blysmus rufus, Centaurium littorale, Frankenia laevis, Limonium bellidifolium* and, though also associated with damp shingle, *Suaeda fruticosa*). This 'sandwich zone' as it might be called from the characteristic alternating soil types deserves special study in its own right as a separate habitat complex.

Maarel and Leertouwer (1967) used ordination and classification of con-tiguous quadrats on a dune gradient at Schiermonnikoog, Holland based on an index distinguishing floristic difference between adjacent quadrats. This showed continuous variation of vegetation which was correlated with variation in pH value and vertical height of the ground (Fig. 64). The remarkable pH gradient they found from *Drosera* areas on soil with pH 4 to *Schoenus* areas on soil of pH 7 over a very short distance is clearly similar to that in the dune heath situation studied at Newborough (Ranwell 1959).

While it is true that these studies emphasize the continuum nature of dune slack transitions, Leeuwen (1965) points out that the presence of a fluctuating water table near the surface marks out a zone on the gradient between dune and slack which is characterized by instability (in regard to the water factor) in time. This gives a specialized habitat which appears to suit orchids for example which are characteristic of (though not necessarily confined to) gradient situations like this and path sides. Freijsen's (1967) work (see below) shows that *Centaurium littorale* is best developed where the fluctuating influence of the water table is maximal.

For practical purposes it is necessary to draw boundaries and preferably ones which can be readily distinguished on the ground or on aerial photo-graphs. Crawford and Wishart (1968) note the distinctive appearance of certain physiognomic dominants like *Erica tetralix, Glyceria maxima, Carex nigra* or *Juncus effusus* on photographs of the Tentsmuir dune slacks. Individual species of this type have special value for mapping when it comes to monitoring the rapid vegetation changes that occur in coastal systems.

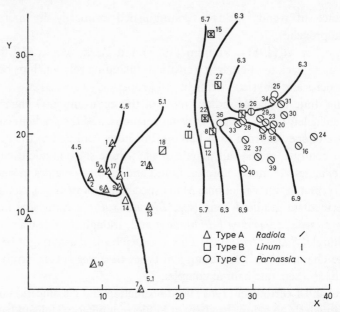

Fig. 64. Ordination of 40 quadrats in a 10 × 4 m transect laid down in the transition between *Schoenus nigricans* associes on base-rich ground at low elevations, and *Drosera rotundifolia* associes on base-deficient ground at slightly higher elevations, with isonomes of pH superimposed. Species number was taken as a measure of species diversity and was found to be related to range of pH and height. Results suggest a continuum-like variation in vegetation types mainly governed by pH variation itself governed by variation in height (from Maarel and Leertouwer 1967).

Similarly we need practical and workable divisions of the apparent continuum from the aquatic habitat to the dune in the vertical plane, and the next section outlines a system suitable for this purpose.

Water Table Limits as a Basis for Defining Slack Plant Community Limits

Studies at Newborough Warren and subsequent observations suggest that four distinctive levels of plant growth in relation to the water table can be distinguished (Ranwell 1959 and 1960 *a*). They are levels which appear to be significant in a number of ways which are biologically meaningful, but it is highly desirable that their delineation should be based on more objective criteria. In particular, one would like to see comparative study of the rooting depths of all species and study of the nutrient economy within and between the different zones. At the present time the literature on sand dune vegetation seems especially confusing in relation to the levels variously referred to as 'dune pasture', 'dune grassland', 'fixed dune', and 'grey dune'. Judging from the species composition and descriptions, many of these landscape types have more in common with what is defined below as the dry slack level than they do with the dune level. Perhaps the following classification may serve as a useful basis for clearing up such problems:

(1) *Semiaquatic habitat*

The water table is never more than 0·5 m below the soil surface and floods the surface from autumn to spring or later; plant roots are almost permanently waterlogged. Amphibious hydrophytes like *Littorella uniflora*, *Polygonum amphibium* or *Ranunculus aquatilis* are represented in the flora.

(2) *Wet slack habitat*

The water table never falls below 1 m below the soil surface and plants have their roots within reach of adequate moisture supplies at all seasons. Bryophytes are particularly abundant, the bulk of the flora is mesophytic and relatively few grass species occur.

(3) *Dry slack habitat*

The water table lies between 1 and 2 m below the surface at all seasons. Shallower rooted species are beyond the influence of the water table, but deeper rooted species benefit from its influence in summer drought. Phreatophytes and grasses are especially abundant and under rabbit-grazed conditions lichens may be locally abundant.

(4) *Dune habitat*

The water table never rises above 2 m below the surface and most of the plant growth is independent of it and wholly dependent on pendular water. Xerophytes and therophytes are common and vegetation tends to remain open.

In connection with the paucity of grasses in wet slacks, Jones and Etherington (1971) found from pot experiments that the dune grasses (*Agrostis stolonifera* and *Festuca rubra*) showed reduced tiller production and stunted roots in water-logged conditions. Growth of sedges (*Carex flacca and Carex nigra*) was less affected by water-logging.

It is true that Boerboom (1963) found that the presence of moisture indicator plants was found to be ordered by the quality (humus content) of the topmost soil layer rather than by the depth of the groundwater level and concluded that the field moisture capacity of the soil surface layers during drought was a better standard for the presence of moisture indicators than total pore space or the moisture content at various tensions. It is also true that as Vose *et al* (1957) showed there may be a higher moisture retentiveness in the surface layers in more humid areas such as the Tiree machairs off the western seaboard of Scotland. Also species like *Empetrum nigrum* normally dependent on groundwater survive at higher levels on north slopes (Westhoff 1947). Nevertheless, the broad distinctions outlined above seem to hold in European dunes at least, and it is very much easier to determine the approximate position of the water table within 2 m of the surface at any season with an auger than it is to measure field moisture capacities in drought periods.

Goethart *et al* (1924) have worked out the vertical ranges in relation to the water table of 91 species of flowering plants in several Dutch dune systems, but this work has been overlooked by most later workers.

Minor slack habitats

Within the main slack levels which are generally flat, secondary biotopographic units may be developed locally. They include: wet flushes; man-made pools and turf or peat cuts; low hummocks associated with clonal patches of such species as *Agropyron junceiforme* and *Salix repens*; mole-hills; ant-hills; and rabbit-disturbed ground. Each of these surface irregularities may show zonal sequences with characteristic communities varying according to salinity, moisture and physico-chemical soil factors. They are minor habitats found again and again in different dune systems wherever dune slacks occur, and they are worthy of detailed comparative study. To take one example, Freijsen (1967) has made a special study of the low *Agropyron junceiforme* hummocks of the Boschplat on the island of Terschelling. These form characteristic circular or horseshoe-shaped isolates on the floor of coastal slacks. He investigated the performance and regeneration of *Centaurium littorale*, a plant characteristic of the wet-dry gradient, on these hummocks. His studies (see below) are of considerable interest in helping us to understand the problems of plant establishment and growth in this sub-habitat of dune slacks. These *Agropyron* hummocks are especially characteristic of rapidly prograding phases of dune systems and are also found at Tentsmuir, Fife; Morrich More, Ross; Towyn Burrows, Carmarthen, and Newborough Warren, Anglesey.

Establishment and Growth in the Slack Habitat

Migration into the slack

Salisbury (1952) concluded that the flora of wet slacks is chiefly composed of marsh plants commonly found outside the dune system. Very few species are confined to the dune slack habitat. Apart from being a relatively rare habitat, slacks are isolated among the drier dunes and only in direct communication with other wet habitats such as a salt marsh during relatively short periods when they are formed at the coast or with other fresh-water bodies via temporary streams during flooding. Once the slack is isolated by the growth of dunes, migration into it must come largely via wind-borne seeds, by birds, or by human activities.

The open damp slack surface exposed in the wake of eroding dunes becomes warm and moist in late spring or early autumn and ideal for seedling establishment, but only for very short and irregular periods. Where the slack surface is level, Martin (1959) failed to find any obvious environmental gradients of soil moisture, salinity, or soil physico-chemical factors in Island Beach, New Jersey. Yet there were striking differences from point to point in the vegetation (e.g. locally pure stands of *Dryopteris thelypteris* up to 40 m in diameter). Blanchard (1952) found similar point to point variation and large pure stands of a variety of species in a relatively young slack at Ainsdale, Lancashire. Martin concluded that chance factors of migration and establishment must play a big part in the colonization of slacks to account for the variety found. At Newborough Warren a few large clones of *Juncus maritimus* occur in certain landward slacks. During a 20 year period of observation only one new seedling of this species became established in these slacks. The seeds of this species are small enough to be carried in mud on the feet of birds, but unlikely to be distributed far by wind. Now there is a 200 acre (80 ha) *Juncus maritimus* marsh within a distance of 3 flight miles (4·48 km) of these slacks. This example suggests that bird-induced migration of plant species into slacks is likely to be of very rare occurrence indeed, a conclusion also reached by Westhoff (1947) in relation to colonization of the West Friesian Islands off the Dutch coast. Westhoff concluded that cattle were an important agent of dissemination within dune systems in addition to the main agents, water and the wind.

Establishment problems

The presence of such relict salt marsh species as *Glaux maritima* which establish in seaward slacks and persist in landward ones long since cut off from the sea, often gives the impression that there is a persistent saline influence in landward slacks operating through the water table. This is not necessarily so and many authors (Lambinon 1956, Ranwell 1959, Martin 1959, Duvigneaud 1947) have confirmed that the saline groundwater influence is limited to coastal slacks affected by tidal influence either by occasional tidal flooding or via percolation through a permeable shingle base. Pioneer species like *Centaurium littorale*, *Agrostis stolonifera* and *Juncus articulatus* are able to tolerate temporary periods of high salinity and even *Salix repens* can germinate in 25 per cent sea water (Ranwell 1960 *a*).

Submergence in wet slacks limits the period of establishment of most species to late spring or summer when the flood waters recede. Freijsen (1947) found that *Centaurium littorale* occurs on a level just reached by the capillary fringe (c. 55 cm above the water table). Germination in this species occurred when the mean afternoon temperature exceeded the critical temperature for germination (13°C) and was at a maximum when the temperature reached 24°C. The effect of the sun's altitude is important in autumn when slack surfaces become warmer than north slopes. Shallow water acts as a heat reservoir during the night and warms slacks to slope temperatures in spring. Experimental sowings of *Centaurium littorale* showed that germination was inhibited where the surface soil was saturated (Freijsen).

The lower limit of many species in slacks appears to be controlled by submergence though precisely how is not clear. Blanchard (1952) made detailed observations of the duration of fresh-water submergence in dune slacks at Ainsdale, Lancashire.

Birse (1958) carried out experiments on the tolerance of mosses to flooding and showed that species characteristic of dry slacks like *Ceratodon purpureus* and *Climacium dendroides* could tolerate up to 4 months flooding and survive. Westhoff (1947) found that in dune slacks with open water the strip along the shores is almost always water-logged, while elsewhere the soil is drier even though the water table is at the same depth. As Freijsen (1967) points out this is because the capillary rise is higher in wet than in dry soil where large pore spaces limit the rise of capillary threads. Westhoff observed that species requiring water-logged soil (e.g. *Littorella uniflora* can only thrive in the neighbourhood of open water and hence are particularly sensitive to drainage.

The density of vegetation in fully-vegetated slacks is persistently very high and this makes it difficult for other plants to establish. The only sites where *Calluna vulgaris* seedlings were found at Newborough were in turf cut areas where the vegetation had been temporarily opened up. *Calluna* does not enter the succession until a late phase at Newborough where leaching provides a sufficiently acid soil. There is of course no such problem for this species in lime-deficient dune slacks such as Good (1935) described at Studland, Dorset as *Calluna* can enter the slacks in the open phase.

Freijsen (1967) demonstrated how populations of *Centaurium vulgare* (syn. *Centaurium littorale*) oscillated in their vertical distribution from year to year according to the depth of the soil water table in spring (Fig. 65). Drought was clearly limiting both germination and establishment at the upper vertical limit of the populations. At the wetter, lower limit *Centaurium* showed delayed development up to three years though it is normally a biennial plant. As in *Aster* we have here another good example of the 'close-tracking' of the environment (see Chapter 6) shown by a short-lived perennial.

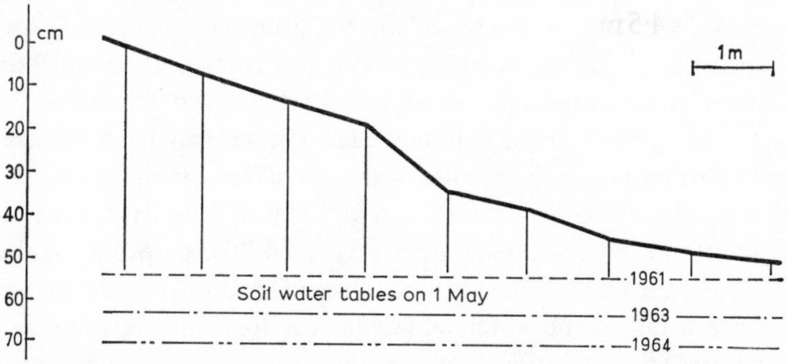

Sample plot	A1	A2	B1	B2	C1	C2	D1	D2	
length in cm	18	—	11	—	3	—	4·5	—	⎤
fruits (av.)	5·3	—	2·1	—	1	—	1	—	⎬ 1961
plants on 2m²	170	—	375	—	350	—	130	—	
fruits on 2m²	885	—	800	—	370	—	130	—	⎦
length in cm	15	14	13	10	4	6	0	0	⎤
fruits (av.)	15	8	4	4·3	1	1	0	0	⎬ 1963
plants on 2m²	1	19	42	33	10	3	0?	0?	
fruits on 2m²	15	153	170	141	10	3	0	0	⎦
diameter of rosettes (mm)	0	0	15	8	5	5	2	2	⎤ 1964
plants on 2m²	0	0	120	2500	1250	1250	250	100	⎦

Fig. 65. Variations in properties of *Centaurium vulgare* (syn. *C. littorale*) populations across a transect in a dune slack on Terschelling, West Friesian Islands, Netherlands (from Freijsen 1967).

It is of interest that these gradient environments favour the development of hybrids between *Agrostis stolonifera* (which occurs in wet slacks and semi-stable dune) and *Agrostis tenuis* (confined to drier sites) on the older dry slacks at Newborough (Bradshaw 1958). Anderson and Stebbins (1964) have pointed out the significance of habitat gradients for survival of hybrids.

Species of dune slack plants show very extreme morphological modifications in reaction to excess or deficiency of water. Non-flowering and very flaccid-leaved forms of *Myosotis scorpioides* occur in slacks submerged until summer. Reduced terrestrial forms of aquatic species like *Polygonum amphibium* occur in areas normally flooded but exposed in drought. As we have seen, submergence causes dwarfing in *Centaurium littorale* and *Salix repens* while as Salisbury (1952) demonstrates, drought has a similar effect on *Samolus valerandi* and *Plantago coronopus*. It is not surprising that with the two opposed extremes of too much and too little water constantly oscillating that very few species like *Centaurium littorale* have become adapted for growth specifically in the gradient zone between wet and dry slacks.

Westhoff (1946) observed that only a few species may have contact with the groundwater or capillary zones to depths of 3 m. At the dry slack level (as defined above) many species do so and it would be desirable to know more about the evapo-transpiration powers of these species. Robinson (1952) quotes the extraordinarily high figure of an annual discharge equivalent to a 2 m fall in the water table per year for *Tamarix* growing on a shallow water table at Safford Valley, Arizona. By contrast where the water table depth is 4·5 m the annual water loss from transpiration is equivalent to a fall in the water table of only 5 cm. There is no doubt that with the spread of such species as *Hippophaë rhamnoides* since myxomatosis, wet slacks will dry out and marsh species will suffer, but this effect has not yet been measured.

Community Transformations

It may seem a surprising omission that diagrams showing how plant communities of salt marsh or sand dunes are linked to one another to form successional series are completely absent from this book. There are two reasons: first, it is a fact that there is extraordinarily little direct evidence based on frequent and long term observations of marked plots in support of the assumptions made in such diagrams; second, two-dimensional diagrams are inadequate for the expression of the complexity of communities that can arise at any one location according to its history and subsequent treatment.

Successional diagrams not only oversimplify the many directions in which a particular community can develop, but they tend to falsify the reality of the situation in the minds of student ecologists. Successions do not end at the point where man's influence becomes dominant, they are simply modified by it. Many of the earlier accounts of dune succession stop at the first fence-line and ignore the fact that beyond it in the sandy pastures, the golf links or the conifer plantations, a high proportion of the dune flora and fauna continues to exist and develop under the imposed conditions of management. Some account of these various forms of more intensive management are discussed in the last chapter.

Physiographic changes (Chapter 8) and soil changes (Chapter 9) in space and time have already been discussed. These exert primary control on the type of communities present at any particular time and in any particular place on a dune system. As we have seen, the seaward edge of a dune system tends to undergo alternating change from the strandline community through embryo to open dune community and back again. Within the mobile dunes another type of alternation or cycle may occur from the open wet slack community to a more species rich, but still open dune community which erodes right down to damp bare sand to start the next phase in the cycle. And finally only when the dunes are worn down at the landward side of the dune system to near the dry slack level is there persistent stability. Here fully closed vegetation maintained as turf with dwarf shrubs under grazing, or developing towards some type of woodland, can develop.

Thus as in an estuarine series of marshes, we must think in terms of several quite distinct successional series operating persistently at different points in the system and not in terms of units of the spatial sequence from seaward to landward succeeding one another in time.

Coastal slacks

These are usually very transient features liable to sea water flooding or to obliteration by the growth of embryo dunes. They usually contain very open communities of scattered strandline species and a few salt marsh plants tolerant of well-drained soils. Where the dune system is prograding in alternating bands of low dunes and intervening coastal slacks they can develop more stable communities in which individual clones of halophytic and wet dune slack perennials close up to form a mosaic. The development of these communities has received little study and it would be interesting to establish long term observations on such sites as Morrich More, Ross or Tentsmuir, Fife to see how persistent the halophytic elements are with time and to find out just how perennials characteristic of later stages establish.

Blanchard (1952) made a detailed map of semi-aquatic plant communities associated with a coastal slack in Ainsdale dunes, Lancashire. She

o

found these formed a mosaic, the elements of which were evidently laid down at the time of establishment and subsequently formed a pattern of very persistent form. It is interesting that although this slack has been cut off from the sea for many years, now some 20 years after Blanchard's study the sea is threatening to break through again. If this is allowed to happen the existing vegetation of tall fresh water marsh species may well be destroyed leaving a bare surface for a new pattern, stemming from chance factors affecting establishment, to be set up.

Wet slacks

Where these are created by the erosion of a mobile dune as at Newborough, Anglesey, each new crescent of newly exposed wet sand in the wake of the eroding dune carries a slightly different seed complement from that of the previous year. Consequently banded communities commonly occur across the slacks often at slightly different levels according to the depth of the water table and the intensity of wind erosion at the time of their formation.

Among mobile dunes these slacks may persist with relatively open vegetation for 50 years or more. It was interesting to find at Newborough Warren that even with the reduction in rabbit grazing following myxomatosis that the existing vegetation of these wet slacks remain short although the flowering of many species (especially terrestrial orchids) was much improved. Evidently the adverse effects of summer drought for some species and winter flooding for others and not grazing are the main factors restricting growth.

However Westhoff (1946) records that since about 1910 the Dutch government has been active in controlling rabbits, and scrub has come up in the dune slacks. This led Westhoff to conclude that biotic rather than climatic factors have limited the spread of dune woodland in the past. Tansley (1949) suggested that the lack of tree seed parents in the neighbourhood of the coast was mainly responsible for absence of native forest on coastal dunes.

Now of course we are witnessing the post-myxomatosis transformation and *Alnus* and *Salix* are developing extensively in wet slacks and especially where they are close to afforested areas where rabbits were controlled prior to myxomatosis. Nevertheless in some of the bigger systems still remote from tree seed parents, tree seedlings have not yet appeared in wet slacks.

Dry slacks

Open vegetation communities at the dry slack level, like coastal slacks, are usually very transient habitats. They occur either at the base of the lee slope of advancing mobile dunes or occasionally over wider areas where shifts in the dune contours have led to re-erosion of a low dune area. Hummocks of *Salix repens, Ligustrum vulgare* or other shrub species are especially characteristic of such sites and they usually carry a rather sparse associated flora in which annual species are common, at least in the more stable areas.

The dune system comes to rest at the closed dry slack to dune level, and it is here that biological, as opposed to other environmental influences, become paramount in controlling community changes.

Prior to myxomatosis it was shown that there was strong evidence from sequences in the mosaic of vegetation that turf and dwarf shrub communities alternated with one another in time at Newborough Warren, Anglesey (Ranwell 1960 *a*). In this particular example a defoliating beetle (*Lochmea capreæ*) and the drought effect from rabbit-burrowing beneath *Salix repens* were believed to be responsible for its death. The occasional chance establishment of *Salix* seedlings in rabbit-disturbed turf started the cycle of shrub growth and ultimate death and decay again.

In this more stable zone it is legitimate to equate seral relations in time and space in local areas. From a study of serally related transects on dry slack turf at Newborough before and three years after myxomatosis, it was shown that while no seral trends were reversed, significant changes did occur in the frequency of species which were serally static. In particular there was a marked increase in the growth and flowering of most grasses and sedges. Turf 1 cm high grew to 15 cm in 3 years, low growing herbs and lichens were much reduced, but mosses remained abundant (Ranwell 1960 *b*). Now 15 years later the grassland has formed a 'rough' 40 to 50 cm high, mosses are much reduced, lichens are absent and scattered shrubs are overtopping the grassland.

Even more dramatic effects are evident on the dunes where rabbits no longer graze in any numbers. The vastly increased seed output has filled up the gaps in many formerly mobile dune areas and effectively locked the moving dunes into place.

The future clearly lies with the newly developing shrub communities, especially those associated with *Hippophaë rhamnoides* in European systems, unless active management takes a hand.

PART FOUR   Human Influences

12 Management of Salt Marsh Wildlife Resources

Salt marshes are the product of land erosion and therefore an expanding resource. It is no accident that the greater part of the world's population derives its food from the great deltas, largely in the form of fish and rice. No other habitat has sufficient natural fertility to support it. According to Grist (1959) possibly over 600 million people in Asia derive 50 per cent or more of their food calories from rice.

For centuries human beings have settled at the head of deltas and estuaries and expanded cropping and port facilities in pace with the seaward thrust of siltation. Yet it is extraordinary how even today in the most highly civilized countries this elementary geographical process seems to catch unawares the local authorities or other coastal landowners who suddenly find that their creek or tidal flat frontages are no longer open but clothed with salt marsh vegetation. Similarly, the significance of the dredger off-shore or the coastal engineering works on the other side of the estuary is rarely grasped by those whose coastal facilities will suffer in 10, 20 or 50 years time, until it is too late to do anything about it.

Rather more subtle changes associated with isostatic adjustment may be equally significant over periods of 50 or 100 years in those areas where the rate of coastal sinking is nearly balanced by the rate of salt marsh accretion. As we have seen this appears to be happening on parts of the south and south-east coasts of England at the present time.

Human influence on the salt marsh environment is increasing. The ecologist and the physiographer have an important responsibility to inform themselves of the directions and time scales of change relating to salt marsh formation, development and destruction. They also have the responsibility to pass on their knowledge in intelligible form to those who need to act on it.

An excellent account of human influences on general estuarine processes and the animals inhabiting estuaries is given by Cronin (in Lauff 1967); the following is chiefly concerned with human influence on salt marsh vegetation, and its management.

External Human Influences

Catchment activities

Land cultivation and mining activities have big effects on water and silt inflow into estuarine basins and hence on the life cycle of salt marshes.

It is claimed that the hydraulic mining in operation from 1850 until it was banned in 1884 added a metre of silt to the Suisan and San Pablo parts of San Francisco Bay (Gilliam 1957).

If silt is added in quantity to an estuary it increases the turbidity and raises the lower vertical limit to which salt marsh plants can grow. At the same time the rate of accretion of the levels which can support marsh growth will increase. These opposing effects result in a tendency to extensive cliffing at the seaward edge of the marsh which is very persistent even after the silt input is subsequently reduced. No one has measured these effects yet recent changes in land cultivation have been on a vast scale and must have had a profound influence on salt marsh development. Equally if cultivation demands improved drainage, then a greater volume of fresh water enters the estuary and this on meeting tidal waters will cause an increase in the height to which the tide will rise and consequently a reduction in the depth at which salt marsh can establish.

The need for data relating to these input factors is now recognized in relation to current studies on estuarine barrage schemes (Anon 1966 *a* to *c*, 1967, and 1970 *a*).

Pollution

In addition to the relatively innocuous effects of increased water and sediment input there may come along with it a frighteningly complex array of chemical substances derived from agricultural operations, industry, and sewage. This pollution approaches the salt marshes from landward and seaward. There is also a vertical component from air pollution.

In industrialized estuaries the sediment of which marshes are built may contain a high proportion of man-made detritus. Cinders, siliceous and metallic fly ash, slag, and coal were found in the sand-size fractions from the top 35 cm of a core in bottom sediment from the centre section of the Hudson estuary, New York State (McCrone 1966).

With the possible exception of oil, we are again very ignorant of both the nutritive or toxic effects of these substances on the life of salt marshes. No one has measured for example changes in the deathline for salt marsh growth in heavily polluted estuaries due to the combined effect of all these influences close to centres of civilization. It has been shown that overall productivity of macro-algal communities on the Adriatic coast remains unimpaired right up to the deathline where macro-algal growth suddenly fails (Golubic 1970). Significantly as this point is approached, the species diversity is reduced from many to only two algal species (*Ulva lactuca* and *Hypnea musciformis*) and one larger animal, the sea hare *Aplysia fasciata*. Beyond this point persistently anaerobic organic-rich mud forms a foul-smelling 'bacterial soup' virtually devoid of higher forms of life.

One of the most noticeable changes in southern English salt marshes over the past 20 years is the extensive growths of green algae (*Enteromorpha* and *Ulva* species) which have developed around the seaward edges of salt marshes. They occur particularly in the more sheltered bays where sewage or industrial effluents in built up areas, or fertilizer outwash in arable farming areas, are likely to accumulate. Now these algae are capable of utilizing nitrogen in the ammonium form and these various effluents must contribute substantial quantities of organic or ammonium nitrogen, which would normally be converted to readily assimilated nitrite and nitrate. But it is significant that under anaerobic conditions, the conversion of organic nitrogen stops with the step of ammonium formation (Black 1968). It seems likely that accumulation of ammonium nitrogen may preferentially benefit algal, rather than salt marsh plant growth. The growths are so extensive that in sheltered bays which could act as nutrient traps in the Blackwater estuary, Essex, or Poole Harbour, Dorset, for example, they appear to smother salt marsh growth and replace it locally. Studies are in progress to test the truth of this hypothesis and to determine the ultimate fate of the algal growths in chronic pollution conditions.

Chronic pollution from oil refinery effluent has much the same effect and the line between apparently normal live *Spartina anglica* marsh and dead marsh at Fawley in Southampton Water for example was found to be very sharp indeed when the site was visited in 1962. Boorman (*pers. comm.*) notes that *Limonium* species disappear from salt marsh in heavily polluted estuaries. It is important that studies should be made of the more subtle effects of pollution: sub-lethal damage, nutritional disturbance and, in the case of invertebrates, behavioural disturbance due to chemo-sensitivity, but there is much to be said for concentrating first on gross effects of total pollution as described above.

Heavy but isolated oil pollution may be tolerated without serious harm by salt marsh plants like *Spartina anglica* (Ranwell and Hewett 1964), indeed marsh growth forms a valuable trapping surface for oil in estuaries and strains it from the tidal water where it is so harmful to birds. However, most vegetation including salt marsh is rapidly killed by emulsifiers used to disperse oil (Ranwell and Stebbings 1967), so it is pointless to use them on an oiled salt marsh.

A recent bibliography by Nelson-Smith (1968) gives a valuable key to the literature on oil pollution and outstanding contributions have been made on the effects of oil (Plate 5) and emulsifiers on salt marsh plants and salt marshes by Baker (1970 *a* to *i*). This work is incidentally a model example of the experimental approach and its presentation. It has demonstrated the relatively high resistance of *Puccinellia* marsh turf to repeated oil sprayings, clearcut differences in the tolerance of different salt marsh species to oil pollution, and a (possibly indirect) nutritive effect of oil on salt marsh vegetation.

Baker (1970 *c*) also tested the effect of emulsifiers used to disperse oil pollution on *Puccinellia maritima/Festuca rubra* turves and found that emulsifiers in current use killed plants in concentrations above 10 per cent (Fig. 66). In a field trial where emulsifier (B.P. 1002) was used to clean oil, no decrease in damage to *Puccinellia* or *Spartina* marsh was noted and it was concluded that oiled salt marshes are best left to recover naturally (Baker 1970 *i*).

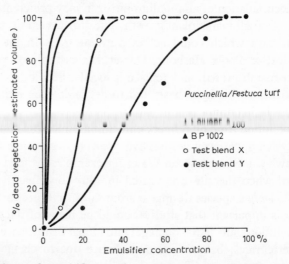

Fig. 66. Effects of emulsifiers and a solvent on *Puccinellia maritima/Festuca rubra* turf (from Baker 1970 *c*).

The effects of air pollution on salt marshes are probably minimal because of regular tidal flooding. However, there is evidence (McCrone 1966) that algae and silt accumulate radio-isotopes and Preston (1968) has shown that radionuclide concentrations decrease exponentially with depth from the surface in silt cores taken from the Ravenglass estuary, Cumberland. By contrast there was little significant change in radionuclide concentrations, in cores taken in nearby beach sands.

Introduced species

One of the most powerful human influences on salt marshes in Europe has been the deliberate introduction of *Spartina anglica* to particular sites and its subsequent uncontrolled spread to other sites from them (Ranwell 1967 *a*). This plant has also been established in Australia, Tasmania and New Zealand and recently planted in Puget Sound, Washington State, U.S.A. where it seems to be flourishing (Table 25). It has partially replaced *Zostera* and algal communities on high level mudflats and temporarily reduces variety where it becomes dominant in salt marshes. The rationale of many of the introductions is questionable and many attempts have been made to eradicate it locally. In most cases they have failed because of the high reproductive potential of this species. Currently work is in progress in Northern Ireland and elsewhere to determine the population level at which effective control can be achieved at reasonable cost.

Table 25. World resources of *Spartina anglica* marsh (from Ranwell 1967).

Country	Date of first record*	Area	
		Acres	Hectares
Great Britain	1870	30,000	12,000
Ireland	1925	500–1,000	200–400
Denmark	1931	1,230	500
Germany	1927	1,000–2,000	400–800
Netherlands	1924	9,800–14,300	4,000–5,800
France	1906	10,000–20,000	4,000–8,000
Australia	1930	25–50	10–20
Tasmania	1927	50–100	20–40
New Zealand	1913	50–100	20–40
United States	1960	< 1	< 1
Total		52,400–68,500	21,000–27,700

* Dates refer to the first recorded appearance, or first known introduction, to a country. All British material before 1892, when the fertile form was first recorded, is of the sterile form. Area estimates are of ground covered 50 % or more by *Spartina* and must be considered as very approximate.

The introduction of *Tamarix gallica* from the Mediterranean to the salt marshes of the southern United States has had more serious consequences. Martin (1953) records that its uncontrolled spread from wind and water dispersed seed has interfered with drainage, promoted flooding, reduced the value of grazing and waterfowl habitat, and resulted in extensive losses of irrigation water through evapo-transpiration. The latter has the effect of increasing ground water salinity in brackish areas. This limits the extent of rice cultivation and other salt-sensitive crops in the delta areas. The growth of deep-rooted phreatophytes like *Tamarix* is primarily a problem associated with marshlands in the warmer and more arid parts of the world.

Much of the literature on this subject relates to inland growths of *Tamarix*. Fletcher and Elmendorf (1955) for example quote annual water losses of up to 5 acre – feet due to *Tamarix* in the Pecos river delta, New Mexico. They give a useful review of the significance of phreatophytes in water control and the effect of attempts to limit their growth.

Internal Human Influences

The mildest forms of human influence on salt marshes result from sporadic direct cropping of the plants and animals which live on them (e.g. the gathering of 'samphire' (*Salicornia* sp.) or wildfowling). Indirect cropping with domestic grazing animals has a stronger influence as it changes the physical environment and the species composition. Draining and spraying activities produce even more profound changes in hydrological, chemical and biological parts of the environment. Both the creation and extermination of salt marshes may be caused by coast protection activities, reclamation, or other coastline modifying activities such as estuarine barrage or airport construction.

It is useful to consider these activities as given above in the sequence of increasingly strong human influence and we have to bear in mind there is often a hidden legacy from past activities, such as salt panning or derelict reclamation schemes which have left their mark on the marsh. Directly or indirectly, the character of most salt marshes throughout the world today has been largely determined by human activities past or present just as in other habitats.

Direct cropping

Spartina marshes on the north-east coast of North America were formerly mown for hay and Burkholder (1956) records an amusing energy chain from Georgia, U.S.A. where 'in former years marsh grass was harvested as the sole feed for mules that were used to haul fuel for the wood-burning steam locomotives on the Old Brunswick and Florida Railroad.' *Spartina patens* was formerly cut for hay in Delaware and *Spartina pectinata* (said to be dominant over some 28,000 acres (11,3000 ha) of marsh around the Bay of Fundy, Nova Scotia) is under investigation at the present time for use as hay and pasture (Nicholson and Longille 1965). Hubbard and Ranwell (1966) demonstrated that it was possible to cut *Spartina anglica* marsh in dry weather using a light tractor at Bridgwater Bay, Somerset and to make palatable and digestible silage for sheep. No information has been found on the effect of regular mowing of salt marshes on their botanical composition. It seems unlikely that mowing was practised in the native short grass or herb-rich marshes on European coasts, though reed (*Phragmites*) cutting is still an important activity in the larger deltas like that of the Danube.

Most of the *Spartina anglica* planting stocks used in different parts of the world were derived from a small bay in Poole Harbour, Dorset (Ranwell 1967) and seed stocks of *Festuca rubra* are currently harvested from Lancashire marshlands. Both this species and *Agrostis stolonifera* are being propagated for use on embankments on the German North Sea coast (Wohlenberg 1965). The selection and breeding of coastal grasses for use in specialized habitats of this type has hardly begun, and there is great scope for further work in this field and for their use as pasture plants on inland salinized soils.

Turf cutting is practised on the sheep-grazed Lancashire and Solway marshes. Usually 2 in (5 cm) strips are left between cuts to improve regeneration and within 5 years the same areas may be cut again. Experiments are in progress in the Bridgwater Bay National Nature Reserve, Somerset to determine the botanical changes of this cycle and to see if it is possible to reverse succession from coarse and relatively unpalatable *Festuca rubra* marsh to *Puccinellia* marsh, more palatable for wildfowl (Plate 8).

Wintering flocks of wildfowl on tidal marshes have been cropped for centuries. While in general this has developed in an uncontrolled manner particularly in Europe, the controlled cropping of wildfowl and muskrat on Delaware marshes has been combined with the application of sophisticated habitat management techniques. These include the excavation of flight pools, the planting of wildfowl foods, and spraying or burning to control tall marsh growths (Lynch 1941; Schmidt 1950 and Steenis *et al* 1954).

There is another less tangible 'crop' of increasing importance from salt marshes and that is the education and recreation derived by students, naturalists, yachtsmen and anyone who seeks to explore the life of the marshes or derives pleasure from the subtle contours and colours of their remote landscapes.

Indirect cropping

By far the most widespread use of salt marshes has involved indirect cropping by open range grazing with domestic animals. On the Gulf and Atlantic coasts of North America cattle graze the coarse *Spartina* marsh growths and older breeds of sheep do so in the British Isles. Williams (1955, 1959) has shown how access to the marshes can be improved by provision of cattle walkways (Plate 7). These are ridges of spoil bull-dozed from the marsh and spaced half a mile (0·8 km) apart where they provide refuge for cattle at high tide. The borrow pits from which the soil is dug, flood, and attract wildfowl. *Spartina* and *Distichalis* marshes will support a cow for every 2 to 4 acre (0·8 to 1·6 ha) during the 6 month grazing season. Burning is practised widely by stockmen to stimulate succulent new growth, but during drought, fire can reach plant crowns and severely damage the marsh vegetation (Williams 1955).

Salt marshes of the European seaboard are used for cattle, but more generally for sheep-grazing. Very extensive salting pastures are found in Northern France (e.g. the Baie de St. Michel) and on a smaller scale in most of the estuaries and bays of the west coast of England and Wales from the Solway to the Bristol Channel. European saltings are composed of three principal grasses, *Agrostis stolonifera*, *Festuca rubra*, and *Puccinellia maritima*. They support 2 to 3 sheep to the acre (0·4 ha) for most of the year when the marshes are free of tides. It has been shown that high level *Spartina anglica* marsh can be converted to *Puccinellia maritima* marsh by sheep grazing (Ranwell 1961). Experimental studies (Plate 6) indicate that on high level *Spartina* marsh growing on firm silt this can be achieved in about 5 to 10 years. With the development of intensive agriculture and loss of inland pasture for running sheep at high tide, or in mid winter, sheep-grazing has declined on many coast marshes in southern England. This has led to the spread of unpalatable tufted growths of *Festuca rubra* or *Agropyron pungens* which accrete silt more rapidly than close-grazed salting, quickly replacing succulent *Puccinellia* marsh. Chippindale and Merricks (1965) have shown how gang-mowing can help to maintain reclaimed salting pasture at times when sheep are in short supply. Wohlenberg (1965) records that turf cutting on salting pasture on the West German coast may enable *Agropyron pungens* to establish. Once established this coarse, unpalatable species can rapidly invade high level salting pasture.

There is a very critical stage near the upper limit of *Puccinellia* growth where coarser grasses can invade but at this level sheep-trampling helps to offset the very small but significant accretion brought by the few tides that reach these high level salting pastures. This compaction, aided by the normal settlement due to drying, can hold the marsh at a level suitable for *Puccinellia* growth for decades longer than it would otherwise be able to survive, providing it continues to be hard-grazed by sheep (Ranwell 1968 *a*).

Drainage

Large scale residential development near tidal marshes in the warmer parts of the world invariably promotes activities associated with mosquito control; in particular drainage and spraying.

Bourn and Cottam (1950) record that ditching for mosquito control began in New Jersey in 1912; greatly expanded in 1933 when relief labour (organized as a result of the economic depression) became available, and by 1938 had encompassed 90 per cent (562,500 acre (227,700 ha)) of the original tidewater lands lying between Maine and Virginia. Inevitably there was a clash with sporting and conservation interests, but by the time this became vociferous enough to achieve action most of the marshes had been criss-crossed by a network of drainage channels.

Taylor (1937) testified to the effectiveness of mosquito control on newly ditched marshes in comparison with unditched marshes and concluded from a superficial study of the vegetation that the only significant changes were in the development of secondary vegetation on ditch banks, notably the spread of *Iva ovaria*. However Bourn and Cottam (1950) carried out a much more detailed study over a period of 12 years on ditched Delaware marshes and found that shrubby growths of *Baccharis halimifolia* and *Iva Frutescens* had largely replaced the marshes natural grass associations and resulted in serious reductions in populations of marshland inverte-brates important as food for wildfowl and waders. There is no mention of reduction in grazing or hay cutting on these marshes with the advent of ditching, but inevitably this would result from reduced access due to the ditches and must have contributed to the spread of taller vegetation. In addition to the serious loss of wildlife habitat, Bourn and Cottam (1950) note that mosquito control has not been effective in many areas due to lack of maintenance on the ditches.

A great deal of literature exists relating to the use of brackish water for crop irrigation in coastal areas (see Gallatin *et al* 1962 and numerous publications of the U.S. Salinity Laboratory, Riverside, California), but very little study has been given to the effects of changing water quality on the wildlife of tidal marshlands. However, valuable studies have been carried out on this subject in the Camargue marshes of the Rhône delta, France by biologists at the Tour du Valat Biological Station. For example, Aguesse and Marazanof (1965) have studied changes in salt marsh and brackish water populations of invertebrates over a period of some 30 years in relation to climate, the effects of irrigation for rice cultivation, and habitats modified by salt production. Of particular interest is their conclusion that all the changes observed are reversible. But one should not assume that this would be true for larger vertebrates. As we have seen the spread of phreatophytes like *Tamarix* species may contribute to increasing the salinity of ground water, while the development of desalination plants will increase the salinity of superficial waters flooding estuarine marshes. Presumably this will result in a partial reversal of the normal salinity gradient in estuaries and encourage the spread of more salt tolerant species further up the estuary.

Spraying

In the past 30 years insecticide or herbicide spraying has been used increasingly on coastal marshes for management purposes in relation to wildlife cropping. Spraying has been used also for mosquito control, for oil pollution decontamination purposes, and in mangrove swamp for clearance for military purposes.

In general the use of herbicides for wildlife management is a responsible activity carried out or supervised by well-informed people who are primarily interested in protecting wildlife rather than destroying it. Certain herbicides like Dalapon (sodium salt, 2, 2 – dichloropropionic acid) are not known to be significantly harmful to life on tidal marshes other than the grass species like *Spartina* or *Phragmites* they are used to control. However, it is not possible to use sprays effectively in marshland washed daily by the tides and in the control of *Spartina anglica* in such sites the use of pelleted substituted urea compounds such as Fenuron (3 phenyl 1,1 dimethylurea) has been found effective (Ranwell and Downing 1960). These of course are soil sterilents and non-specific. It would be desirable to know more about their side effects on invertebrates and the risks of promoting erosion before they are used on a wide scale.

The aerial spraying of tidal marshland for mosquito control has had serious consequences and Springer and Webster (1951) have demonstrated the more immediate effects of aerial spraying on experimental plots in the New Jersey marshes. Plots were 50 acre (20 ha) or 100 acre (40 ha) and were treated with dosages ranging from 0·2 (0·09 kg) to 1·6 lb (0·7 kg) DDT per acre (0·4 ha) and results measured against untreated controls. Birds were not obviously affected, but heavy losses of fish were recorded in dosages above 0·8 lb per acre (0·36 kg/ha) and crabs were almost completely killed, these effects being greater in ponds than in creeks or ditches. Effects on smaller invertebrates were variable; shrimps and amphipods were seriously affected, insects, spiders and worms less so, and mites and molluscs not apparently harmed.

Now of course, we are aware of the more subtle dangers that accrue through the build up of chlorinated hydrocarbon residues from substances like DDT in food chains. Haderlie (1970) records the death of hundreds of fish-eating marine birds and some sea lions, believed to have accumulated lethal doses of DDT off the Monterey Bay coast, California. He is currently studying the accumulation of this substance and its derivatives in the estuary of the Salinas River draining the Salinas valley. Here, during the past 10 years it is estimated that 125,000 lb (56,700 kg) of DDT has been sprayed on agricultural land each year.

Tschirley (1969) estimates that the regeneration of mangrove forest to its original condition following defoliant spraying in Vietnam for military purposes with 2, 4–D and 2,4,5–T (normal butyl esters of 2,4–dichlorophenoxy – acetic acid and 2,4,5 – trichlorophenoxyacetic acid) or with triisopropanolamine salts of 2,4–D and picloram (4 – amino – 3,5,6 – trichloropicolinic acid) will require about 20 years. Fish yields have increased during a period of intensive defoliation, but this could be a temporary phenomenon due to release of nutrients.

Reclamation and coastal transformation

Reduction in the tidal area of Poole Harbour, Dorset through natural siltation and reclamation is estimated to have increased within the past 150 years to a rate 12 times that of the previous 6,000 years (May 1969). This gives some idea of the accelerated pace at which salt marshes are being diminished. In San Francisco Bay less than a quarter of the original marshland survives (Harvey 1966). Much depends on how the reclamation is achieved, and there is convincing evidence that embankment of marshland around the Wash in England has in the past stimulated the formation of new salt marsh to replace that reclaimed (Inglis and Kestner 1958 a and Kestner 1962). Dalby (1957) estimates that some 80,000 acre (32,400 ha) have been embanked around the Wash since the seventeenth century and estimated that embankment could continue at a rate of some 15 000 acre (6 100 ha) per century. This reclaimed land has produced some of the most highly fertile agricultural soils in the world, but only at a controlled rate of reclamation which does not exceed the rate of new marsh formation. In fact,

P

Inglis and Kestner (1958 *b*) give evidence which suggests that supplies of silt which had taken thousands of years to accumulate in the Wash may already be so depleted as a result of reclamation that little of the progressive silting expected seaward of a recent embankment has occurred.

The pace of salt marsh formation has been increased on the Dutch, German and Danish wadden coasts by means of ditched and groyned sedimentation fields and an excellent account of the techniques involved is given by Kamps (1962).

Unfortunately, in many industrialized estuaries, land prices are so high and the need for new land so urgent that it becomes economic and expedient to infill marshes with rubble and rubbish directly to make up the level at a rate faster than there is time for new marsh to form. Obviously this brings a serious risk of pollution especially if the tipping is not done behind bunds which effectively keep the sea from re-working the rubbish.

Reclaimed marshland used as pasture and intersected by drainage ditches may retain elements of the salt marsh flora for at least 100 years (Petch 1945). It provides grazing and roost for wildfowl at high tide and the dykes and ditches extend the habitat of many rare species normally localized at the salt marsh upper limit and in brackish flushes. This habitat has never received proper ecological study although it probably carries almost as high species diversity as the sand dune and slack gradient. The present trend towards arable farming is rapidly destroying reclaimed pastureland at a time when its wildlife potential is only beginning to be recognized and valued.

The needs of coastal protection, improved navigation and wholesale transformation for fresh water reservoirs behind estuarine barrages, or coastally sited airports, all result in re-structuring of coastal sediments and the marshes derived from them. It is not always appreciated that foreshore amenity may be lost in a few decades as a result of siltation and marsh formation at sites apparently remote from newly constructed works. For example the training of the low water channel to the south shore of the Dee Estuary, Flint is the indirect cause of the loss of coastal waterfront at Parkgate, Cheshire on the north shore.

Kestner (in Thorn 1966) has reviewed the effects of dredging, barrages and training walls, on the tidal and siltation regime in estuaries. He concludes that the most successful schemes have been those in which the estuary as a whole has been modified. Half measures have usually not been successful and have produced undesirable side effects.

Gilson (in Lowe-McConnell 1966) has discussed some of the biological implications of proposed barrages in Morecambe Bay, Lancashire and the

Solway Firth to the north of it. More specifically Gray (in Perring 1970) who has completed a two year study of the Morecambe Bay salt marshes, draws attention in an interim report to the hazards of ecological prediction and to the probably ill-founded assumption that the present ecological behaviour of a given species is a reliable guide to its reaction to new situations. Most likely it is not, and the explosive spread of *Typha* in possibly new genetic combinations on the pseudo-delta of the Niger estuary (Trochain *pers. comm.*) may well be a pointer to the sort of biological reactions we should expect.

Integrated Management

It should be apparent from this account that the human impact on the salt marsh environment has not in general been based on informed understanding or consideration for the wildlife resources it contains. It follows that we are not fully aware of the value of these resources. Somewhat frantic efforts are being made at the present time to bring to the attention of authorities a fuller understanding of what is being lost and what might be gained by combined planning for the use of existing resources and the deliberate design of new salt marsh resources. For example, the creation of the Rømo dam joining the mainland to the island of Romø in Denmark, has been foreseen to encourage the formation of new salt marshes in its sheltered angles. Their formation is actively aided by ploughing drainage ditches in high level mudflats to seaward so that salt marsh growth is improved on the intervening ridges.

The activities of the San Francisco Bay Conservation and Development Commission (Harvey 1966 *a* and *b*) are spreading wider understanding of the value of existing wildlife resources to the people that live around the shores of the Bay. Steenis *et al* (1954) have done the same for the Delaware marshes and Goodwin *et al* (1961) for Connecticut's coastal marshes where significant advances in legislation have provided valuable protection to these habitats.

Fresh water reservoir proposals in the inter-tidal zone of estuaries are under joint investigation by engineers, hydrologists, fisheries, biologists, limnologists and all who are directly concerned with the protection and production of wildlife. All these activities are leading towards integrated management proposals which should enable the living things on salt marshes space to exist and should no longer allow the marsh to be treated as a convenient potential rubbish dump.

But they cannot only exist. They must be made to produce in common with other land for our crowded societies. Work in the larger nature reserves must evolve new management techniques, the full value of marshes in coastal protection must be assessed and the value of a fully utilized marsh set against any reclamation proposals for other purposes.

One example of the seasonal cycle of use that might be more fully developed is as follows. In the spring when migratory wildfowl have left, marshes may be rested for a few weeks to allow vegetation to recover and resident marshland birds to breed. Turf cutting could commence on suitable sites and stock return to graze. In summer, marshland areas could be increasingly used for recreation and education at a time when least harm will be done to wildlife resources. Mowing can be carried out to preserve the quality of salting pasture and in preparation for autumn turf cutting. In winter the migratory wildfowl will take up residence and could be cropped on a regulated permit system as at Caerlaverock National Nature Reserve, Dumfries, or fully protected as in the case of diminishing species such as the Brent Goose as at Scolt Head Island, Norfolk.

Only when we have tried to dove-tail these various forms of management can we hope to set a proper value on the salt marsh.

13 Management of Sand Dune Wildlife Resources

Sand dunes, unlike salt marshes, are effectively a diminishing resource around the coasts of lowland Europe and North America. Not only is their regeneration limited by what is believed to be a diminishing bank of off-shore sand supplies, but their rate of destruction under development of various kinds is almost certainly exceeded by their rate of formation. Expansion in area of a dune system is a much slower process than that associated with salt marsh formation. No figures are available for the proportion of sandy prograding coasts where the rate of formation is maximal as opposed to systems where the coastline is static or eroding, but it seems likely that if dune coastline lengths were scored for these properties, prograding sandy coasts would be in the minority.

While a certain amount of re-cycling of material goes on, this is primarily of a very local nature and most of the sand of a dune system being above the inter-tidal zone is out of circulation anyway. So, while there may be considerable internal mobility, dune systems as a whole are much more static in position on the coastline than salt marshes. They also tend to be more isolated one from another than salt marshes and this accounts for the distinctiveness of each individual dune flora. This is well illustrated by the colour variants of *Viola tricolor* sub-species *curtisii* on European dunes. Only yellow-flowered forms may occur on one system, on another, both yellow and blue-flowered forms are found, presumably evidence of isolation in terms of gene flow.

As we have seen, the low fertility of dune soils coupled with much open ground for casual colonization produces an immensely rich flora. This, combined with the distinctive landscape and shorelines ideal for recreation, attracts people in ever increasing numbers.

Sand dunes were among the earliest of sites settled by primitive man.

They have often been used with little understanding and disastrous results when the dunes, re-mobilized by over-cropping, have overwhelmed adjoining land settlements. More enlightened management policies followed and the value of dunes in coast protection was recognized. Some of the larger systems were afforested in the eighteenth and nineteenth century. As land became scarce dune systems were levelled for industry, housing, and airport needs. Now we are beginning to realize the special virtues of the diminishing dune landscape for recreation and the need for protecting these resources from further despoliation.

External Influences

Water extraction

The effect of water extraction on the dune flora has received little study except in the Netherlands. Here, Westhoff (1964) records that the dune area has 'to a large extent been dried up by the extraction of drinking water'. The Wassenaar dunes near the Hague have been exploited as a catchment area since 1874 and from about 1885 onward this has caused a serious fall in the level of the ground water table (Boerboom 1960). Many moisture-loving plants disappeared and the plant communities dependent on a high water table level were almost destroyed except in a few small man-made hollows formerly used as wells. Even a small permanent fall in the water table of about 10 cm can be fatal especially to the plants and animals of sub-aquatic and wet dune slacks (Voo 1964). In their place, common species such as *Molinia caerulea* or *Calamagrostis canescens* have spread over these habitats in the Netherlands. Uncontrolled water extraction from sites close behind the coastal dune can also lead to contamination of fresh-water supplies with brackish water.

Fortunately the dangers have been recognized in time and artificial fresh-water infiltration has been started in the Wassenaar dunes since 1955. Boerboom (1960) has been recording the floristic changes as the water table began to rise again. These changes are not necessarily a straight reversal to the original damp and wet slack communities, partly because of loss of parent material and partly because rabbit-grazing has diminished so altering the floristic balance. Studies on changes due to falling water tables are urgently needed in British dunes and especially those where there is little immediate prospect of new slack formation at the coast (as at Ainsdale, Lancashire for example). Any new slacks would of course result from wind excavation down to the new water table level.

Pollution

In a low-lying country like the Netherlands, there is a serious problem in maintaining oligotrophic communities like those found in lime-deficient dune slacks for they are enriched by nutrients from fertilizer residues washed out of agricultural land. Westhoff (1964) points out that a high proportion of the rare flowering plant species found in European dune slacks are characteristic of leached soils developed in the Atlantic climate zone. These are the first to diminish as soil enrichment progresses. This enrichment effect is proceeding only slowly in the Netherlands according to Voo (1964). Nevertheless from samples of about 900 oligotrophic waters throughout the Netherlands, it was found that significant changes in communities attributed to enrichment occurred in 42 per cent of them. Much depends on the way drainage from the agricultural catchment impinges on the dune water table. High-lying arable land directly to landward of the dune system is likely to have the most serious effects. In mesotrophic dune systems, incipient oligotrophic dune heath develops at the landward edge of the system. Such areas, lying closest to cultivated land, are particularly susceptible. For this reason it is essential to control drainage or at least to have a buffer zone to landward where high fertility cultivation is discouraged if oligotrophic systems are to be preserved as nature reserves.

Oil pollution does not have such serious effects on dune systems as on salt marshes, but where it does reach coastal dune slacks such species as *Euphorbia paralias* may be damaged by combinations of oil and emulsifiers (Ranwell 1968 *b*). It has been observed that up to 10 per cent of wind blown sand grains may be contaminated with oil and emulsifiers (Elliston – *pers. comm.*) after a serious pollution incident. We have no measure of the background oil contamination levels on sandy shores, but this will be maximal at the backshore, the source of dune sand, where conditions may often be too dry for effective bacterial breakdown of oil residues.

An increasing quantity of litter of all types is brought to the shores by tides and into the dune system by tourists. Teagle (1966) has analysed the weekly quantities of litter collected at Studland dunes, Dorset over a two-year period and finds the summer values about ten times greater than the winter quantities with peak values of thirty times the winter values on public holidays. The bulk of the litter is paper, but food remains attract gulls, and empty milk bottles trap small mammals in alarming quantities e.g. 48 mammals in 15 bottles in 1 year.

The possible consequences of air pollution on the mineral deficient soils of dune systems has been referred to earlier, but remains open for study.

Voo (1964) notes that shelter belts have been planted along the borders of nature reserves in the Netherlands to reduce the effects of airborne pollution and Bernatsky (1969) has demonstrated the importance of design of protective plantations in reducing air pollution.

Introduced species

Because of the need to control sand dune movement species like *Ammophila arenaria* have been deliberately introduced from Europe to the United States, South Africa, Australia and New Zealand. *Hippophaë rhamnoides* has now been planted on more dune systems within the British Isles than there are in its native range. The presence of this species (frequently planted in gardens), within a radius of about 5 miles (8 km) of a dune system brings a persistent risk of invasion via the agency of birds. A vigilant management policy is needed to check sporadic appearances and subsequent spread if the dune flora is not to be shaded out by its growth. This is a serious problem in some sand dune native reserves (e.g. Ainsdale Lancashire and Gibraltar Point, Lincolnshire). The rare sterile hybrid grass *Ammocalamagrostis baltica* was widely planted to new stations on Norfolk and Suffolk coasts during a dune re-planting programme following damage to the coast by floods in 1953 (Ellis 1960).

Afforestation is by far the most powerful agent for introduction of new species on to sand dunes and Holder (1953) records that following afforestation at Ainsdale, Lancashire the flora became far richer than it was originally. Similarly at Newborough, Anglesey the introduction of trees and shrubs for stabilization purposes, the use of roadside verge cuttings and forestry 'brash' to still the sand, and the introduction of weeds with hop manure in nursery beds, increased the flowering plant species total of the system by at least one third in about 10 years.

Teagle (1966) found little evidence that increasing numbers of tourists had added to the introduced flora of Ainsdale. However but since 1953 the New Zealand alien, *Acaena anserinifolia* has become well established in car park areas and in heavily trampled pathways. This species has hooked burrs on the fruiting head and is readily transported on the fur of animals or on clothes. The burrs may so clog the feathers of fledgling ground-nesting birds that they are unable to move effectively and die of starvation. This has been observed at Holy Island dunes, Northumberland where *Acaena* is abundant in *Ammophila* dunes.

Garden rubbish dumping adds to the dune flora and bulb cultivation on the Isles of Scilly has produced a remarkable assortment of aliens on many of the small dune systems there.

Internal Influences

Direct cropping of sand

The sand itself is mined locally for mineral extraction or building purposes. Mineral-bearing sands are widespread on the shores and dunes throughout the New South Wales coast and also on the south and central Queensland coasts of Australia (Sless 1956). Sand-winning for building purposes occurs sporadically around the British coast e.g. at Ainsdale, Lancashire and Druridge Bay, Northumberland. In many areas it has been discontinued (e.g. at Rock dunes, Cornwall) because of the risks to coast protection and loss of amenity beaches.

Other direct cropping

With the exception of the cranberry bogs associated with some of the North America dune systems, there is little available evidence that dune floras have so far yielded plants of any significant economic value. However, it is interesting that *Elymus arenarius* has been successfully hybridized with wheat (Pissarev and Vinogradova 1944), and with barley (Tsitsin 1946). Tsitsin considers that the hybrids thus obtained are 'of very great import-ance indeed' and should lead to big increases in crop yield.

In the past, marram grass (*Ammophila arenaria*) was regularly cut for thatching as at Newborough Warren, Anglesey (Ranwell 1959), but with increased availability of straw and development of plastics this is now dis-continued in most areas.

Sand dune-building plants (especially *Ammophila* species) are cropped for stabilization purposes, but only on a small scale as a few strong tussocks will produce a great many planting units (Plate 15).

Rabbit cropping

Sand dunes were used extensively in medieval times as rabbit warrens, at least in Britain. They have also been used for centuries as open range graz-ing for stock. Warrens were effectively managed at first, but wild popula-tions established and spread without control. Tansley (1949) records that rabbits were little known in Scotland until as late as the nineteenth century when their numbers rapidly increased. The structure of sand dune com-munities in Europe prior to myxomatosis was effectively the product of intensive rabbit-grazing.

Stock cropping

There is little information about the effect of stock grazing on dunes and this has never received experimental study. Frame (1971) records that a cow's hoof exerts a pressure of 40 to 60 lb per in^2 and that an acre of pasture would be trodden some three or four times in a year at normal stocking. By contrast sheep hooves exert a pressure of about 25 to 35 lb per in^2 and tread an acre of pasture six to ten times in a year. It becomes immediately clear from this why sheep have been found to be particularly damaging to dune pasture. However the low-lying lime-rich dune pastures (machairs) of Scotland have a relatively high moisture-holding capacity and have supported sheep for centuries without serious erosion. Elsewhere the uncontrolled mobility of many European dune systems which developed in stormy periods was undoubtedly triggered off by over-grazing by rabbits and stock in the past. All forms of large mammal grazing have now declined in many dune areas though it is still possible to see the typical grazed sward flora in pockets where rabbits have survived. At Whiteford Burrows, Glamorgan, ponies graze the dunes (in addition to sheep) and with little apparent harm to the dune turf which they crop almost as closely as rabbits.

Golf links

The use of sand dunes as golf links involves heavy local fertilizing, extensive mowing, some drainage, and local shrub clearance. Small areas are intensively managed as greens, tees or bunkers, but for the most part a modified, fairly varied dune flora and fauna survives unharmed. Wallace (1953) recorded some 350 species of flowering plants on Dawlish Warren, Devon a small dune system of about 100 acre (c.40 ha) partly used as a golf links. Beeftink (1966) found no less than 220 species on only one hectare of the Heveringen dunes formerly grazed by horses and goats and afterwards used as a golf links. Experimental studies on the effects of mowing dune vegetation are now in progress in the Newborough Warren (Anglesey), and Holkham and Winterton (Norfolk) National Nature Reserves.

No one has yet brought together the very considerable practical experience obtained by golf links management on sand dunes. Ecologists need to relate this knowledge to the modified, but locally species-rich plant and animal communities produced. It may well help in the design of field experimental studies required for effective management of sand dune nature reserves. It is probably true to say that this relatively benign use has done more to preserve the dune flora and fauna near built up areas than any other factor. In doing so it has helped to keep open the lines of migration between one dune system and another for recruitment of flora and fauna.

Afforestation

The primary reason for planting trees on sand dunes has always been to protect the surface of shifting sands which in the past have overwhelmed coastal settlements in many parts of the world on more exposed dune coasts. Plantings have also been made for amenity purposes, as at Holkham, Norfolk. Afforestation is not the best means of protecting dunes from coastal erosion as the trees shade out *Ammophila* and other plants capable of recruiting new coastal dunes at the strandline. Timber production is only significant on the very largest dune plantations, and then only behind the shelter of protection forest consisting of wind-deformed trees, themselves useless for timber production.

At Les Landes in France 250,000 acre (101,075 ha) of dune were afforested during the nineteenth century mainly with *Pinus maritima* (Macdonald 1954). English (1969) has described the technique developed on this coast by the French engineer Bremontier. A shallow sloping littoral dune is created with fences and *Ammophila* planting, and behind this lies the protection forest itself protecting the production forest. In 1949 forest fires destroyed 200,000 acre (80,940 ha) of this woodland and 82 people died. However, the speed of the fire was so rapid that seeds survived intact in cones and pine regenerated in the burnt areas (English 1969).

In Denmark 75,000 acre (30,352 ha) of coastal dune have been afforested and are managed by the State primarily as amenity woodlands. *Pinus mugo* is used as both *Pinus nigra* and *Pinus maritima* (widely used on dunes elsewhere) were found to be attacked and destroyed by the fungus *Crumenula pinea* after 15 to 20 years growth. Careful attention is paid to thatching felled areas with cut heather or to planting with *Ammophila* before new plantations are started (Thaarup 1954). Trees on dunes are very deep-rooted and not readily subject to wind throw.

Some 10,000 acre (4,047 ha) have been planted chiefly with *Pinus nigra* var. *calabrica* and some *P. maritima* and *P. sylvestris* in Great Britain (Macdonald 1954).

The immediate effect of afforestation is to increase the diversity of flowering plant species largely through introduction as mentioned earlier. As the trees mature they shade out the ground flora almost completely although certain species like *Goodyera repens* at Culbin, Moray (not present in the unplanted dunes), are widespread in the plantations.

Ovington (1950 and 1951) has studied changes in the soil environment due to afforestation on dunes. He found that the water table was lowered by 17 cm in 20 year old conifer plantations compared with unplanted areas at Tentsmuir, Fife. At both Culbin and Tentsmuir, the nutrient content decreased with afforestation and the soil acidity increased (Fig. 67) while the organic matter at the surface and the manganese content increased in plantations over a 20 year period. Nutrients are bound up in the tree crop and when this is removed the impoverished soil is highly vulnerable to erosion.

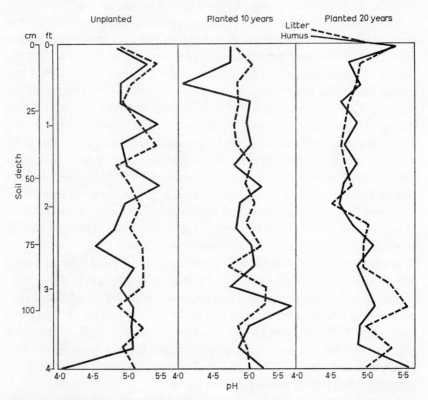

Fig. 67. The effect of Conifer planting upon soil pH at various depths in dune soil from Culbin Sands, Morayshire. Two profiles for each area are shown (from Ovington 1950).

Wright (1955) extended Ovington's studies in a wider variety of tree species and age classes at Culbin and recorded soil moisture and temperature in plantation soils using gypsum soil moisture blocks and thermistor techniques. The growth of trees dried out upper sand layers considerably although the surface organic layers of older plantations had a high moisture-holding capacity.

Little is known about the ecology of these dune forests or the young plantations. Where seedling pines invade dune nature reserves as at Tentsmuir, Fife they have to be cut out regularly, to protect the native fauna and flora.

Coast protection and amenity use

Ever since the stormy periods of the fourteenth and fifteenth centuries *Ammophila* has been planted to stabilize sand surfaces. Brown and Hafenrichter (1948) in an important series of papers describe experiments on the influence of date of planting, density, and different combinations of fertilizers on the growth of *Ammophila breviligulata*, *A. arenaria* and *Elymus mollis*. Charlton (in Anon 1970 *b*) has also carried out fertilizer trials on the growth of *Ammophila arenaria* and *Elymus arenarius* in Scotland. Thornton and Davis (1964) have selected and propagated genotypes of *Ammophila breviligulata* and studied germination of this species. Organic material of various kinds (e.g. forestry trimmings, roadside verge cuttings) is regularly used to protect bare sand from erosion. Haas and Steers (1964) describe a latex spray technique for stilling sand surfaces and Zak (1967) experimented with the use of hydraulically sprayed mulches and seed mixtures for stabilization purposes (Plate 16).

There is now a very extensive world literature on dune stabilization techniques and as this is being reviewed elsewhere it is not appropriate to deal with it here. Perhaps of more direct interest to the ecologist is the effect of the treatments on the plants and animals, the effect that the recent upsurge in tourist use of dunes is having upon them, and the techniques being used to study this.

Hewett (1970) has recorded the re-establishment of the dune flora within a 100 acre (40 ha) *Ammophila* plantation at Braunton Burrows, Devon and found that 53 species of flowering plants, two mosses and one lichen had colonized the bare sand in 15 years or less. These were all plants characteristic of the existing dune system and included several of the less common species. *Festuca rubra* was beginning to close up the gaps in the plantations and leguminous species were becoming increasingly common 10 to 15 years after stabilization.

No studies have yet been made on grasslands established on dunes by hydraulic seeding using cultivated grass seed. Where this has been done successfully, at Camber, Sussex for example, the dunes have been artificially graded before seeding to produce uniform slopes. Some habitat diversity has therefore already been lost and it may be many years before native species are able to reinvade. In fact this system of some 250 acre (100 ha), part of which is used as a Golf Links, may receive up to 17,000 people a day in summer and it seems likely there will be a constant need for repair of trampled turf by seeding and fertilizing. Shrub planting is now in progress and the system is clearly moving towards a very artificial habitat specifically designed for recreational use. Nevertheless it may still harbour many native species alongside the introduced ones.

Where human population pressures are rather lower as on parts of the East Lothian sand dune coast, dune restoration with native species, *Elymus arenarius* and *Ammophila arenaria*, and the judicious clearance of pathways through invasive growths of *Hippophaë rhamnoides*, help to retain much of the original character of the dune systems while still allowing large numbers of people access to the shores. (Tindall 1967 and Anon 1970 *b*.)

Low level aerial photography from a captive balloon coupled with quadrat ground survey has been used to record the distribution of people and plants at Whitesands and Yellowcraig, East Lothian (Duffield in 1970 *b*). Here a very detailed picture is being built up from which future changes can be measured.

Quinn (in Anon 1970 *b*) used conventional air photography to study recreational use over a 230 acre (85 ha) dune system at Brittas Bay, Wicklow, Ireland and recorded a maximum of 250 people per 50 m^2, falling to 120 to 80 people per 50 m^2 at 100 to 150 m distance from paths.

Goldsmith *et al* (1970) have studied the effect of trampling on dune vegetation in the Isles of Scilly. Schofield (in Duffey 1967) used electronic counters for monitoring the movement of people on dunes at Gibraltar Point, Lincolnshire, while Bayfield (1971) has shown how short soft metal wires can be set in paths and used to measure trampling by the proportion of wires that get bent flat.

These studies are just beginning, but it is clear that the ecologist is at last beginning to treat man as a highly significant animal in the dune landscape worthy of objective study.

Integrated Management

Because dune systems are now recognized as a valuable and limited resource not only for wildlife but also as recreational land, each country with dune resources clearly needs to develop a national plan for their protection and use. Such a plan would record the distribution and size of dune resources and designate those areas in which there is a priority for coast protection, recreational use or for protection of wildlife.

Any dune sites which are managed primarily for coast protection or recreation will still contain significant wildlife resources. Their protection is clearly relevant to the maintenance of the system for both these uses. Nevertheless the initiative to protect specific populations of rare or local species on such systems must lie with local naturalists or voluntary bodies. They can do much to help avoid unnecessary destruction by providing owners and planners with maps showing location of sites for which protection is desirable or by actually transplanting species to nearby safe areas from those which must be disturbed. The recording of such transplanting activities is clearly desirable.

Management for coast protection

Where coast protection is the primary aim any sand-winning activities should be gradually phased out, growth of trees should not be allowed to shade out dune-forming grasses near the coast and a regular maintenance commitment accepted at the coast. Air photography should be commissioned on a regular 3 to 5 year basis to record the success of management activities and to help understand the structural development of the system in relation to adjoining coastal changes. Instant stabilization can be employed in serious trouble spots with modern techniques referred to above. Elsewhere the principle of developing an aerodynamically stable shallow-sloping seaward face to the coast dune should be followed with conventional fencing and planting techniques using selected strains of appropriate grasses with use of fertilizers to aid establishment.

Management for recreation

Where recreational use is the primary object it is essential to provide convenient access to the shore where most people want to be, via specified pathways which effectively protect the sand from erosion. Where visitors are few natural vegetated pathways can be protected by rotational use. With increasing numbers of visitors fertilizing and regular repair of pathways by seeding becomes essential. Where large numbers of people need access to the shore artificially surfaced paths (plastic netting, wood, shells or gravel) must be provided.

The extent to which people penetrate back into the dunes from the shore is under active study at the present time. Many factors are involved here including the orientation of the dune coast, the freedom of the shore from pollution, the weather, and the type of vegetation on or behind the coast dune. Much could be done by judicious management of the grass/ shrub balance to accommodate more people within dunes in relative privacy from one another, but there is a limit and at the present time we do not have the facts and figures which will tell us the optimum design for maximum acceptable densities.

While coast protection is primarily concerned with dune maintenance at the coast itself, a more comprehensive dune maintenance programme over the whole dune system is required where it is under intensive recreational use. Air photo monitoring may be required more frequently to detect changes in pathway patterns pointing to the need for closer access control or urgent restoration activities. Car park capacities must be related to holding capacity of the dune system for people and uncontrolled parking on dune turf is bound to lead to expensive control measures or ultimate abandonment of the site. The siting of car parks and caravan sites to the landward of the dunes should be designed to avoid releasing large numbers of people where the shore is narrow and sand supply for dune building minimal.

Management for wildlife protection

The objectives of management for coast protection and recreation are simply defined. They are to keep the sea out and to enable as many people as possible to enjoy the dune amenity without destroying it.

The objectives of management for wildlife protection are more complex and less easily defined and achieved. The British series of dune National Nature Reserves has been chosen to include representative physiographic and soil and climate-determined biological types throughout the country. Broadly speaking the objectives of management in these systems is to maintain the plant and animal communities for which they were originally selected, to utilize them for educational and research purposes and, where there is scope for this, to increase the diversity of habitats within them by controlled disturbance.

The maintenance of dune communities produced by a long history of intensive rabbit grazing, now much reduced since myxomatosis, presents special problems. It may be possible on one or two larger systems to enclose a captive rabbit population within rabbit-proof fencing. This would in fact be a return to the way in which these communities presumably started in specially created warrens. However, because of costs and the general undesirability of building up rabbit populations this could not be a generally acceptable policy. Cutting out of invasive trees and shrubs at least in selected areas is more generally acceptable and practicable where invasion is still in an early stage. This policy is already in practice in a number of reserves e.g. at Whiteford Burrows, Glamorgan where *Hippophaë* is removed and at Tentsmuir, Fife where unwanted pines are cut out.

Mowing could only be used on a limited scale and while it may help to maintain populations of certain low-growing species threatened by under-grazing. it will produce different communities to those characteristic of rabbit grazing. Carefully controlled sheep and pony grazing may be more generally applicable, but imply control of dogs which is not easily achieved near centres of population.

It seems inevitable that we must accept major changes towards scrub and woodland communities in some reserves where invasion is already well-advanced as at Ainsdale, Lancashire or Gibraltar Point, Lincolnshire. These new communities may eventually become as diverse and interesting as the species-rich dune grasslands they replace. However, it seems likely that they will themselves tend to be controlled by fire, as already happens at Studland, Dorset. It follows therefore, that specially designed fire-breaks will have to be created and maintained if fire control is not to become too destructive and lead to massive erosion.

As we have seen the problem of falling water tables can and has been tackled in Dutch dune reserves by active management of the water table. This again is costly and probably only applicable to few selected areas. The deliberate creation of pools by excavation can help to recreate late stage hydroseres where these have been lost by drying up or where as at New-borough Warren, Anglesey it was done to diversify the system. But this does bring the risk of attracting Herring Gulls which may in turn attack the young of other ground-nesting species such as terns. Wherever possible the natural formation of new slacks at the coast should be allowed to proceed unhindered to replenish those which in the normal course of development become drier as they mature.

Unlike the salt marsh habitat there is little opportunity for zoning differ-ent activities in time on dune systems, but there is a great deal to be gained from spacial zonation. The principle of resting sections from intensive edu-cational or recreational use with temporary fencing can improve both coast protection and restoration of a trampled strand-line flora. Afforestation designed for recreational use can develop side by side with undisturbed wildlife sectors running from the coast to the landward limits in the bigger dune systems. Educational use can be separated from remoter research sites to cut down disturbance to the latter to a minimum.

It is already apparent in the British sand dune reserve series that systems showing a high recreational use are more appropriate for intensive educa-tional use (e.g. Studland, Dorset) those readily accessible to research stations with lighter recreational use are more appropriate for research use (e.g. Holkham, Norfolk), while small remote systems with climatically distinctive communities (e.g. Invernaver, Sutherland) are best left undis-turbed as much as possible.

We begin to see a pattern emerging which should be applicable not just to nature reserves, but to dune systems generally whatever their use: appropriate use of different systems; appropriate use of parts within the systems, joint care for the needs of people and of wildlife.

Q

References

ADAMS, D. A. (1963), 'Factors influencing vascular plant zonation in North Carolina salt marshes', *Ecology*, **44**, 445–456.

ADRIANI, E. D. (1945), 'Sur la Phytosociologie, la Synécologie et le bilan d'eau de Halophytes de la région Néerlandaise Méridionale, ainsi que de la Mediterranee Française.' *S.I.G.M.A.*, *Groningen*, **88**, 1–217.

AGUESSE, P. and MARAZANOF, F. (1965), 'Les modifications des milieux aquatiques de Camargues au cours des 30 dernières annés', *Ann. de Limiol.*, **1**, 163–190.

ALLEN, S. E., CARLISLE, A., WHITE, E. J. and EVANS, C. C. (1968), 'The plant nutrient content of rainwater'. *J. Ecol.*, **56**, 497–504.

ALVIN, K. L. (1960), 'Observations on the lichen ecology of South Haven Peninsula, Studland Heath, Dorset', *J. Ecol.*, **48**, 331–339.

ANDERSON, E. and STEBBINS, G. L. (1954), 'Hybridization as an evolutionary stimulus', *Evolution*, 8, 378–388.

ANON (1966 *a*), *Solway Barrage*, Water Resources Board Report, London: H.M.S.O.

ANON (1966 *b*), *Morecambe Bay Barrage*, Water Resources Board Report, London: H.M.S.O.

ANON (1966 *c*), *Morecambe Bay and Solway Barrages*, Water Resources Board Report, London: H M S O

ANON (1967), *Dee crossing study. Phase 1.* Ministry of Housing and Local Government Report, London: H.M.S.O.

ANON (1970 *a*), *The Wash: estuary storage*, Water Resources Board Report, London: H.M.S.O.

ANON (1970 *b*) *Dune conservation 1970*, North Berwick Study Group Rep, North Berwick: East Lothian County Council.

ANON (1970 *c*), *Modern Farming and the Soil*, London: H.M.S.O.

ARDÖ, P. (1957), 'Studies in the marine shore dune ecosystem with special reference to the dipterous fauna', *Opusc. ent. Suppl.*, **14**, 1–255.

ARNOLD, A. (1955), Die Bedeutung der Chlorionen für die Pflanze. Bot. Stud. 2. Jena.

AUGUSTINE, M. T., THORNTON, R. B., SANBORN, J. M. and LEISER, A. T. (1964),

'Response of American Beachgrass to fertilizer', *J. Soil and Water Consvn.*, **19**, 112–116.

BAGNOLD, R. A. (1941), *The Physics of Blown Sand and Desert Dunes*, London; Methuen.

BAKER, J. M. (1970 *a*), 'Oil and salt marsh soil', Institute of Petroleum Symposium on the ecological effects of oil pollution on littoral communities. London, Morning Session 1–10.

BAKER, J. M. (1970 *b*), 'Growth stimulation following oil pollution', *Ibid*, 11–16. (1970 *c*), 'Comparative toxicities of oils, oil fractions and emulsifiers', *Ibid*, 17–26.

(1970 *d*), 'The effects of oils on plant physiology', *Ibid*, 27–37.

(1970 *e*), 'The effects of a single oil spillage', Institute of Petroleum Symposium on the ecological effects of oil pollution on littoral communities. London, Afternoon Session, 1–5.

(1970 *f*), 'Successive spillages', *Ibid*, 7–18.

(1970 *g*), 'Refinery effluent', *Ibid*, 19–29.

(1970 *h*), 'Seasonal effects', *Ibid*, 31–38.

(1970 *i*), 'Effects of cleaning', *Ibid*, 39–44.

BAKKER, D., TER BORG, S. J. and OTZEN, D. (1966), 'Ecological research at the Plantecology Laboratory, State University, Groningen', *Wentia*, **15**, 1–24.

BALL, P. W. and BROWN, K. G. (1970), 'A biosystematic and ecological study of *Salicornia* in the Dee estuary', *Watsonia*, **8**, 27–40.

BARKLEY, S. Y. (1955), 'The morphology and vegetation of the sands of Forvie with reference to certain related areas', Ph.D. Thesis, Aberdeen.

BARNES, B. M. and BARNES, R. D. (1954), 'The ecology of the spiders of maritime drift lines', *Ecology*, **35**, 25–35.

BAYFIELD, N. G. (1971), 'A simple method for detecting variations in walker pressure laterally across paths', *J. appl. Ecol.*, **8**, 533–535.

BEEFTINK, W. G. (1962), 'Conspectus of the phanerogamic salt plant communities in the Netherlands', *Biol. Jaarb. Antwerp*, 325–362.

BEEFTINK, W. G. (1965), De zoutvegetatie van ZW – Nederland beschouwd in Europees Verbaud. Wageningen.

BEEFTINK, W. G. (1966), 'Vegetation and habitat of the salt marshes and beach plains in the south-western part of the Netherlands', *Wentia*, **15**, 83–108.

BERNATZKY, A. (1969), Die Bedeutung von Schutzpflanzungen gegen Luftverunreinigungen. Air Pollution. Proc. 1st. Europ. Congr. on Influence of Air Pollution on Plants and Animals, Wageningen 1968, 383–395.

BERNSTEIN, L. and PEARSON, G. A. (1956), 'Influence of exchangeable sodium on the yield and chemical composition of plants. 1. Green beans, garden beans, clover and alfalfa', *Soil Sci.*, **82**, 247–258.

BIEDERMAN, E. W. Jr. (1962), 'Distinction of shoreline environments in New Jersey', *J. Sediment. Petrol.*, **32**, 181–200.

BIGOT, M. L. (1958), Les grands caractères écologiques des milieux terrestes de Camargue, 3° Congr. Soc. Sav., 533–539.

BINET, P. (1964 *a*), 'Action de la température et de la salinité sur la germination des graines de *Plantago maritima* L.', *Bull. Soc. bot. Fr.*, **111**, 407–411.

BINET, P. (1964 b), 'La germination des semences des halophytes', *Bull. Soc. Fr. Physiol. Vég.*, **10**, 253–263.

BINET, P. (1965 a), Etudes d'écologie expérimentale et physiologique sur *Cochlearia anglica* L. I Etudes dans l'estuaire de l'Orne.' *Oecol Planta.*, **1**, 7–38.

BINET, P. (1965 b), 'Action de la température et de la salinité sur la germination des graines de *Cochlearia anglica* L.', *Revue gen. Bot.*, **72**, 221–236.

BINET, P. (1965 c), 'Action de divers rhythmes thermiques journaliers sur la germination des semences de *Triglochin maritima* L.', *Bull. Soc. Linn. Normandie Series* 10, **6**, 99–102.

BINET, P. (1965 d), 'Action de la température et de la salinité sur la germination des graines de *Glaux maritima* L'., *Bull. Soc. bot. Fr.*, **112**, 346–350.

BINET, P. (1965 e), 'Aptitude a germer en milieu salé de trois espèces de *Glyceria*: *G. borreri* Bab., *G. distans.* Wahlb. et *G. maritima* Wahlb.', *Bull Soc. bot. Fr.*, **113**, 361–367.

BIRSE, E. L. and GIMINGHAM, C. H. (1955), 'Changes in the structure of bryophytic communities with the progress of succession on sand dunes', *Trans. Br. Bryol. Soc.*, **2**, 523–531.

BIRSE, E. L., LANDSBERG, S. Y. and GIMINGHAM, C. H. (1957), 'The effects of burial by sand on dune mosses', *Trans. Br. Bryol. Soc.*, **3**, 285–301.

BIRSE, E. M. (1958), 'Ecological studies on growth-form in Bryophytes. III. The relationship between the growth-form of mosses and ground-water supply', *J. Ecol.*, **46**, 9–27.

BLACK, C. A. (1968), *Soil-plant Relationships*. 2nd edn. Chichester: J. Wiley.

BLANCHARD, B. (1952), An ecological survey of the vegetation of the sand dune system of the South West Lancashire coast, with special reference to an associated marsh flora. Ph.D. Thesis, Liverpool.

BLOCK, R. J. (1945), 'Amino acid composition of food proteins', Adv. Protein Chemistry. **2**, 119–134.

BÖCHER, T. W. (1952), 'Vegetationsudvikling iforhold til marin akkumulation', *Bot. Tidsskr.*, **49**, 1–32.

BOERBOOM, J. H. A. (1960), 'De plantengemeenschappen van de Wassenaarse duinen', *Meded. LandbHoogesch. Wageningen*, **60**, 1–135.

BOERBOOM, J. H. A. (1963), 'Het verband tussen bodem en vegetatie in de Wassenaarse duinen', *Meded. en Stede*, **12**, 120-155.

BOERBOOM, J. H. A. (1964), 'Microklimatologiese observasie in the Wassenaarse dunes', *Meded. LandbHoogesch. Wageningen*, **64**, 1–28.

BOLLARD, E. G. and BUTLER, G. W. (1966), 'Mineral nutrition of plants', *A. Rev. Pl. Physiol.*, **17**, 77–112.

BOND, G., MACCONNELL, J. T. and MCCULLUM, A. H. (1956), 'The nitrogen nutrition of *Hippophaë rhamnoides*, L.', *Ann. Bot. (N.S.)*, **20**, 501–512.

BOND, T. E. T. (1952), '*Elymus arenarius.* Biological Flora of the British Isles', *J. Ecol.*, **40**, 217–227.

BOORMAN, L. A. (1967, '*Limonium vulgare* Mill. and *L. humile* Mill, Biological flora of the British Isles', *J. Ecol.*, **55**, 221–232.

BOORMAN, L. A. (1968), 'Some aspects of the reproductive biology of *Limonium vulgare* Mill. and *Limonium humile* Mill.', *Ann. Bot.*, **32**, 803–824.

BOURN, W. S. and COTTAM, C. (1950), Some biological effects of ditching tide-water marshes. U.S. Fish and Wildlife Service, Rep., **19**, 1–30.

BOYCE, S. G. (1954), 'The salt spray community', *Ecol. Mongr.*, **24**, 29–67.

BOYD, J. M. (1957), 'The Lumbricidae of a dune – machair soil gradient in Tiree, Argyll', Ann. Mag. nat. Hist., Ser. 12, **10**, 274–282.

BRADSHAW, A. D. (1958), 'Natural hybridization of *Agrostis tenuis* Sibth. and *A. stolonifera* L.', *New Phyt*, **57**, 66–84.

BRADSHAW, A. D. (1965), 'Evolutionary significance of phenotypic plasticity in plants', *Adv. Genet.*, **13**, 115–155.

BRAUN-BLANQUET, J. (1932), *Plant Sociology*, London: McGraw-Hill.

BRAYBROOKS, E. M. (1958), The general ecology of *Spartina townsendii* (*sic. S. anglica*) with special reference to sward build-up and degradation. M.Sc. Thesis, Southampton.

BRERETON, A. J. (1965). Pattern in salt marsh vegetation. Ph.D. Thesis, Univ. of Wales.

BRERETON, A. J. (1971), 'The structure of the species populations in the initial stages of salt-marsh succession', *J. Ecol.*, **59**, 321–338.

BROOKS, C. E. P. (1949), *Climate Through the Ages*. London: Ernest Benn.

BROWN, D. H. and BROWN, R. M. (1969), 'Lichen communities at Blakeney Point, Norfolk', *Trans. Norfolk Norwich Nat. Soc.*, **21**, 235–250.

BROWN, J. C. (1958), 'Soil fungi of some British sand dunes in relation to soil type and succession', *J. Ecol.*, **46**, 641–664.

BROWN, J. S. (1925), A study of coastal ground water. U.S. Geol. Survey Water Supply Paper 537, 16–17.

BROWN, R. L. and HAFENRICHTER, A. L. (1948), 'Factors influencing the production and use of beach-grass and dune-grass clones for erosion control. I. Effect of date of planting. II. Influence of density of planting. III. Influence of kinds and amounts of fertilizer on production', *J. Am. Soc. Agron.*, **40**, 512–521; 603–609; 677–684.

BROWNELL, P. F. (1965), 'Sodium as an essential micronutrient element for a higher plant (*Atriplex vesicaria*)', *Pl. Physiol.*, **40**, 460–468.

BURKHOLDER, P. R. (1956), Studies on the nutritive value of *Spartina* grass growing in the marsh areas of coastal Georgia', *Bull. Torrey bot. Club*, **83**, 327–334.

BURKHOLDER, P. R. and BURKHOLDER, L. M. (1956), 'Vitamin B_{12} in suspended solids and marsh muds collected along the coast of Georgia', *Limnol. Oceanogr.*, **1**, 202–208.

BURKHOLDER, P. R. and BORNSIDE, G. H. (1957), 'Decomposition of marsh grass by aerobic marine bacteria', *Bull. Torrey bot. Club*, **84**, 366–383.

BURNETT, J. H. (ed.) (1964), *The Vegetation of Scotland*. Edinburgh: Oliver and Boyd.

CAREY, A. E. and OLIVER, F. W. (1918), *Tidal Lands*. London: Blackie.

CHAPMAN, V. J. (1938), 'Studies in salt marsh ecology. Sections I–III', *J. Ecol.*, **26**, 144–179.

CHAPMAN, V. J. (1940), Succession on the New England salt marshes. *Ecology*, **21**, 279–282.

CHAPMAN, V. J. (1942), 'The new perspective in the Halophytes, *Q. Rev. Biol.*, **17**, 291–311.

CHAPMAN, V. J. (1944), 'Cambridge University expedition to Jamaica', *J. Linn. Soc.* (Bot), **52**, 407–533.

CHAPMAN, V. J. (1959), 'Studies in salt marsh ecology. IX. Changes in salt marsh vegetation at Scolt Head Island, Norfolk', *J. Ecol.*, **47**, 619–639.

CHAPMAN, V. J. (1960), *Salt Marshes and Salt Deserts of the World.* London: Leonard Hill.

CHAPMAN, V. J. and RONALDSON, J. W. (1958). The mangrove and salt marsh flats of the Auckland Isthmus. N.Z. Dept. Sci. and Indust. Res., Bull. 125, 1–79.

CHIPPINDALE, H. G. and MERRICKS, R. W. (1965), 'Gang-mowing and pasture management', *J. Br. Grassld Soc.*, **11**, 1–9.

CLAPHAM, A. R., PEARSALL, W. H. and RICHARDS, P. W. (1942), '*Aster tripolium.* Biological flora of the British Isles'. *J. Ecol.*, **30**, 385–395.

CLARKE, L. D. and HANNON, N. J. (1967), 'The mangrove swamp and salt marsh communities of the Sydney district. I Vegetation, soils and climate', *J. Ecol.*, **55**, 753–771.

CLARKE, L. D. and HANNON, N. J. (1969), 'The mangrove swamp and salt marsh communities of the Sydney district. II The Holocoenotic complex with particular reference to physiography', *J. Ecol.*, **57**, 213–234.

CLARKE, L. D. and HANNON, N. J. (1970), 'The mangrove swamp and salt marsh communities of the Sydney district. III. Plant growth in relation to salinity and waterlogging', *J. Ecol.*, **58**, 351–369.

CLARKE, S. M. (1965), Some aspects of the autecology of *Elymus arenarius* L. Ph.D. Thesis, Hull.

COTTON, M. J. (1967), 'Aspects of the ecology of sand dune arthropods', *Entomologist*, **100**, 157–165.

COOPER, W. S. (1958), 'Coastal sand dunes of Oregon and Washington', Geol. Soc. America Memoir, **72**. Baltimore.

COTTAM, C. and MUNRO, D. A. (1954), 'Eelgrass status and environmental relations', *J. Wildl. Mgmt*, **18**, 449–460.

COULL, J. (1968), 'Crofting townships and common grazings', *Agr. Hist. Rev.*, 16.

COWLES, H. C. (1899), 'The ecological relations of the vegetation on the sand dunes of Lake Michigan', *Bot. Gaz.*, **27**, 95–117; 167–202; 281–308; 361–391.

COWLES, H. C. (1911), 'A fifteen year study of advancing sand dunes', Rep. Br. Ass. 1911, 565.

CRAWFORD, R. M. M. and WISHART, D. (1966), 'A multivariate analysis of the development of dune slack vegetation in relation to coastal accretion at Tentsmuir, Fife', *J. Ecol.*, **54**, 729–743.

CRAWFORD, R. M. M. and WISHART, D. (1967), 'A rapid multivariate method for the detection and classification of groups of ecologically related species', *J. Ecol.*, **55**, 505–524.

CRAWFORD, R. M. M. and WISHART, D. (1968), 'A rapid classification and ordination method and its application to vegetation mapping', *J. Ecol.*, **56**, 385–404.

DAHL, R. G. (1959), 'Studies on Scandinavian *Ephydridae* (*Diptera, Brachycera*)', Opusc. ent. suppl., **15**, 1–224.

DALBY, D. H. (1962), 'Chromosome number, morphology and breeding behaviour in the British *Salicorniae*', *Watsonia*, **5**, 150–162.

DALBY, D. H. (1963), 'Seed dispersal in *Salicornia pusilla*', *Nature*, **199**, 197–198.

DALBY, D. H. (1970), 'The salt marshes of Milford Haven, Pembrokeshire', *Field Studies*, **3**, 297–330.

DALBY, R. (1957), 'Problems of land reclamation. 5. Salt marsh in the Wash', *Agric. Rev.*, **2**, 31–37.

DAVIS, J. H. (1940), The ecology and geologic role of mangroves in Florida. Carnegie Inst. Publ. 517, 303.

DAVIS, L. V. and GRAY, I. E. (1966), Zonal and seasonal distribution of insects in North Carolina salt marshes. Ecol. Monogr., **36**, 275–295.

DAY, J. H. (1951), 'The ecology of South African estuaries Pt. I. A review of estuarine conditions in general', *Trans. Roy. Soc. S. Afr.*, **33**, 53–91.

DEFANT, A. (1964), *Ebb and Flow*. New York: University of Michigan Press.

DUFF, S. and TEAL, J. M. (1965), Temperature change and gas exchange in Nova Scotia and Georgia salt marsh muds. Woods Hole Oceanographic Inst. Contrib. No. 1501, 67–73.

DUFFEY, E. (1967), The biotic effects of public pressure on the environment. Nature Conservancy, Monks Wood Experimental Station Symposium, **3**, 1–178.

DUFFEY, E. (1968), 'An ecological analysis of the spider fauna of sand dunes', *J. Anim. Ecol.*, **37**, 641–674.

DUVIGNEAUD, P. (1947), 'Remarques sur la végétation des pannes dans les dunes littorales entre La Panne et Dunkerque', *Bull. Soc. roy. Bot. Belg.*, **79**, 123–140.

EHRLICH, P. R. and RAVEN, P. H. (1969), 'Differentiation of populations', *Science*, **165**, 1128–1232.

ELLIS, E. A. (1960), 'The purple (hybrid) Marram, *Ammocalamagrostis baltica* (Fluegge) P. Fourn. in East Anglia', *Trans. Norfolk Norwich Nat. Soc.*, **19**, 49–51.

ELTON, C. S. (1966), '*The pattern of Animal Communities*'. London: Methuen.

ELZAM, O. E. and EPSTEIN, E. (1969), 'Salt relations of two grass species differing in salt tolerance. I. Growth and salt content at different salt concentrations', *Agrochimica*, **13**, 187–195.

ENGLISH, N. (1969), 'Les Landes', Nature Conservancy unpubld. typescript, 1–20.

EVANS, H. J. and SORGER, G. J. (1966), 'Role of mineral elements with emphasis on the univalent cations', *A. Rev. Pl. Physiol.*, **17**, 47–76.

FAEGRI, K. (1958), 'On the climatic demands of Oceanic plants', *Bot. notiser*, 3, 325–332.

FAEGRI, K. (1960), *The Distribution of Coast Plants*. Oslo: Oslo University Press.

FAIRBRIDGE, R. W. (1961), 'Eustatic changes in sea level', *Phys. Chem. Earth*, **4**, 99–185.

FLETCHER, H. C. and ELMENDORF, H. B. (1955), 'Phreatophytes – a serious problem in the West. U.S.', *Yearb. Agric.*, **1955**, 423–429.

FRAME, J. (1971), 'Fundamentals of grassland management. 10. The grazing animal', *Scottish Agric.*, **50**, 1–17.

FREIJSEN, A. H. J. (1967), *A Field Study of the Ecology of Centaurium vulgare* Rafn., Tilburg: H. Gianotten.

FOWDEN, L. (1959), *Physiologia Pl.*, **12**, 657–664.

GALLATIN, M. H., LUNIN, J. and BATCHELDER, A. R. (1962), 'Brackish water sources for irrigation along the eastern seaboard of the United States', *U.S. Dept. Agric. Prod. Resour Rep.*, **61**, 1–28.

GARRET, P. (1971), The sedimentary record of life on a modern tropical tidal flat, Andros Island, Bahamas. Ph. D. thesis John Hopkins Univ., Baltimore.

GATES, F. C. (1950), 'The disappearing Sleeping Bear Dune', *Ecology*, **31**, 386–392.

GEMMELL, A. R., GREIG-SMITH, P. and GIMINGHAM, C. H. (1953), 'A note on the behaviour of *Ammophila arenaria* (L.) Link in relation to sand-dune formation', *Trans. bot. Soc. Edinb.*, **36**, 132–136.

GIGLIOLI, M. E. C. and THORNTON, I. (1965), 'The mangrove swamps of Keneba, Lower Gambia river basin. I. Descriptive notes on the climate, the mangrove swamps and the physical conditions of their soils', *J. appl. Ecol.*, **2**, 81–103.

GILLHAM, M. E. (1957), 'Coastal vegetation of Mull and Iona in relation to salinity and soil reaction', *J. Ecol.*, **45**, 757–778.

GILLHAM, M. E. (1964), 'The vegetation of local coastal gull colonies', *Trans. Cardiff Nat. Soc.*, **91**, 23–33.

GILLIAM, H. T. (1957), *San Francisco Bay*. New York: Doubleday.

GILLNER, V. (1965), 'Salt marsh vegetation in Southern Sweden', *Acta Phytogeogr. Suecica*, **50**, 97–104.

GIMINGHAM, C. H. GEMMELL, A. R. and GREIG-SMITH, P. (1948), 'The vegetation of a sand dune system in the Outer Hebrides', *Trans. Proc. Bot. Soc. Edinb.*, **35**, 82–96.

GIMINGHAM, C. H. (1951), 'Contributions to the maritime ecology of St. Cyrus, Kincardineshire. Part II. The sand dunes', *Trans. Proc. Bot. Soc. Edinb., 35, 387–414.*

GIMINGHAM, C. H. (1955), 'Contributions to the maritime ecology of St. Cyrus, Kincardineshire. III. The salt marsh', *Trans. Proc. Bot. Soc. Edinb.*, **36**, 137–164.

GINSBURG, R. N., ISHAM, L. B., BEIN, S. J. and KUPERBERG, J. (1954), Laminated algal sediments of south Florida and their recognition in the fossil record: unpublished Rep. No. 54–21, Marine Laboratory, University of Miami, Coral Gables, Florida.

GINSBURG, R. N. and LOWENSTAM, H. A. (1958), 'The influence of marine bottom communities on the depositional environment of sediments', *J. Geol.*, **66**, 310–318.

GLOPPER, R. J. de (1964), 'About the water content and shrinkage of some Dutch lacustrine and marine sediments', *Neth. J. agric. Sci.*, **12**, 221–226.

GODWIN, H. SUGGATE, R. P. and WILLIS, E. H. (1958), 'Radiocarbon dating of the eustatic rise in ocean level', *Nature*, **181**, 1518–1519.

GOETHART, J. W. C., TESCH, P., HESSELINK, E. and DIJT, M. D. (1924), 'Cultuur-en waterleidingbelangen wittreksel uit het rapport inzake het verband tusschen wateronttrekking en plantengroei', *Meded. Rijksboschb Proefstn. s'Gravenhage*, 1/3, 5, 5–28.

GOLDSMITH, F. B., MUNTON, R. J. C. and WARREN, A. (1970), 'The impact of reacreation on the ecology and amenity of semi-natural areas: methods of investigation used in the Isles of Scilly', *Biol. J. Linn. Soc.*, **2**, 287–306.

GOLUBIC, S. (1970), 'Effect of organic pollution on benthic communities', Marine Pollut. Bull. 1 (N.S.), 56–57.

GOOD, R. (1935), 'Contributions towards a survey of the plants and animals of South Haven Peninsula, Studland Heath, Dorset. II General ecology of the flowering plants and ferns', *J. Ecol.*, **23**, 361–405.

GOOD, R. (1964), *The Geography of the Flowering Plants*. (3rd edn.) London: Longman.

GOODMAN, P. J. and WILLIAMS, W. T. (1961), 'Investigations into 'die-back' in *Spartina townsendii* agg. III. Physiological correlates of 'die-back', *J. Ecol.*, **49**, 391–398.

GOODWIN. R. H. (ed.) (1961), 'Connecticut's coastal marshes. A vanishing re-source', *The Connecticut Arboretum Bull.*, **12**, 1–36.

GORHAM, A. V. and GORHAM, E. (1965), 'Iron, manganese, ash and nitrogen in some plants from salt marsh and shingle habitats', *Ann. Bot.*, **19**, 571–577.

GORHAM, E. (1958 *a*), 'Soluble salts in dune sands from Blakeney Point in Nor-folk', *J. Ecol.*, **46**, 373–379.

GORHAM, E. (1958 *b*), 'The influence and importance of daily weather conditions in the supply of chloride, sulphate and other ions to fresh waters from atmos-pheric precipitation', Phil. Trans. Roy. Soc. Series B, **241**, 147–178.

GOTTSCHALK, L. C. and JONES, V. H. (1955), 'Valleys and hills, erosion and sedi-mentation', *Yearb. U.S. Dep. Agric.*, 135–143.

GRAY, A. J. (1971), 'Variation in *Aster tripolium* L., with particular reference to some British populations'. Ph.D. Thesis, University of Keele.

GREEN, F. H. W. (1964), 'A map of annual average potential water deficit in the British Isles', *J. appl. Ecol.*, **1**, 151–158.

GREEN, R. D. and ASKEW, G. P. (1965), 'Observations on the biological develop-ment of macropores in soils of Romney Marsh', *J. Soil. Sci.*, **16**, 342–349.

GREENSMITH, J. T. and TUCKER, E. V. (1966), 'Morphology and evolution of in-shore shell ridges and mud-mounds on modern intertidal flats, near Bradwell, Essex', *Proc. Geol. Ass.*, **77**, 329–346.

GRIM, R. E. (1953), *Clay Mineralogy*. New York: McGraw-Hill.

GRIME, J. P. (1965), 'Comparative experiments as a key to the ecology of flowering plants', *Ecology*, **46**, 513–515.

GRIST, D. H. (1959), *Rice*, London.

GUILCHER, A. and BERTHOIS, L. (1957), 'Cinq années d'observations sédimento-logiques dans quartre estuaires-témoins de l'ouest de la Bretagne', *Rev. de Géomorph. Dynamique*, **5–6**, 67–86.

GUNKEL, W. (1968), 'Bacteriological investigations of oil-polluted sediments from the Cornish coast following the Torrey Canyon disaster. The biological effects of oil pollution on littoral communities', *Field Studies 2, suppl.*, 151–158.

GUTNECHT, J. and DAINTY, J. (1968), 'Ionic relations of marine algae', *Oceanogr. Mar. Biol. Ann. Rev.*, **6**, 163–200.

HAAS, J. A. and STEERS, J. A. (1964), 'An aid to stabilization of sand dunes: experiments at Scolt Head Island', *Geogr. J.*, **130**, 265–267.

HADERLIE, E. C. (1970), 'Influence of pesticide run-off in Monterey Bay', *Mar. Pollut. Bull.* **1** (*N.S.*), 42–43.

HANNON, N. and BRADSHAW, A. D. (1968), 'Evolution of salt tolerance in two co-existing species of grass', *Nature*, **220**, 1342–1343.

HARBERD, D. J. (1961), 'Observations on population structure and longevity of *Festuca rubra*', *New Phytol.*, **60**, 184–206.

HARVEY, H. T. (1966 *a*), 'Marshes and mudflats of San Francisco Bay', San Francisco Bay Conserv. and Dev. Comm., San Francisco.

HARVEY, H. T. (1966 *b*), 'Some ecological aspects of San Francisco Bay', San Francisco Bay Conserv. and Dev. Comm., San Francisco.

HASSOUNA, M. G. and Wareing, P. F. (1964), 'Possible role of rhizosphere bacteria in the nitrogen nutrition of *Ammophila arenaria*', *Nature*, **202**, 467–469.

HEERDT, P. F. VAN and MÖRZER BRUYNS, M. F. (1960), 'A biocoenological investigation in the yellow dune region of Terschelling', *Tijdschr. Ent.*, **103**, 225–275.

HEIMANN, H. (1958), 'Irrigation with saline water and the ionic environment', 'Potassium-symposium'. 1958. Berne, 173–220.

HESSE, P. R. (1961), 'Some differences between the soils of *Rhizophora* and *Avicennia* mangrove swamps in Sierra Leone', *Pl. Soil*, **14**, 335–346.

HESSE, P. R. (1963), 'Phosphorus relationships in a mangrove swamp mud with particular reference to aluminium toxicity', *Pl. Soil*, **19**, 205–218.

HEWETT, D. G. (1970), 'The colonization of sand dunes after stabilization with Marram grass ' (*Ammophila arenaria*), *J. Ecol.*, **58**, 653–668.

HEWETT, D. G. (1971), 'The effects of the cold winter of 1962/63 on *Juncus acutus* at Braunton Burrows, Devon'. Devon Assoc. Adv. Sci. Lit. Art Rep. Trans., 1970, **102**, 193–201.

HIGGINS, L. S. (1933), 'An investigation into the problem of the sand dune areas on the South Wales coast', *Arch. Camb.*, June 1933.

HILL, T. G. and HANLEY, J. A. (1914), 'The structure and water content of shingle beaches', *J. Ecol.*, **7**, 11–50.

HINCKS, W. D., MICHAELIS, H. N., SHAW, S., BRAHAM, A. C., MURGATROYD, J. H. and BUTLER, P. M. (1951–4), 'The entomology of Spurn Peninsula', *Naturalist*, 1951: 75–86, 139–46, 183–90; 1952: 131–8, 169–76; 1953: 125–40, 157–72; 1954: 74–8, 95–109.

HINDE, H. P. (1954), 'Vertical distribution of salt marsh phanerogams in relation to tide levels', *Ecol. Mon.*, **24**, 209–225.

HITCHCOCK, A. S. (1904), 'Methods used for controlling and reclaiming sand dunes', U.S. Department of Agriculture, Bureau of Plant Industry Bull. No. 57.

HOLDER, F. W. (1953), 'Changing flora of the South Lancashire dunes', *N.West. Nat.*, **1** (N.S.), 451–452.

HOPE-SIMPSON, J. F. and JEFFERIES, R. L. (1966), 'Observations relating to vigour and debility in Marram grass (*Ammophila arenaria* (L.) Link)', *J. Ecol.*, **54**, 271–274.

HOPKINS, B. (1962), 'The measurement of available light by the use of *Chlorella*', *New Phyt.*, **61**, 221–223.

HUBBARD, C. E. (1968), *Grasses*. (2nd edn.), Harmondsworth: Penguin.

HUBBARD, J. C. E. (1965), '*Spartina* marshes in Southern England. VI. Pattern of invasion in Poole Harbour', *J. Ecol.*, **53**, 799–813.

HUBBARD, J. C. E. (1969), 'Light in relation to tidal immersion and the growth of *Spartina townsendii* (s.l.)', *J. Ecol.*, **57**, 795–804.

HUBBARD, J. C. E. (1970), 'Effects of cutting and seed production in *Spartina anglica*', *J. Ecol.*, **58**, 329–334.

HUBBARD, J. C. E. and RANWELL, D. S. (1966), 'Cropping *Spartina* salt marsh for silage', *J. Br. Grassld Soc.*, **21**, 214–217.

HUBBARD, J. C. E. and STEBBINGS, R. E. (1968), '*Spartina* marshes in Southern England. VII Stratigraphy of the Keysworth marsh, Poole Harbour', *J. Ecol.*, **56**, 707–722.

HUGHES, G. P. (1953), 'The effect on agriculture of the East Coast floods', Unpublished report by the National Agricultural Advisory Service, Ministry of Agriculture Fisheries and Food, 1–262.

HULME, B. A. (1957), 'Studies on some British species of *Atriplex* L.', Ph.D. Thesis, University of Edinburgh.

HUNT, O. J. (1965), 'Salt tolerance in intermediate wheatgrass *Agropyron intermedium*', *Crop Sci.*, **5**, 407–409.

INGLIS, C. C. and ALLEN, F. H. (1957), 'The regimen of the Thames Estuary as affected by currents, salinities and river flow', *Proc. Instn Civ. Engrs*, **7**, 827–878.

INGLIS, C. C. and KESTNER, F. J. T. (1958 a), 'Changes in the Wash as affected by training walls and reclamation works', *Proc. Instn Civ. Engrs.*, **11**, 435–466.

INGIS, C. C. and KESTNER, F. J. T. (1958 b), 'The long-term effects of training walls, reclamation, and dredging on estuaries', *Proc. Instn Civ. Engrs*, **9**, 193–216.

IVERSON, J. (1936), *Biologische Pflanzentypen als Hilfsmittel in der Vegetationsforschung*. Copenhagen: Medd. Fra. Skalling-Labor. Bd., 4.

IVERSON, J. (1954), 'The zonation of the salt marsh vegetation of Skallingen in 1931–4 and in 1952', *Meddr Skalling – Lab.*, **14**, 113–118.

JACOBSEN, N. K. (1960), 'Types of sedimentation in a drowned delta region', *Geogr. Tidsskr.*, **59**, 58–69.

JACOBSEN, N. K. (1964), 'Troek af Tøndermarskens naturgeografi med saerligt henblik på morfogenesen', *Folia Georgr. Dan.*, **7**, 1–350.

JAKOBSEN, B., JENSEN, K. M. and NIELSEN, N. (1955), 'Forlag til landvindingsarbejder langs den sømderjyske vadehavskyst', *Geogr. Tidsskr.*, **55**, 62–87.

JAKOBSEN, B. (1961), 'Vadehavets sedimentomsoetning belyst ved kvantitative målinger', *Geogr. Tidsskr.*, **60**, 87–103.

JAKOBSEN, B. (1964), 'Vadehavets morfologi', *Folia Geogr. Dan.*, **11**, 1–176.

JENNINGS, J. N. (1964), 'The question of coastal dunes in tropical, humid climates', *Z. Geomorph.*, **8**, 150–154.

JOHNSON, C. G. and SMITH, L. P. (Eds.) (1965). *The Biological Significance of Climatic Changes in Britain*. London: Institute of Biology and Academic Press.

JOHNSON, D. S. and YORK, H. H. (1915), The relation of plants to tide levels, Carnegie Institute Washington Publication, 206.

JONES, R. and ETHERINGTON, J. R. (1971), Comparative studies of plant growth and distribution in relation to water-logging IV. The growth of dune and slack plants, *J. Ecol.*, **59**, 793–801.

JOSEPH, A. F. and OAKLEY, H. B. (1929), 'The properties of heavy alkaline soils containing different exchangeable bases', *J. agric. Sci.*, **19**, 121–131.

KALLE, K. (1958), Sea water as a source of mineral substances for plants, Nature Conservation (London) Translation No. 11.

KAMPS, L. F. (1962), 'Mud distribution and land reclamation in the eastern Wadden shallows', *RijkswatSt. Commun.*, No. 4, 1–73.

KASSAS, M. (1957), 'On the ecology of the Red Sea coastal land', *J. Ecol.*, **45**, 187–203.

KELLEY, W. P. (1951), *Alkali Soils: their Formation, Properties and Reclamation*. Monograph No. 111. New York: Rheinhold.

KESTNER, F. J. T. and INGLIS, C. C. (1956), 'A study of erosion and accretion during cyclic changes in an estuary and their effect on reclamation of marginal land', *J. Agric. Engng. Res.*, **1**, 63–67.

KESTNER, F. J. T. (1961), 'Short term changes in the distribution of fine sediments in estuaries', *Proc. Instn. Civ. Engrs.*, **19**, 185–208.

KESTNER, F. J. T. (1962), 'The old coastline of the Wash', *Geogr. J.*, **128**, 457–478.

KESTNER, F. J. T. (1963), The supply and circulation of silt in the Wash. 10th Congr. International Association Hydraulic Research, London, 231–238.

KIDSON, C. and CARR, A. P. (1961), 'Beach drift experiments at Bridgwater Bay, Somerset', *Proc. Bristol Nat. Soc.*, **30**, 163–180.

KING, C. A. M. (1972), *Beaches and Coasts* (2nd edn.), London: Edward Arnold.

KRINSLEY, D. H. and FUNNELL, B. M. (1965), 'Environmental history of quartz sand grains from the Lower and Middle Pleistocene of Norfolk, England', *Q J. Geol. Soc. Lond.*, **121**, 435–461.

KRUMBEIN, W. C. and SLACK, H. A. (1956), 'The relative efficiency of beach sampling methods', *Tech. Memo. Beach Eros. Bd U.S.*, **90**, 1–34.

LAING, C. (1954), The ecological life history of the marram grass community on Lake Michigan dunes. Ph.D. dissertation, University of Chicago.

LAMB, H. H. (1969), 'The new look of climatology', *Nature*, **223**, 1209–1215.

LAMB, H. H. (1970), The variability of climate. Met. Office, Bracknell, unpublished typescript, 1–22.

LAMBINON, J. (1956), 'Aperçu sur les groupements végétaux du district maritime Belge entre La Panne et Coxyde', *Bull. Soc. Roy. Bot. Belg.*, **88**, 107–127.

LANDSBERG, S. Y. (1956), 'The orientation of dunes in relation to wind', *Geogr. J.*, **122**, 176–189.

LANDSBERG, H. and RILEY, N. A. (1943), Wind influences on the transportation of sand over a Michigan sand dune. Proceedings 2nd. Hydraulics Conference Bulletin 27, Univ. Iowa Studies in Engineering.

LARSEN, H. (1967), 'Biochemical aspects of extreme Halophilism', *Adv. Microb. Physiol.*, 1, 97–132.

LAUFF, G. H. (ed.) (1967), Conference on estuaries. Jekyll Island (Ga.), 1964. Washington.

LEEUWEN, C. G. van (1965), 'Het verband tussen naturrlijke en anthropogene landschapsvormen, bezien vanuit de betrekkingen in grenzmilieu's', *Gorteria*, 2, 93–105.

LINES, R. (1957), 'Estimation of exposure by flags', Report on Forestry Research, H.M.S.O. London 1957, 47–48.

LOPEZ-GONZALEZ, J. de and JENNY, H. (1959), 'Diffusion of strontium in ion-exchange membranes', *J. Colloid Sci.*, 14, 533–542.

LOWE-McCONNELL, R. H. (ed.) (1966), *Man-made Lakes*. London: Institute of Biology and Academic Press.

LUGG, J. W. H. (1949), 'Plant Proteins', *Adv. Protein Chem.*, 5, 230–295.

LUXTON, M. (1964), 'Some aspects of the biology of salt marsh Acarina', *Acaralogia*. C.R. 1er Congrès Int. d'Acaralogie, Fort Collins, Colorado, U.S.A. 1963, 172–182.

LYNCH, J. J. (1941), 'The place of burning in management of the Gulf Coast refuges', *J. Wildl. Mgmt.*, 5, 454–458.

LYNCH, J. J., O'NEIL, T. and LANG, D. W. (1947), 'Management significance of damage by geese and muskrats to Gulf Coast marshes', *J. Wildl. Mgmt.*, 2, 50–76.

MAAREL, E. VAN DER (1966), 'Dutch studies on coastal sand dune vegetation, especially in the delta region', *Wentia*, 15, 47–82.

MAAREL, E. VAN DER and LEERTOUWER, J. (1967), 'Variation in vegetation and species diversity along a local environmental gradient', *Acta. Bot. Neerl.*, 16, 211–221.

MAAREL, E. VAN DER and WESTHOFF, V. (1964), 'The vegetation of the dunes near Oostvoorne', *Wentia*, 12, 1–61.

MACDONALD, J. (1954), 'Tree planting on coastal sand dunes in Great Britain', *Adv. Sci.*, 11, 33–37.

MACDONALD, K. B. (1969), 'Quantitative studies of salt marsh mollusc faunas from the North American Pacific coast', *Ecol. Mongr.*, 39, 33–60.

MACNAE, W. (1966), 'Mangroves in eastern and southern Australia', *Aust. J. Bot.*, 14, 67–104.

MACNAE, W. (1968), 'A general account of the fauna and flora of mangrove swamps and forests in the Indo-West-Pacific Region', *Adv. Mar. Biol.*, 6, 73–270.

MARCHANT, C. J. (1967), 'Evolution in *Spartina* (Graminae) I. The history and morphology of the genus in Britain', *J. Linn. Soc. (Bot.)*, 60, 1–24.

MARCHANT, C. J. (1968), 'Evolution in *Spartina* (Graminae) II. Chromosomes, basic relationships and the problem of *S. x townsendii* agg.,' *J. Linn. Soc. (Bot.)*, 60, 381–409.

MARPLES, T. G. (1966), 'A radionuclide tracer study of Arthropod food chains in a *Spartina* salt marsh ecosystem', *Ecology*, **47**, 270–277.

MARSHALL, J. K. (1965), '*Corynephorus canescens* (L.) P. Beauv. as a model for the *Ammophila* problem', *J. Ecol.*, **53**, 447–463.

MARTIN, A. C. (1953), 'Improving duck marshes by weed control. U.S. Fish and Wildlife Service Circular', **19**, 1–49.

MARTIN, W. E. (1959), 'The vegetation of Island Beach State Park, New Jersey', *Ecol. Mongr.*, **29**, 1–46.

MATTHEWS, J. R. (1937), 'Geographical relationships of the British Flora', *J. Ecol.*, **25**, 1–90.

MAY, V. J. (1969), 'Reclamation and shore line change in Poole Harbour, Dorset', *Proc. Dorset Nat. Hist. Archaeol. Soc.*, **90**, 141–154.

McCRONE, A. (1966), 'The Hudson river estuary. Hydrology, sediments and pollution', *Geogr. Rev.*, **56**, 175–189.

McROY, C. P. (1969), 'Eelgrass under Arctic winter ice', *Nature*, **224**, 818–819.

MOBBERLEY, D. G. (1956), 'Taxonomy and distribution of the genus *Spartina*', *Iowa St. J. Sci.*, **30**, 471–574.

MØLLER, J. T. (1963), 'Accumulation and abrasion in a tidal area', *Geogr. Tidsskr.*, **62**, 56–79.

MØLLER, J. T. (1964), *Fladkystems og Flodens Morfologiske Elementer*, Copenhagen: K. G. Wingstrand.

MONTFORT, C. and BRANDRUP, W. (1927), 'Physiologische und Pflanzengeographische Seesalzwirkungen II. Okologische Studien über Keimung und erste Entwicklung bei Halophyten', *Jb. Wiss. Bot.*, **66**, 902–946.

MOORE, P. D. (1971), 'Computer analysis of sand dune vegetation in Norfolk, England, and its implications for convservation', *Vegetatio*, **23**, 323–338.

MÖRZER BRUYNS, M. F. and WESTHOFF, V. (1951), The Netherlands as an environment of insect life. 9th Int. Congr. Entom., Amsterdam.

MYRICK, R. M. and LEOPOLD, L. B. (1963), 'Hydraulic geometry of a small tidal estuary', U.S. Geol. Survey Professional Paper, 422–B, 1–18.

NELSON-SMITH, A. (1968), *A Classified Bibliography of Oil Pollution*, Swansea: University College (typescript 1–51).

POWELL, R. C. (1953), 'The role of calcium in the nutrition of two marine deposit feeders, the Prosobranch *Hydrobia ulvae* and the bivalve *Macoma balthica*', *Proc. Zool. Soc. Lond.*, **144**, 25–45.

NEWMAN, W. S. and RUSNAK, G. A. (1965), 'Holocene submergence of the Eastern shore of Virginia', *Science*, **148**, 1464–1466.

NICHOLSON, I. A. (1952), A study of *Agropyron junceum* (Beauv.) in relation to the stabilization of coastal sand and the development of sand dunes. M.Sc. Thesis, University of Durham.

NIELSEN, N. (1935), 'Eine methode zur exakten sedimentations-messung studien über die marschbildung auf der halbinsel Skalling. Danske Videnskabernes Selskab', *Biol. Meddr.*, **12**, 1–96.

NOBUHARA, H. (1967), 'Analysis of coastal vegetation on sandy shore by biological types in Japan', *Jap. J. Bot.*, **19**, 325–351.

NORTHFIELD, J. (1960), 'The bryophyte flora of Studland Heath', *Durham Colleges Nat. Hist. Soc. J.*, **7**, 38–45.

ODUM, E. P. (1961), 'The role of tidal marshes in estuarine production', N.Y. State Conservationist Information Leaflet.

ODUM, E. P. (1962), 'Relationship between structure and function in the ecosystem', *Jap. J. Ecol.*, **12**, 108–118.

ODUM, E. P. (1963), 'Primary and secondary energy flow in relation to ecosystem structure', Proceedings of XVI International Congr. Zool., **4**, 336–338.

ODUM, E. P. and CRUZ, A. A. de la (1967), 'Particulate organic detritus in a Georgia salt marsh – estuarine ecosystem'. Estuaries. Publication No. 83 American Association for the Advancement of Science, Washington, 383–388.

ODUM, E. P. and SMALLEY, A. E. (1959), 'Comparison of population energy flow of a herbivorous and deposit-feeding invertebrate in a salt marsh ecosystem', *Proc. Natn. Acad. Sci., U.S.A.*, **45**, 617–622.

OKUDA, A. and Takahashi, E. (1965), The role of silicon, in *Mineral Nutrition of the Rice Plant*, Ch. 10, 123–146 (Proc. Intern. Conf. Rice Res. Inst., Los Bañjos, Philippines, 1964. John Hopkins Press, Baltimore).

OLIVER, F. W. (1929), 'Blakeney Point Reports', *Trans. Norfolk Norwich Nat. Soc.*, **12**, 630–653.

OLSON, J. S. (1958 *a*), 'Rates of succession and soil changes on Southern Lake Michigan sand dunes', *Bot. Gaz.*, **119**, 125–170.

OLSON, J. S. (1958 *b*), 'Lake Michigan dune development. 1. Wind-velocity profiles', *J. Geol.*, **66**, 254–263.

OLSON, J. S. (1958 *c*), 'Lake Michigan dune development. 2. Plants as agents and tools in geomorphology', *J. Geol.*, **66**, 345–351.

OLSSON-SEFFER, P. (1909), 'Hydrodynamic factors influencing plant life on sandy sea shores', *New Phytol.*, **8**, 37–49.

OOSTING, H. J. (1954), Ecological processes and vegetation of the maritime strand in the United States. *Bot. Rev.*, **20**, 226–262.

OSBORN, T. G. B. and ROBERTSON, R. N. (1939), 'A reconnaissance survey of the vegetation of Myall Lakes', *Proc. Linn. Soc. N.S.W.*, **64**, 279–296.

OVINGTON, J. D. (1950), 'The afforestation of the Culbin sands', *J. Ecol.*, **38**, 303–319.

OVINGTON, J. D. (1951), 'The afforestation of Tentsmuir Sands', *J. Ecol.*, **39**, 363–375.

PACKHAM, J. R. and LIDDLE, M. J. (1970), 'The Cefni salt marsh, Anglesey and its recent development', *Fld Stud.*, **3**, 331–356.

PARHAM, M. R. (1970), A Comparative study of the mineral nutrition of selected halophytes and glycophytes. Ph.D. Thesis University of East Anglia.

PAVIOUR-SMITH, K. (1956), 'The biotic community of a salt meadow in New Zealand', *Trans. Roy. Soc. N.Z.*, **83**, 525–554.

PAYNE, K. T. (1972 – in press), 'A survey of the *Spartina* feeding insects in Poole Harbour, Dorset', *Entomologist's mon. Mag.*

PERKINS, E. J., WILLIAMS, B. R. H. and BAILEY, M. (1963), 'Some preliminary notes on the bottom currents of the Solway Firth and North East Irish sea', *Trans. Dumfries and Galloway Nat. Hist. and Antiq. Soc. Ser.* 3, **41**, 45–51.

PERKINS, E. J. and WILLIAMS, B. R. H. (1965), 'Some results of an investigation of the biology of the Solway Firth in relation to radioactivity', *Trans. J. Dumfries. Galloway nat. Hist. Antiq. Soc., Ser.* 3, **42**, 1–5.

PERRING, F. (1970), 'The flora of a changing Britain', *Bot. Soc. British Isles Rep.* No. 11. Hampton, Middlesex.

PERRING, F. H. and WALTERS, S. M. (1962), 'Atlas of the British Flora', London: Nelson.

PESTRONG, R. (1965), 'The development of drainage patterns on tidal marshes', Stanford University Publication Geological Science, 10, 1–87.

PETCH, C. P. (1945), 'Reclaimed lands of West Norfolk', *Trans. Norfolk Norwich Nat. Soc.*, **16**, 106–109.

PETERSEN, C. G. J. (1915), 'A preliminary result of the investigations on the valuation of the sea', *Rep. Dan. biol. Stn.*, **23**, 29–32.

PETERSEN, C. G. J. (1918), 'The sea bottom and its production of fish food', *Rep. Dan. biol. Stn.*, **25**, 1–62.

PETTERSSON, O. (1914), 'Climatic variations in historic and prehistoric time', *Svenska hydrogr.-biol. Kommn. Skr.*, **5**.

PHILLIPS, A. W. (1964), 'Some observations on coast erosion studies at South Holderness and Spurn Head', *Dock Harb. Auth.*, **45**, 64–66.

PISSAREV, V. E. and VINOGRADOVA, N. M. (1944), 'Hybrids between wheat and *Elymus*', C.r. *Dokl. Proc. Acad. Sci. U.S.S.R.*, **45**, 129–132.

POEL, L. W. (1960), 'The estimation of oxygen diffusion rates in soils', *J. Ecol.*, **48**, 169–177.

POMEROY, L. E. (1959), 'Algal productivity in salt marshes of Georgia', *Limnol. Oceanogr.*, **4**, 386–395.

POORE, M. E. D. and ROBERTSON, V. C. (1964), An approach to the rapid description and mapping of biological habitats. International Biological Programme Publication. London.

PORTER, J. J. (1962), 'Electron microscopy of sand surface textures', *J. Sedim. Petrol.*, **32**, 124–135.

PRAEGER, R. L. (1913), 'On the buoyancy of the seeds of some Brittanic plants', *Proc. Roy. Dub. Soc.*, **14**, 13–62.

PRESTON, A. (1960), radioecology and radiobiology, Annual Report Fisheries Laboratory, Ministry of Agriculture, Fisheries and Food, London. 108.

PRICE, W. A. and KENDRICK, M. P. (1963), 'Field model investigation into the reasons for silting in the Mersey estuary', *Proc. Inst. Civ. Engrs.*, **24**, 273–518.

PURER, E. A. (1942), 'Plant ecology of the coastal salt marshes of San Diego County, California', *Ecol. Mon.*, **12**, 81–111.

RAGOTSKIE, R. A. (1959), Proc. Salt Marsh Conf. Marine Inst. University of Georgia Publication, Athens, Georgia.

RAMALEY, F. (1918), 'Notes on dune vegetation at San Francisco, California', *Pl. Wld*, **21**, 191–201.

RANWELL, D. S. (1955), Slack vegetation, dune system development and cyclical change at Newborough Warren, Anglesey. Ph.D. Thesis, University of London.

RANWELL, D. S. (1958), 'Movement of vegetated sand dunes at Newborough Warren, Anglesey', *J. Ecol.*, **46**, 83–100.

RANWELL, D. S. (1959), 'Newborough Warren, Anglesey. I. The dune system and dune slack habitat', *J. Ecol.*, **47**, 571–601.

RANWELL, D. S. (1960 *a*), 'Newborough Warren, Angelsey. II. Plant associes and succession cycles of the sand dune and dune slack vegetation', *J. Ecol.*, **48**, 117–141.

RANWELL, D. S. (1960 *b*), 'Newborough Warren, Anglesey. III. Changes in the vegetation on parts of the dune system after the loss of rabbits by myxomatosis', *J. Ecol.*, **48**, 385–395.

RANWELL, D. S. (1961), '*Spartina* salt marshes in Southern England. I. The effects of sheep grazing at the upper limits of *Spartina* marsh in Bridgwater Bay', *J. Ecol.*, **49**, 325–340.

RANWELL, D. S. (1964 *a*), '*Spartina* salt marshes in Southern England. II. Rate and seasonal pattern of sediment accretion', *J. Ecol.*, **52**, 79–94.

RANWELL, D. S. (1964 *b*), '*Spartina* salt marshes in Southern England. III. Rates of establishment, succession and nutrient supply at Bridgwater Bay, Somerset', *J. Ecol.*, **52**, 95–105.

RANWELL, D. S. (1967), 'World resources of *Spartina townsendii* (*sensu lato*) and economic use of *Spartina* marshland', *J. Appl. Ecol.*, **4**, 239–256.

RANWELL, D. S. (1968 *a*), Coastal marshes in perspective. Regional studies Group Bull. Strathclyde No. 9, 1–26.

RANWELL, D. S. (1968 *b*), 'Extent of damage to coastal habitats due to the Torrey Canyon incident', Fld Stud., **2** (Suppl,), 39–47.

RANWELL, D. S. (ed.) (1972), The Management of Sea Buckthorn (*Hippophaë rhamnoides* L.) on selected sites in Great Britain. Nature Conservancy Report. London.

RANWELL, D. S., BIRD, E. C. F., HUBBARD, J. C. E. and STEBBINGS, R. E. (1964), '*Spartina* salt marshes in Southern England. V. Tidal submergence and chlorinity in Poole Harbour', *J. Ecol.*, **52**, 627–641.

RANWELL, D. S. and DOWNING, B. M. (1959), 'Brent goose (*Branta bernicla* L.) winter feeding pattern and *Zostera* resources at Scolt Head Island, Norfolk', *Anim. Behav.*, **7**, 42–56.

RANWELL, D. S. and DOWNING, B. M. (1960), 'The use of Dalapon and Substituted Urea herbicides for control of seed-bearing *Spartina* (Cord-grass) in inter-tidal zones of estuarine marsh', *Weeds*, **8**, 78–88.

RANWELL, D. S. and HEWETT, D. (1964), 'Oil pollution in Poole Harbour and its effect on birds', *Bird Notes*, **31**, 192–197.

RANWELL, D. S. and STEBBINGS, R. E. (1967), Report on the effects of Torrey Canyon oil pollution and decontamination methods in Cornwall and Brittany, March to April 1967. Nature Conservancy (London) Unpublished rep., 1–12.

RATCLIFFE, D. A. (1968), 'An ecological account of Atlantic Bryophytes in the British Isles', *New Phytol.*, **67**, 365–439.

REDFIELD, A. C. (1965), 'Ontogeny of a salt marsh estuary', *Science*, **147**, 50–55.

REDFIELD, A. C. and RUBIN, M. (1962), 'The age of salt marsh peat and its relation to recent changes in sea level at Barnstable, Massachusetts', *Proc. natn. Acad. Sci. U.S.A.*, **48**, 1728–1735.

REID, C. (1913), *Submerged Forests*. Cambridge: University Press.

RENGER, M. (1965), 'Berechnung der Austanchkapazität der organischen und anorganischen Anteile der Böden', *Z. Pfl-ernähr. Düng. Bodenk.*, **110**, 10–26.

REYNOLDSON, T. B. (1955), 'Observations on the earthworms of North Wales', *N. West Nat.*, Sept./Dec., 291–304.

REZK, M. R. (1970), 'Vegetation change from a sand dune community to a salt marsh as related to soil characters in Mariut District, Egypt', *Oikos*, **21**, 341–343.

RICHARDS, F. J. (1934), 'The salt marshes of the Dovey estuary. IV. The rates of vertical accretion, horizontal extension and scarp erosion', *Ann. Bot.*, **48**, 225–259.

RICHARDS, P. W. (1929), 'Notes on the ecology of the bryophytes and lichens at Blakeney Point, Norfolk', *J. Ecol.*, **17**, 127–140.

RIDLEY, H. N. (1930), *The Dispersal of Plants throughout the World*, Ashford: L. Reeve.

RILEY, G. A. (1963), 'Organic aggregates in sea water and the dynamics of their formation and utilization', *Limnol. Oceanogr.*, **8**, 373–381.

RITCHIE, W. and MATHER, A. (1969), *The Beaches of Sutherland*, Aberdeen: Dept. Geography, Univ. of Aberdeen.

RITCHIE, W. and MATHER, A. S. (1971), 'Conservation and use: Case-study of Beaches of Sutherland, Scotland', *Biol. Consvn.*, **3**, 199–207.

ROBERTSON, D. A. (1955), The ecology of the sand dune vegetation of Ross Links, Northumberland with special reference to secondary succession in the blow-outs. Ph.D. Thesis, Durham University.

ROBINSON, A. H. W. (1966), 'Residual currents in relation to shoreline evolution of the East Anglian coast', *Mar. Geol.*, **4**, 57–84.

ROBINSON, T. W. (1952), 'Phreatophytes and their relation to water in Western United States. Symposium on Phreatophytes', *Trans. Am. geophys. Un.*, **33**, 57–61.

ROBSON, M. J. and JEWISS, O. R. (1968), 'A comparison of British and North African varieties of tall Fescue (*Festuca arundinacea*) II. and III.', *J. appl. Ecol.*, **5**, 179–190 and 191–204.

RORISON, I. H. (ed.) (1969), *Ecological Aspects of the Mineral Nutrition of Plants*, Oxford: Blackwell.

SAKAI, A. (1970), 'Freezing resistance in willows from different climates', *Ecology*, **51**, 485–491.

SALISBURY, E. J. (1925), 'Note on the edaphic succession in some dune soils with special reference to the time factor', *J. Ecol.*, **13**, 322.

SALISBURY, E. J. (1934), 'On the day temperatures of sand dunes in relation to the vegetation at Blakeney Point, Norfolk', *Trans. Norfolk Norwich Nat. Soc.*, **13**, 333–355.

SALISBURY, E. J. (1952), *Downs and Dunes*, London: Bell.

SCHMIDT, F. V. (1950), 'An evaluation of practical tidal marsh management on state and private marshes. Proceedings of the North-East Fish and Wildlife Conference.

SCHRATZ, E. (1934), 'Beiträge zur Biologie der Halophyten I. Keimungsphysiologie', *Jb. wiss. Bot.*, **80**, 112–142.

SENECA, E. D. (1969), 'Germination response to temperature and salinity of four dune grasses from the Outer Banks of North Carolina', *Ecology*, **50**, 44–53.

SETCHELL, W. A. (1920), 'Geographical distribution of the marine spermatophytes', *Bull. Torrey bot. Club.*, **47**.

SHAW, R. H. (Ed.) (1967), *Ground Level Climatology*. Baltimore: American Assocn. for Advancement of Science.

SHIELDS, L. M. (1957), 'Algal and lichen floras in relation to nitrogen content of certain volcanic and arid range soils', *Ecology*, **38**, 661–663.

SIIRA, J. (1970), 'Studies in the ecology of the sea shore meadows of the Bothnian Bay with special reference to the Limnika area', *Aquila Ser. Bot.*, **9**, 1–109.

SLATYER, R. O. (1967), *Plant-water Relationships*, London: Academic Press.

SLESS, J. B. (1956), 'Control of sand drift in beach mining', *J. Soil. Conserv. Serv. N.S. W.*, **12**, 164–176.

SLOET V. OLDRUITENBORGH, C. J. M. (1969), 'On the contribution of air-borne salt to the gradient character of the Voorne dune area', *Acta bot. neerl.*, **18**, 315–324.

SPARLING, J. H. (1967), 'The occurrence of *Schoenus nigricans* L. in blanket bogs. II. Experiments on the growth of *S. nigricans* under controlled conditions', *J. Ecol.*, **55**, 15–31.

SPRINGER, P. F. and WEBSTER, J. R. (1951), 'Biological effects of DDT application on tidal salt marshes', *Mosquito News*, **2**, 67–74.

STEARNS, L. A. and MACCREARY, D. (1957), 'The case of the vanishing brick dust', *Mosquito News*, **17**, 303–304.

STEBBINGS, R. E. (1971), 'Some ecological observations on the fauna in a tidal marsh to woodland transition', *Proc. Trans. Brit. Entom. Soc.*, **4**, 83–88.

STEENIS, C. G. G. J. VAN (1958), Discrimination of tropical shore vegetation. Proceedings of the symposium on humid tropics vegetation, 215–217, New Delhi, UNESCO.

STEENIS, J. H., WILDER, N. G., COFER, H. P. and BECK, R. A. (1954), 'The marshes of Delaware, their improvement and preservation. Delaware Board of Game and Fish Commissioners', *Pittman-Robertson Bull.*, **2**, 1–42.

STEERS, J. A. (1939), 'Sand and shingle formations in Cardigan Bay', *Geogrl. J.*, **94**, 209–227.

STEERS, J. A. (Ed.) (1960), *Scolt Head Island*, Cambridge: Heffer.

STEERS, J. A. (1964), *The Coastline of England and Wales.* (2nd edn.), Cambridge: University Press.

STEVENSON, R. E. and EMERY, K. O. (1958), Marshlands at Newport Bay, California. Allan Hancock Foundation Publication No. 20. Los Angeles.

STEWART, G. R., LEE, J. A. and GREBAMJO, T. O. (1972), *Nitrogen Metabolism of Halophytes.* I. Nitrate reductase activity in *Suaeda* maritima,' *New Phyt.* **71**, 263–167.

STEWART, W. D. P. (1967), 'Transfer of biologically fixed nitrogen in a sand dune slack region', *Nature*, **214**, 603–604.

STUBBINGS, H. G. and HOUGHTON, D. R. (1964), 'The ecology of Chichester Harbour', *Int. Rev. ges. Hydrobiol., Syst. beih.*, **49**, 233–279.

STOUTJESDIJKE, Ph. (1961), 'Micrometeorological measurements in vegetations of various structures', *Proc. K. ned. Akad. Wet., Amsterdam. section C*, **64**, 1–207.

TANSLEY, A. G. (1949), *The British Islands and their Vegetation*, Cambridge: University Press.

TASCHDJIAN, E. (1954), 'A note on *Spartina* protein', *Econ. Bot.*, **8**, 164–165.

TAYLOR, M. C. and BURROWS, E. M. (1968), 'Studies on the biology of *Spartina* in the Dee estuary, Cheshire', *J. Ecol.*, **56**, 795–809.

TAYLOR, N. (1937), 'A preliminary report on the relation of mosquito control ditching to Long Island salt marsh vegetation', *Proc. New Jers. Mosq. Exterm. Ass.*, **24**, 211–217.

TAYLOR, N. (1939), Salt tolerance of Long Island salt marsh plants. New York State Museum Circular No. 23, 1–42.

TEAGLE, W. G. (1966), Public pressure on South Haven Peninsula and its effect on Studland Heath National Nature Reserve, Nature Conservancy, Unpublished typescript, 1–89.

TEAL, J. M. (1962), 'Energy flow in the salt marsh ecosystem of Georgia', *Ecology*, **43**, 614–624.

THAARUP, P. (1954), 'The afforestation of the sand dunes of the western coast of Jutland', *Advmt. Sci. Lond.*, **11**, 38–41.

THORN, R. B. (1966), *River Engineering and Water Conservation Works*, London: Butterworth.

THORNTON, R. B. and DAVIS, A. G. (1964), Development and use of American Beachgrass for dune stabilization. Paper to American Society of Agronomy Meeting, Missouri, 1–21.

TINDALL, F. P. (1967), 'The care of a coastline', *J. Tn Plan. Inst.*, **53**, 387–392.

TROLL, C. (1963), *Seasonal Climates of the Earth. The Seasonal Course of Natural Phenomena in the Different Climatic Zones of the Earth. World maps of Climatology*, Berlin: Springer.

TSCHIRLEY, F. H. (1969), 'Defoliation in Vietnam', *Science*, **163**, 779–786.

TSITSIN, A. N. (1946), 'Perennial wheats', *Discovery*, **7**, 180.

TSOPA, E. (1939), La végétation des halophytes du nord de la Roumanie en connexion avec celle du reste du pays', *SIGMA*, **70**, 1–22.

TÜXEN, R. (1957), 'Die Pflanzengesellschaften des Aussendiechslandes von Neuwerk', *Mitt. flor.-soz. Arbgemein.*, **6/7**

TYLER, G. (1971), 'Studies in the ecology of Baltic sea-shore meadows III. Hydrology and salinity of Baltic sea shore meadows', *Oikos*, **22**, 1–20.

VOO, E. E. van der (1964), Danger to scientifically important wetlands in the Netherlands by modification of the surrounding environment. Proceedings of the MAR Conference, I.U.C.N. Publication. N.S. **3**, 274–278.

VOSE, P. B., POWELL, H. G. and SPENCE, J. B. (1957), 'The machair grazings of Tiree, Inner Hebrides', *Trans. Proc. bot. Soc. Edinb.*, **37**, 89–110.

WALLACE, T. J. (1953), 'The plant ecology of Dawlish Warren Pt. 1, *Rep. Trans. Devon. Ass. Advmt. Sci. Lit. Art*, **85**, 86–94.

WATT, A. S. (1947), 'Pattern and process in the plant community', *J. Ecol.*, **35**, 1–22.

WEBBER, H. J. (1895), The two freezes of 1894–95 in Florida, and what they teach. U.S. Department of Agriculture Year Book 1895, 159–174.

WEBLEY, D. M., EASTWOOD, D. J. and GIMINGHAM, C. H. (1952), 'Development of a soil microflora in relation to plant succession on sand dunes, including the 'rhizosphere' flora associated with colonizing species', *J. Ecol.*, **40**, 168–178.

WELBOURN, R. M. E. and LANGE, R. T. (1969), 'An analysis of vegetation on stranded coastal dune ranges between Robe and Naracoorte, South Australia', *Trans. Roy. Soc. S. Aust.*, **92**, 19–25.

WEST, R. C. (1956), 'Mangrove swamps of the Pacific coast of Colombia', *Ann. Ass. Am. Geogr.*, **46**, 98–121.

WESTHOFF, V. (1947), The vegetation of dunes and salt marshes on the Dutch islands of Terschelling, Vlieland and Texel. S. Gravenhage.

WESTHOFF, V. (1952), Gezelschappen met houtige gewassen in de duinen en langs de binnenduinrand. Dendrol. Jaarbk. 1952, 9–49.

WESTHOFF, V. (1962), Plant species characteristic of wetland habitats in the Netherlands. Proceedings of the MAR Conference I.U.C.N. Publication. N.S., **3**, 122–129.

WESTHOFF, V., LEEUWEN, C. G. van and ADRIANI, M. J. (1961), 'Enkele aspecten van vegetatie en bodem der duinen van Goeree, in het bizonder de contactgordels tussen zout en zoet milieu', *Jaarb. Wet. Genot. Goeree-Overflakke*, 46–92.

WESTLAKE, D. F. (1968), The biology of aquatic weeds in relation to their management. Proceedings of the 9th British Weed Control Conference, 372–381.

WESTON, R. L. (1964), 'Nitrogen nutrition in *Atriplex hastata* L.', *Pl. Soil*, **20**, 251–259.

WHITE, D. J. B. (1961), 'Some observations on the vegetation of Blakeney Point, Norfolk, following the disappearance of the rabbits in 1954', *J. Ecol.*, **49**, 113–118.

WHITE, D. J. B. (1967), *An Annotated List of the Flowering Plants and Ferns on Blakeney Point, Norfolk.* (2nd edn) Norwich: The National Trust.

WIEHE, P. O. (1935), 'A quantitative study of the influence of the tide upon populations of *Salicornia europaea*', *J. Ecol.*, **23**, 323–333.

WIEMANN, P. and Domke, W. (1967), 'Pflanzengesellschaften der ostfriesischen Insel Spiekeroog', *Mitt. Staatsinst. Allg. Bot. Hamburg*, **12**, 191–353.

WILLIAMS, R. E. (1955), Development and improvement of coastal marsh ranges. *U.S. Year Book of Agriculture 1955*, 444–449.

WILLIAMS, R. E. (1959), Cattle walkways. U.S. Department of Agriculture Leaflet, 459, 1–8.

WILLIAMS, W. T. and LAMBERT, J. M. (1959), 'Multivariate methods in plant ecology I. Association-analysis in plant communities', *J. Ecol.*, **47**, 83–101.

WILLIS, A. J. (1963), 'Braunton Burrows: the effects on the vegetation of the addition of mineral nutrients to the dune soils', *J. Ecol.*, **51**, 353–374.

WILLIS, A. J., FOLKES, B. F., HOPE-SIMPSON, J. F. and YEMM, E. W. (1959),

Braunton Burrows: the dune system and its vegetation. I and II. *J. Ecol.*, **47**, 1–24 and 249–288.

WILLIS, A. J. and YEMM, E. W. (1961), 'Braunton Burrows: Mineral nutrient status of the dune soils', *J. Ecol.*, **49**, 377–390.

WILSON, K. (1960), 'The time factor in the development of dune soils at South Haven Peninsula, Dorset', *J. Ecol.*, **48**, 341–359.

WOHLENBERG, E. (1965), 'Deichbau und Deichpflege auf biologischer Grundlage', *Die Kuste*, **13**, 73–103.

WRIGHT, T. W. (1955), 'Profile development in the sand dunes of Culbin Forest, Morayshire I. Physical properties', *J. Soil Sci.*, **6**, 270–283.

YANO, N. (1962), 'The subterranean organ of sand dune plants in Japan', *J. Sci. Hiroshima Univ. Ser. B. Div. 2 (Botany)*, **9**, 139–184.

ZAK, J. M. (1967), 'Controlling drifting sand dunes on Cape Cod', *Massachusetts Agric. Expt. Stn. Bull.*, **563**, 1–15.

ZONNEVELD, I. S. (1960), 'The Brabantse Biesboch. A study of soil and vegetation of a freshwater tidal delta', *Bodenik Stud. No. 4. Wageningen.*

Additional References

These, for the most part, most recent references (not included in the text) are given to render the bibliography as up to date as possible.

BIRD, E. C. F. (1965), *A geomorphological study of the Gippsland Lakes*. Dept. of Geography Pubn. G/1. Australian National University, Canberra.

BIRD, E. C. F. (1971), 'Mangroves as land-builders', *Victorian Nat.*, **88**, 189–197.

BOSTON, K. G. (1971), The physiography of Anderson's Inlet, Victoria, with special reference to early stages in the establishment of *Spartina*. M. A. Thesis, University of Melbourne.

BOUGHEY, A. S. (1957), 'Ecological studies of tropical coastlines. I. The Gold Coast', *West Africa J. Ecol.*, **45**, 665–687.

CAMERON, G. N. (1972), 'Analysis of insect trophic diversity in two salt marsh communities', *Ecology*, **53**, 58–73.

CLARKE, L. D. and HANNON, N. J. (1971), 'The Mangrove swamp and salt marsh communities of the Sydney district. IV. The significance of species interaction', *J. Ecol.*, **59**, 535–553.

DENIEL, J. (1971), 'Un example d'utilisation de l'écologie et de la biometriesur un boisement de protection de l'environnement: La plantation de dunes de Cléder (Finistère)', *Penn Bed*, **8**, 147–159.

EBERSOLE, W. C. (1971), 'Predicting disturbances to the near and offshore sedimentary regime from marine mining'. *Water, Air, and Soil Pollution*, **1**, 72–88.

EVANS, G. (1965), 'Intertidal flat sediments and their environments and deposition in the Wash', *Q. Jl geol. Soc. Lond.*, **121**, 209–245.

FREIJSEN, A. H. J. (1971), 'Growth-physiology, salt tolerance and mineral nutrition of *Centaurium littorale* (Turner) Gilmour: Adaptations to its oligotrophic and brackish habitat', *Acta bot. neerl.*, **20**, 577–588.

GLUE, D. E. (1971), 'Saltmarsh reclamation stages and their associated bird-life', *Bird Study*, **18**, 187–198.

GRAY, A. J. (1972), 'The ecology of Morecambe Bay. V. The salt marshes of Morecambe Bay'. *J. appl. Ecol.*, **9**, 207–220.

GRAY, A. J. (1972), 'The ecology of Morecambe Bay. VI. Soils and vegetation of the salt marshes: A multivariate approach', *J. appl. Ecol.*, **9**, 221–234.

GRIMES, B. H. and HUBBARD, J. C. E. (1971), 'A comparison of film type and the importance of season for interpretation of coastal marshland vegetation', *Photogramm. Rec.*, **7**, 213–222.

JEFFRIES, R. L. (1972) *Aspects of salt-marsh ecology with particular reference to inorganic plant nutrition.* The Estuarine Environment, Barking, England: Applied Science Publishers Ltd., 61–85.

JENNINGS, J. N. (1965), 'Further discussion of factors affecting coastal dune formation in the tropics', *Aust. J. Sci.*, **28**, 166–167.

JONES, R. (1972), 'Comparative studies of plant growth and distribution in relation to waterlogging. V. The uptake of iron and manganese by dune and dune slack plants', *J. Ecol.*, **60**, 131–139.

JONES, R. (1972), *Ibid.* VI. 'The effect of manganese on the growth of dune and dune slack plants', *J. Ecol.*, **60**, 141–145.

JONES, R. and ETHERINGTON, J. R. (1971), *Ibid.* IV. 'The growth of dune and dune slack plants', *J. Ecol.*, **59**, 793–801.

LANGLOIS, J. (1971), 'Influence du rythme d'immersion sur la croissance et le métabolisme proteique de *Salicornia stricta* Dumort'. *Oecologia Plantarum*, **6**, 227–245.

MCGUINESS, J. L., HARROLD, L. L. and EDWARDS, W. M. (1971), 'Relation of rainfall energy streamflow to sediment yield from small and large watersheds', *J. Soil Wat. Conserv.*, **26**, 233–234.

MORTON, A. (1970), A study of some factors affecting the structure of grassland vegetation, Ph.D. Thesis, University of Bangor, N. Wales.

MORTON, J. K. (1957), 'Sand dune formation on a tropical shore', *J. Ecol.*, **45**, 495–497.

NEWTON, L. E. (1965), Taxonomic studies in the British species of *Puccinellia*, M.Sc. Thesis, University of London.

OWEN, M. (1971), 'The selection of feeding site by White-fronted geese in winter', *J. appl. Ecol.*, **8**, 905–917.

OWEN, M. (1972), 'Some factors affecting food intake and selection in White-fronted geese', *J. Anim. Ecol.*, **41**, 79–92.

OWEN, M. (1971), 'On the autumn food of Barnacle geese at Caerlaverock National Nature Reserve', *Rep. Wildfowl Trust*, **22**, 114–119.

PEAKE, J. F. (1966), 'A salt marsh at Thornham in N.W. Norfolk', *Trans. Norfolk Norwich Nat. Soc.*, **19**, 36–62.

PETHICK, J. S. (1968), The ecology of the Tunni estuary, M.A. Thesis, University of Cambridge.

PETHICK, J. S. (1971), Salt marsh morphology, Ph.D. Thesis, University of Cambridge.

PONS, L. Z. and ZONNEVELD, I. S. (1965), *Soil ripening and soil classification.* Initial soil formation in alluvial deposits and a classification of the resulting soils. Wageningen: H. Veenman and Zonen, 1–128.

SIIRA, J. and HAAPALA, H. (1969), 'Studies in the distribution and ecology of *Puccinellia phryganodes* (Trin.) Scribn. and Merr. in Finland', *Aquilo, Serie bot.* **8**, 1–24.

SMITH, E. R. (1970), *Evaluation of a leveed Louisiana marsh.* Trans. N. Am. Wildl. Conf., No. 35, 265–275.

THALEN, D. C. P. (1971), 'Variation in some salt marsh and dune vegetations in the Netherlands with special reference to gradient situations', *Acta. bot. neerl.*, **20**, 327–342.

TYLER, G. (1971), 'Studies in the ecology of Baltic sea-shore meadows. IV. Distribution and turnover of organic matter and minerals in a shore meadow ecosystem', *Oikos*, **22**, 265–291.

VAN STRAATEN, L. M. J. (1961), 'Sedimentation in tidal flat areas'. *J. Alberta Soc. Petrol. Geol.*, **9**, 203–226.

WILLIS, A. J. and JEFFERIES, R. L. (1961), 'Investigations on the water relations of sand-dune plants under natural conditions. The water relations of plants', *Brit. Ecol. Soc. Symp. No. 3.* Oxford, 168–189.

Index

This index should be used in conjunction with the contents list at the beginning of the volume.

Evolution of Desert Biota

Evolution of
Desert Biota

Edited by David W. Goodall

University of Texas Press Austin & London

Publication of this book was financed in part by
the Desert Biome and the Structure of Ecosystems programs of
the U.S. participation in the International
Biological Program.

Library of Congress Cataloging in Publication Data
Main entry under title:

Evolution of desert biota.

   Proceedings of a symposium held during the First
International Congress of Systematic and Evolution-
ary Biology which took place in Boulder, Colo.,
during August, 1973.
   Bibliography: p.
   Includes index.
   1. Desert biology—Congresses. 2. Evolution—
Congresses. I. Goodall, David W., 1914–
II. International Congress of Systematic and Evolu-
tionary Biology, 1st, Boulder, Colo., 1973.
QH88.E95   575'.00915'4   75-16071
ISBN 0-292-72015-7

Contents

Evolution of Desert Biota

1. Introduction   David W. Goodall

In the broad sense, "deserts" include all those areas of the earth's surface whose biological potentialities are severely limited by lack of water. If one takes them as coextensive with the arid and semiarid zones of Meigs's classification, they occupy almost one-quarter of the terrestrial surface of the globe. Though the largest arid areas are to be found in Africa and Asia, Australia has the largest proportion of its area in this category. Smaller desert areas occur in North and South America; Antarctica has cold deserts; and the only continent virtually without deserts is Europe.

When life emerged in the waters of the primeval world, it could hardly have been predicted that the progeny of these first organisms would extend their occupancy even to the deserts. Regions more different in character from the origin and natural home of life would be hard to imagine. Protoplasm is based on water, rooted in water. Some three-quarters of the mass of active protoplasm is water; the biochemical reactions underlying all its activities take place in water and depend on the special properties of water for the complex mechanisms of enzymatic and ionic controls which integrate the activity of cell and organisms into a cybernetic whole. It is, accordingly, remarkable that organisms were able to adapt themselves to environments in which water supplies were usually scanty, often almost nonexistent, and always unpredictable.

The first inhabitants of the deserts were presumably opportunistic. On the margins of larger bodies of water were areas which were alternately wetted and dried for longer or shorter periods. Organisms living there acquired the possibility of surviving the dry periods by drying out and becoming inactive until rewetted, at which time their activity resumed where it had left off. While in the dry state, these organisms

4 DAVID W. GOODALL

—initially, doubtless, Protista—were easily moved by air currents and thus could colonize other bodies of water. Among them were the very temporary pools formed by the occasional rainstorms in desert areas. Thus the deserts came to be inhabited by organisms whose ability to dry and remoisten without loss of vitality enabled them to take advantage of the short periods during which limited areas of the deserts deviate from their normally arid state.

Yet other organisms doubtless—the blue green algae among them —similarly took advantage of the much shorter periods, amounting perhaps to an hour at a time, during which the surface of the desert was moistened by dew, and photosynthesis was possible a few minutes before and after sunrise to an organism which could readily change its state of hydration.

In the main, though, colonization of the deserts had to wait until colonization of other terrestrial environments was well advanced. For most groups of organisms, the humid environments on land presented less of a challenge in the transition from aquatic life than did the deserts. By the time arthropods and annelids, mollusks and vertebrates, fungi and higher plants had adapted to the humid terrestrial environments, they were poised on the springboard where they could collect themselves for the ultimate leap into the deserts. And this leap was made successfully and repeatedly. Few of the major groups of organisms that were able to adapt to life on land did not also contrive to colonize the deserts.

Some, like the arthropods and annual plants, had an adaptational mechanism—an inactive stage of the life cycle highly resistant to desiccation—almost made to order to match opportunistically the episodic character of the desert environment. For others the transition was more difficult: for mammals, whose excretory mechanism assumes the availability of liquid water; for perennial plants, whose photosynthetic mechanism normally carries the penalty of water loss concurrent with carbon dioxide intake. But the evolutionary process surmounted these difficulties; and the deserts are now inhabited by a range of organisms which, though somewhat inferior to that of more favored environments, bears testimony to the inventiveness and success of evolution in filling niches and in creating diversity.

The most important modifications and adaptations needed for life in the deserts are concerned with the dryness of the environment there.

But an important feature of most desert environments is also their unpredictability. Precipitation has a higher coefficient of variability, on any time scale, than in other climatic types, with the consequence that desert organisms may have to face floods as well as long and highly variable periods of drought. The range of temperatures may also be extreme—both diurnal and seasonal. Under the high radiation of the subtropical deserts, the soil surface may reach a temperature which few organisms can survive; and, in the cold deserts of the great Asian land mass, extremely low winter temperatures are recorded. Sand and dust storms made possible by the poor stability of the surface soil are also among the environmental hazards to which desert organisms must become adapted.

Like other climatic zones, the deserts have not been stable in relation to the land masses of the world. Continental drift, tectonic movements, and changes in the earth's rotation and in the extent of the polar icecaps have led to secular changes in the area and distribution of arid land surfaces. But, unlike other climatic zones, the arid lands have probably always been fragmented—constituting a number of discrete areas separated from one another by zones of quite different climate. The evolutionary process has gone on largely independently in these separate areas, often starting from different initial material, with the consequence that the desert biota is highly regional. Elements in common between the different main desert areas are few, and, as between continents or subcontinents, there is a high degree of endemism. The smaller desert areas of the world are the equivalent of islands in an ocean of more humid environments.

These are among the problems to be considered in the present volume. It reports the proceedings of a symposium which was held on August 10, 1973, at Boulder, Colorado, as part of the First International Congress of Systematic and Evolutionary Biology.

2. The Origin and Floristic Affinities of the South American Temperate Desert and Semidesert Regions   Otto T. Solbrig

Introduction

In this paper I will attempt to summarize the existent evidence regarding the floristic relations of the desert and semidesert regions of temperate South America and to explain how these affinities came to exist.

More than half of the surface of South America south of the Tropic of Capricorn can be classed as semidesert or desert. In this area lie some of the richest mineral deposits of the continent. These regions consequently are important from the standpoint of human economy. From a more theoretical point, desert environments are credited with stimulating rapid evolution (Stebbins, 1952; Axelrod, 1967) and, further, present some of the most interesting and easy-to-study adaptations in plants and animals.

Although, at present, direct evidence regarding the evolution of desert vegetation in South America is still meager, enough data have accumulated to make some hypotheses. It is hoped this will stimulate more research in the field of plant micropaleontology in temperate South America. Such research in northern South America has advanced our knowledge immensely (Van der Hammen, 1966), and high rewards await the investigator who searches this area in the temperate regions of the continent.

The Problem

If a climatic map of temperate South America is compared with a phytogeographic map of the same region drawn on a physiognomic basis and with one drawn on floristic lines, it will be seen that they do not coincide. Furthermore, if the premise (not proven but generally held to be true) is accepted that the physical environment is the determinant of the structure of the ecosystem and that, as the physical environment (be it climate, physiography, or both) changes, the structure of the vegetation will also change, then an explanation for the discrepancy between climatic and phytogeographic maps has to be provided. Alternative explanations to solve the paradox are (1) the premise on which they are based is entirely or partly wrong; (2) our knowledge is incomplete; or (3) the discrepancies can be explained on the basis of the historical events of the past. It is undoubtedly true that floristic and paleobotanical knowledge of South American deserts is incomplete and that much more work is needed. However, I will proceed under the assumption that a sufficient minimum of information is available. I also feel that our present insights are sufficient to accept the premise that the ecosystem is the result of the interaction between the physical environment and the biota. I shall therefore try to find in the events of the past the answer for the discrepancy.

I shall first describe the semidesert regions of South America and their vegetation, followed by a brief discussion of Tertiary and Pleistocene events. I shall then look at the floristic connections between the regions and the distributional patterns of the dominant elements of the area under study. From this composite picture I shall try to provide a coherent working hypothesis to explain the origin and floristic affinities of the desert and semidesert regions of temperate South America.

Theory

Biogeographical hypotheses such as the ones that will be made further on in this paper are based on certain theoretical assumptions. In most cases, however, these assumptions are not made explicit; consequently, the reader who disagrees with the author is not always certain whether he disagrees with the interpretation of the evidence or with the assumptions made. This has led to many futile controversies. The fundamental assumptions that will be made here follow from the general theory of evolution by natural selection, the theory of speciation, and the theory of geological uniformitarianism.

The first assumption is that a continuous distributional range reflects an environment favorable to the plant, that is, an environment where it can compete successfully. Since the set of conditions (physical, climatical, and biological) where the plant can compete successfully (the realized niche) bounds a limited portion of ecological space, it will be further assumed that the range of a species indicates that conditions over that range do not differ greatly in comparison with the set of all possible conditions that can be given. It will be further assumed that each species is unique in its fundamental and realized niche (defined as the hyperspace bounded by all the ecological parameters to which the species is adapted or over which it is able to compete successfully). Consequently, no species will occupy exactly the same geographical range, and, as a corollary, some species will be able to grow over a wide array of conditions and others over a very limited one.

When the vegetation of a large region, such as a continent, is mapped, it is found that the distributional ranges of species are not independent but that ranges of certain species tend to group themselves even though identical ranges are not necessarily encountered. This allows the phytogeographer to classify the vegetation. It will be assumed that, when neighboring geographical areas do not differ greatly in their present physical environment or in their climate but differ in their flora, the reason for the difference is a historical one reflecting different evolutionary histories in these floras and requiring an explanation.

Disjunctions are common occurrences in the ranges of species. In a strict sense, all ranges are disjunct since a continuous cover of a species over an extensive area is seldom encountered. However, when similar major disjunctions are found in the ranges of many species whose ranges are correlated, the disjunction has biogeographical significance. Unless there is evidence to the contrary, an ancient continuous range will be assumed in such instances, one that was disrupted at a later date by some identifiable event, either geological or climatological.

It will also be assumed that the atmospheric circulation and the basic meteorological phenomena in the past were essentially similar to those encountered today, unless there is positive evidence to the contrary. Further, it will be assumed that the climatic tolerances of a living species were the same in the past as they are today. Finally, it will be assumed that the spectrum of life forms that today signify a rain forest, a subtropical forest, a semidesert, and so on, had the same meaning in the past too, implying with it that the basic processes of carbon gain and water economy have been essentially identical at least since the origin of the angiosperms.

From these assumptions a coherent theory can be developed to reconstruct the past (Good, 1953; Darlington, 1957, 1965). No general assumptions about age and area will be made, however, because they are inconsistent with speciation theory (Stebbins, 1950; Mayr, 1963). In special cases when there is some evidence that a particular group is phylogenetically primitive, the assumption will be made that it is also geologically old. Such an assumption is not very strong and will be used only to support more robust evidence.

The Semidesert Regions of South America

In temperate South America we can recognize five broad phytogeographical regions that can be classed as "desert" or "semidesert" regions. They are the Monte (Haumann, 1947; Morello, 1958), the Patagonian Steppe (Cabrera, 1947), the Prepuna (Cabrera, 1971), and the Puna (Cabrera, 1958) in Argentina, and the Pacific Coastal Desert in Chile and Peru (Goodspeed, 1945; Ferreyra, 1960). In addition, three other regions—the Matorral or "Mediterranean" region in Chile (Mooney and Dunn, 1970) and the Chaco and the Espinal in Argentina (Fiebrig, 1933; Cabrera, 1953, 1971), although not semideserts, are characterized by an extensive dry season. Finally, the High mountain vegetation of the Andes shows adaptations to drought tolerance (fig. 2-1).

The Monte

The Monte (Lorentz, 1876; Haumann, 1947; Cabrera, 1953; Morello, 1958; Solbrig, 1972, 1973) is a phytogeographical province that extends from lat. 24°35′ S to lat. 44°20′ S and from long. 62°54′ W on the Atlantic coast to long. 69°50′ W at the foothills of the Andes (fig. 2-1).

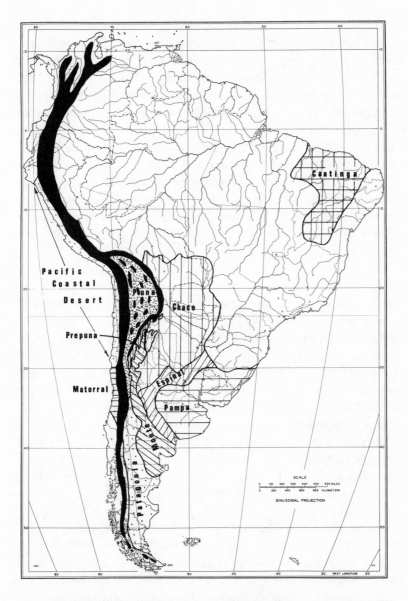

Fig. 2-1. Geographical limits of the phytogeographical provinces of the Andean Dominion (stippled) and of the Chaco Dominion (various hatchings) according to Cabrera (1971). The high cordillera vegetation is indicated in solid black. Goode Base Map, copyright by The University of Chicago, Department of Geography.

Rains average less than 200 mm a year in most localities and never exceed 600 mm; evaporation exceeds rainfall throughout the region. The rain falls in spring and summer. The area is bordered on the west by the Cordillera de los Andes, which varies in height between 5,000 and 7,000 m in this area. On the north the region is bordered by the high Bolivian plateau (3,000–5,000 m high) and on the east by a series of mountain chains (Sierras Pampeanas) that vary in height from 3,000 to 5,000 m in the north (Aconquija, Famatina, and Velazco) to less than 1,000 m (Sierra de Hauca Mahuida) in the south. Physiographically, the northern part is formed by a continuous barrier of high mountains which becomes less important farther south as well as lower in height. The Monte vegetation occupies the valleys between these mountains as a discontinuous phase in the northern region and a more or less continuous phase from approximately lat. 32° S southward.

The predominant vegetation of the Monte is a xerophytic scrubland with small forests along the rivers or in areas where the water table is quite superficial. The predominant community is dominated by the species of the creosote bush or *jarilla* (*Larrea divaricata*, *L. cuneifolia*, and *L. nitida* [Zygophyllaceae]) associated with a number of other xerophytic or aphyllous shrubs: *Condalia microphylla* (Rhamnaceae), *Monttea aphylla* (Scrophulariaceae), *Bougainvillea spinosa* (Nyctaginaceae), *Geoffroea decorticans* (Leguminosae), *Cassia aphylla* (Leguminosae), *Bulnesia schickendanzii* (Zygophyllaceae), *B. retama*, *Atamisquea emarginata* (Capparidaceae), *Zuccagnia punctata* (Leguminosae), *Gochnatia glutinosa* (Compositae), *Proustia cuneifolia* (Compositae), *Flourensia polyclada* (Compositae), and *Chuquiraga erinacea* (Compositae).

Along water courses or in areas with a superficial water table, forests of *algarrobos* (mesquite in the United States) are observed, that is, various species of *Prosopis* (Leguminosae), particularly *P. flexuosa*, *P. nigra*, *P. alba*, and *P. chilensis*. Other phreatophytic or semiphreatophytic species of small trees or small shrubs are *Cercidium praecox* (Leguminosae), *Acacia aroma* (Leguminosae), and *Salix humboldtiana* (Salicaceae).

Herbaceous elements are not common. There is a flora of summer annuals formed principally by grasses.

The Patagonian Steppe

The Patagonian Steppe (Cabrera, 1947, 1953, 1971; Soriano, 1950, 1956) is limited on its eastern and southern borders by the Atlantic Ocean and the Strait of Magellan. On the west it borders quite abruptly with the *Nothofagus* forest; the exact limits, although easy to determine, have not yet been mapped precisely (Dimitri, 1972). On the north it borders with the Monte along an irregular line that goes from Chos Malal in the state of Neuquen in the west to a point on the Atlantic coast near Rawson in the state of Chubut (Soriano, 1949). In addition, a tongue of Patagonian Steppe extends north from Chubut to Mendoza (Cabrera, 1947; Böcher, Hjerting, and Rahn, 1963). Physiognomically the region consists of a series of broad tablelands of increasing altitude as one moves from east to west, reaching to about 1,500 m at the foot of the cordillera. The soil is sandy or rocky, formed by a mixture of windblown cordilleran detritus as well as *in situ* eroded basaltic rocks, the result of ancient volcanism.

The climate is cold temperate with cold summers and relatively mild winters. Summer means vary from 21°C in the north to 12°C in the south (summer mean maxima vary from 30°C to 18°C) with winter means from 8°C in the north to 0°C in the south (winter mean minima 1.5°C to −3°C). Rainfall is very low, averaging less than 200 mm in all the Patagonian territory with the exception of the south and west borders where the effect of the cordilleran rainfall is felt. The little rainfall is fairly well distributed throughout the year with a slight increase during winter months.

The Patagonian Steppe is the result of the rain-shadow effect of the southern cordillera in elevating and drying the moist westerly winds from the Pacific. Consequently the region not only is devoid of rains but also is subjected to a steady westerly wind of fair intensity that has a tremendous drying effect. The few rains that occur are the result of occasional eruptions of the Antarctic polar air mass from the south interrupting the steady flow of the westerlies.

The dominant vegetation is a low scrubland or else a vegetation of low cushion plants. In some areas xerophytic bunch grasses are also common. Among the low (less than 1 m) xerophytic shrubs and cushion plants, the *neneo, Mulinum spinosum* (Umbelliferae), is the dominant form in the northwestern part, while *Chuquiraga avellanedae* (Compositae) and *Nassauvia glomerulosa* (Compositae) are dominant over extensive areas in central Patagonia. Other important shrubs are *Trevoa patagonica* (Rhamnaceae), *Adesmia campestris* (Compositae), *Colliguaja integerrima* (Euphorbiaceae), *Nardophyllum obtusifolium* (Compositae), and *Nassauvia axillaris*. Among the grasses are *Stipa humilis*, *S. neaei*, *S. speciosa*, *Poa huecu*, *P. ligularis*, *Festuca argentina*, *F. gracillima*, *Bromus macranthus*, *Hordeum comosus*, and *Agropyron fuegianum*.

The Puna

The Puna (Weberbauer, 1945; Cabrera, 1953, 1958, 1971) is situated in the northwestern part of Argentina, western and central Bolivia, and southern Peru. It is a very high plateau, the result of the uplift of an enormous block of an old peneplane, which started to lift in the Miocene but mainly rose during the Pliocene and the Pleistocene to a mean elevation of 3,400–3,800 m. The Puna is bordered on the east by the Cordillera Real and on the west by the Cordillera de los Andes that rises to 5,000–6,000 m; the plateau is peppered by a number of volcanoes that rise 1,000–1,500 m over the surface of the Puna.

The soils of the Puna are in general immature, sandy to rocky, and very poor in organic matter (Cabrera, 1958). The area has a number of closed basins, and high mountain lakes and marshes are frequent.

The climate of the Puna is cold and dry with values for minimum and maximum temperatures not too different from Patagonia but with the very significant difference that the daily temperature amplitude is very great (values of over 30°C are common) and the difference between summer and winter very slight. The precipitation is very irregular over the area of the Puna, varying from a high of 800 mm in the northeast corner of Bolivia to 100 mm/year on the southwest border in Argentina. The southern Puna is undoubtedly a semidesert region, but the northern part is more of a high alpine plateau, where the limitations to plant growth are given more by temperature than by rainfall.

The typical vegetation of the Puna is a low, xerophytic scrubland formed by shrubs one-half to one meter tall. In some areas a grassy steppe community is found, and in low areas communities of high mountain marshes are found.

Among the shrubby species we find *Fabiana densa* (Solanaceae), *Psila boliviensis* (Compositae), *Adesmia horridiuscula* (Leguminosae), *A. spinossisima, Junellia seriphioides* (Verbenaceae), *Nardophyllum armatum* (Compositae), and *Acantholippia hastatula* (Verbenaceae). Only one tree, *Polylepis tomentella* (Rosaceae), grows in the Puna, strangely enough only at altitudes of over 4,000 m. Another woody element is *Prosopis ferox*, a small tree or large shrub. Among the grasses are *Bouteloua simplex, Muhlenbergia fastigiata, Stipa leptostachya, Pennisetum chilense*, and *Festuca scirpifolia*. Cactaceae are not very frequent in general, but we find locally abundant *Opuntia atacamensis, Oreocerus trollii, Parodia schroebsia*, and *Trichocereus poco*.

Although physically the Puna ends at about lat. 30° S, Puna vegetation extends on the eastern slope of the Andes to lat. 35° S, where it merges into Patagonian Steppe vegetation.

The Prepuna

The Prepuna (Czajka and Vervoorst, 1956; Cabrera, 1971) extends along the dry mountain slopes of northwestern Argentina from the state of Jujuy to La Rioja, approximately between 2,000 and 3,400 m. It is characterized by a dry and warm climate with summer rains; it is warmer than the Puna, colder than the Monte; and it is a special formation strongly influenced by the exposure of the mountains in the region.

The vegetation is mainly formed by xerophytic shrubs and cacti. Among the shrubs, the most abundant are *Gochnatia glutinosa* (Compositae), *Cassia crassiramea* (Leguminosae), *Aphyllocladus spartioides, Caesalpinia trichocarpa* (Leguminosae), *Proustia cuneifolia* (Compositae), *Chuquiraga erinacea* (Compositae), *Zuccagnia punctata* (Leguminosae), *Adesmia inflexa* (Leguminosae), and *Psila boliviensis* (Compositae). The most conspicuous member of the Cactaceae is the cardon, *Trichocereus pasacana*; there are also present *T. poco* and species of *Opuntia, Cylindropuntia, Tephrocactus, Parodia*, and *Lobivia*. Among the grasses are *Digitaria californica, Stipa leptostachya, Monroa argentina*, and *Agrostis nana*.

The Pacific Coastal Desert

Along the Peruvian and Chilean coast from lat. 5° S to approximately lat. 30° S, we find the region denominated "La Costa" in Peru (Weber-bauer, 1945; Ferreyra, 1960) and "Northern Desert," "Coastal Desert," or "Atacama Desert" in Chile (Johnston, 1929; Reiche, 1934; Goodspeed, 1945). This very dry region is under the influence of the combined rain shadow of the high cordillera to the east and the cold Humboldt Current and the coastal upwelling along the Peruvian coast. Although physically continuous, the vegetation is not uniform, as a result of the combination of temperature and rainfall variations in such an extended territory. Temperature decreases from north to south as can be expected, going from a yearly mean to close to 25°C in northern Peru (Ferreyra, 1960) to a low of 15°C at its southern border. Rainfall is very irregular and very meager. Although some localities in Peru (Zorritos, Lomas de Lachay; cf. Ferreyra, 1960) have averages of 200 mm, the average yearly rainfall is below 50 mm in most places. This has created an extreme xerophytic vegetation often with special adaptations to make use of the coastal fog.

Behind the coastal area are a number of dry valleys, some in Peru but mostly in northern Chile, with the same kind of extreme dry conditions as the coastal area.

The flora is characterized by plants with extreme xerophytic adaptations, especially succulents, such as *Cereus spinibaris* and *C. coquimbanus*, various species of *Echinocactus*, and *Euphorbia lactifolia*. The most interesting associations occur in the so-called *lomas*, or low hills (less than 1,500 m), along the coast that intercept the coastal fog and provide very intensified conditions favorable for plant growth. Almost each of these formations from the Ecuadorian border to central Chile constitutes a unique community. Over 40 percent of the plants in the Peruvian coastal community are annuals (Ferreyra, 1960), although annuals apparently are less common in Chile (Johnston, 1929); of the perennials, a large number are root perennials or succulents. Only about 5 percent are shrubs or trees in the northern sites (Ferreyra, 1960), while shrubs and semishrubs constitute a higher proportion in the Chilean region. From the Chilean region should be mentioned *Oxalis gigantea* (Oxalidaceae), *Heliotropium philippianum* (Boraginaceae), *Salvia gilliesii* (Labiatae), and

Proustia tipia (Compositae) among the shrubs; species of *Poa*, *Eragrostis*, *Elymus*, *Stipa*, and *Nasella* among the grasses; and *Alstroemeria violacea* (Amaryllidaceae), a conspicuous and relatively common root perennial. In southern Peru *Nolana inflata*, *N. spathulata* (Nolanaceae), and other species of this widespread genus; *Tropaeolum majus* (Tropaeolaceae), *Loasa urens* (Loasaceae), and *Arcythophyllum thymifolium* (Rubiaceae); in the *lomas* of central Peru the *amancay*, *Hymenocallis amancaes* (Amaryllidaceae), *Alstroemeria recumbens* (Amaryllidaceae), *Peperomia atocongona* (Piperaceae), *Vicia lomensis* (Leguminosae), *Carica candicans* (Caricaceae), *Lobelia decurrens* (Lobeliaceae), *Drymaria weberbaueri* (Caryophyllaceae), *Capparis prisca* (Capparidaceae), *Caesalpinia tinctoria* (Leguminosae), *Pitcairnia lopezii* (Bromeliaceae), and *Haageocereus lachayensis* and *Armatocereus* sp. (Cactaceae). Finally, in the north we find *Tillandsia recurvata*, *Fourcroya occidentalis*, *Apralanthera ferreyra*, *Solanum multinterruptum*, and so on.

Of great phytogeographic interest is the existence of a less-xerophytic element in the very northern extreme of the Pacific Coastal Desert, from Trujillo to the border with Ecuador (Ferreyra, 1960), known as *algarrobal*. Principal elements of this vegetation are two species of *Prosopis*, *P. limensis* and *P. chilensis*; others are *Cercidium praecox*, *Caesalpinia paipai*, *Acacia huarango*, *Bursera graveolens* (Burseraceae), *Celtis iguanea* (Ulmaceae), *Bougainvillea peruviana* (Nyctaginaceae), *Cordia rotundifolia* (Boraginaceae), and *Grabowskia boerhaviifolia* (Solanaceae).

Geological History

The present desert and subdesert regions of temperate South America result from the existence of belts of high atmospheric pressure around lat. 30° S, high mountain chains that impede the transport of moisture from the oceans to the continents, and cold water currents along the coast, which by cooling and drying the air that flows over them act like the high mountains.

The Pacific Coastal Desert of Chile and Peru is principally the result of the effect of the cold Humboldt Current that flows from south to north; the Patagonian Steppe is produced by the Cordillera de los Andes that traps the moisture in the prevailing westerly winds; while the Monte and the Puna result from a combination of the cordilleran rain shadow in the west and the Sierras Pampeanas in the east and the existence of the belt of high pressure.

The high-pressure belt of mid-latitudes is a result of the global flow of air (Flohn, 1969) and most likely has existed with little modification throughout the Mesozoic and Cenozoic (however, for a different view, see Schwarzenbach, 1968, and Volkheimer, 1971). The mountain chains and the cold currents, on the other hand, are relatively recent phenomena. The latter's low temperature is largely the result of Antarctic ice. But aridity results from the interaction of temperature and humidity. In effect, when ambient temperatures are high, a greater percentage of the incident rainfall is lost as evaporation and, in addition, plants will transpire more water. Consequently, in order to reconstruct the history of the desert and semidesert regions of South America, we also have to have an idea of the temperature and pluvial regimes of the past.

In this presentation I will use two types of evidence: (1) the purely geological evidence regarding continental drift, times of uplifting of mountain chains, marine transgressions, and existence of paleosoils and pedemonts; and (2) paleontological evidence regarding the ecological types and phylogenetical stock of the organisms that inhabited the area in the past. With this evidence I will try to reconstruct the most likely climate for temperate South America since the Cretaceous and deduce the kind of vegetation that must have existed.

Cretaceous

This account will start from the Cretaceous because it is the oldest period from which we have fossil records of angiosperms, which today constitute more than 90 percent of the vascular flora of the regions under consideration. At the beginning of the Cretaceous, South America and Africa were probably still connected (Dietz and Holden, 1970), since the rift that created the South Atlantic and separated the two continents apparently had its origin during the Lower Cretaceous. The position of South America at this time was slightly south (approximate-